THE INVESTOR'S GUIDE TO STOCK QUOTATIONS

and Other Financial Listings

The Investor's Guide to Stock Quotations

and Other Financial Listings

THIRD EDITION

GERALD WARFIELD

PERENNIAL LIBRARY

HARPER & ROW, PUBLISHERS, New York
Grand Rapids, Philadelphia, St. Louis, San Francisco
London, Singapore, Sydney, Tokyo, Toronto

this book is dedicated to
ANNIE CAMPBELL SPENCER
her children, her two other grandchildren,
her great-grandchildren, and her
great-great-grandchildren

THE INVESTOR'S GUIDE TO STOCK QUOTATIONS *(Third Edition).* Copyright © 1990 by Gerald A. Warfield. All rights reserved. Printed in the United States of America. No part of this book may be used or reproduced in any manner whatsoever without written permission except in the case of brief quotations embodied in critical articles and reviews. For information address Harper & Row, Publishers, Inc., 10 East 53rd Street, New York, N.Y. 10022.

First PERENNIAL LIBRARY edition published 1990.

Designer: Sidney Feinberg

Library of Congress Cataloging-in-Publication Data

Warfield, Gerald.
    The investor's guide to stock quotations and other financial listings / Gerald Warfield — 3rd ed.
      p.   cm.
    ISBN 0-06-055196-8 — ISBN 0-06-096492-8 (pbk.)
    1. Stock quotations—Handbooks, manuals, etc.   I. Title.
HG4636.W28   1990
332.63'2042—dc20   89-46128

90 91 92 93 94 **RRD** 10 9 8 7 6 5 4 3 2 1

Contents

Part Four: How to Read Option Quotations

Part Five: How to Read Futures Quotations

Appendixes

Acknowledgments

It is with gratitude that I acknowledge the many sources from which the information in this book has been compiled. In particular, I would like to acknowledge the generous help and cooperation of Mike Millican, Business News Editor of The Associated Press.

The following individuals gave graciously of their time and expertise in reviewing parts of the manuscript:

Michael G. Balestrieri, Manager of Bond Operations, New York Stock Exchange

Anthony J. Calabrese, Registered Representative, Donald Sheldon & Co., Inc.

Marvin A. Caro, Vice President, L. F. Rothschild, Unterberg, Towbin

Angela Cashman, Supervisor, Consolidated Control Center (SIAC), who taught me to read ticker tape

Donald G. Dueweke, Vice President, Systems Support, New York Stock Exchange

Louis Felice, Manager of Market Services, The Associated Press

Monte Gordon, Director of Research, Dreyfus Corporation

Stephen H. Hogan, Investment Advisor, Harrison Management

Peter Lloyd-Davis, staff economist, Board of Governors of the Federal Reserve System

Arthur W. Matthews, economist, Royal Oak, Michigan

Stanley Noval, partner of Benari Noval, New York, N.Y.

Harold Walpole, Citibank, N.A.

Officers and staff of the following institutions were also of service: Carl L. Bolton, Vice President, New York Stock Exchange; Dorothea Brooks, Business Editor of United Press International; Ray Carmichael, Director of Public Relations, Chicago Board of Trade; Walter Clark, Director of Public Relations, Bunker Ramo Corporation; Jay Cohen, Account Executive, Dean Witter Reynolds, Inc.;

Don S. Disner, Marketing Communication, Quotron Systems, Inc.;
Michael Esposito, Office of the Comptroller, City of New York;
Deborah Gardner, Exchange Archivist, New York Stock Exchange;
Gary W. Guinn, Assistant Director of NASDAQ Operations; N. L.
Hobbing, National Association of Securities Dealers, Inc.; Paul M.
O'Brien, Third Deputy Comptroller, Office of the Comptroller, City
of New York; Ed Topple, New York Stock Exchange photographer.

The table on page 30 is courtesy of AP/Media General Financial
Service as printed in and with the permission of the *San Francisco
Examiner & Chronicle.*

The *New York Post* quotation on p. 24 is reprinted by permission
of the New York Post.

Processing and format of the information contained in the quotations is reprinted with the permission of The Associated Press and
United Press International unless otherwise indicated.

All quotation examples are reproduced photographically from and
with the kind permission of the following newspapers:

The Anchorage Times
The Arizona Republic
Barron's
The Boston Globe
Chicago Tribune
The Cincinnati Enquirer
The Columbus Dispatch
The Dallas Morning News
Ft. Worth Star Telegram
The Honolulu Advertiser
Houston Chronicle
Los Angeles Times
The Miami Herald
The National OTC Stock Exchange
New York Post
The New York Times
The Philadelphia Inquirer
St. Louis Post-Dispatch
San Francisco Chronicle
San Francisco Examiner
The Tampa Tribune
The Wall Street Journal
The Washington Post

Photograph of cable TV stock quotations on p. 79 is courtesy of Manhattan Cable TV and Reuters NEWS-VIEW.

Reproduction of commodity quotations appearing on television is courtesy of The Nightly Business Report/Produced by WPBT-Miami.

Futures prices for Liquefied Propane Gas reprinted courtesy of the Petroleum Association of the New York Cotton Exchange, Inc.

Bond rating tables are reprinted by permission of Moody's Investors Service and Standard & Poor's Corporation.

Money Market Funds quotations on p. 147 are courtesy of *The Boston Globe* and Donoghue's Money Fund Report of Holliston Mass. 01746.

I would like to thank Martin Gonzales, Nina Hill, Richard Brooks, Paul Marcontell, Ann Wood, and Tom Farrington for their help with the manuscript, and Perry McLamb for his photography. Special thanks go to Douglas Abeles, a floor trader on the New York Futures Exchange, who helped in the preparation of the section on stock index futures. And finally, my thanks to Georgia Murphy, who first engaged my interest in investing.

For this edition, all photographs of the New York Stock Exchange were furnished by the NYSE. Historical photographs are from the New York Stock Exchange Archives, and current photographs are courtesy of Ed Topple, NYSE photographer.

Introduction

Learning to Read Financial Quotations

Would you like to sit down with a newspaper and make sense of the financial pages? Reading stock quotations is an important part of that process, and that is what this book is about.

Stock tables (and the quotations for other financial instruments) provide a convenient focus for study, and they yield a surprising amount of valuable information. Being able to read financial quotations, for example, will help you keep an eye on your own investments and even enable you to communicate more effectively with your broker. More important, you will also have taken the initial step toward making your own investment decisions.

One of the first things you will notice in reading the financial tables is that yield (i.e., how much money you stand to make) is directly related to risk so that, for example, if you acquire a relatively speculative investment you should expect greater yield than if you were investing with less risk. Otherwise, why bother? You would be better off selecting an investment with the same yield potential where your money is safer.

Nowhere is the relation of yield to risk more clearly demonstrated than in the bond tables. Highly rated corporate bonds, for example, yield less than more speculative lower-rated corporate bonds, and government bonds—the safest of all—yield even less. Should you find a case where government bonds yield *more* than corporate bonds (and there have been times when that has happened) then you have probably discovered an excellent investment opportunity.

The task for the investor is not to eliminate risk (which is impossible) but to avoid unnecessary or inappropriate risk. Part of the reason for studying investing is so that you can decide upon the degree of safety you require and balance it with the yield you should expect. You may decide, for example, on more than one risk level. You could place 90% of your investable income into safe, lower-yielding investments and place 10% into higher-risk ventures with the possibility of higher gains, and, in fact, that is a typical investment strategy.

Obviously, it is easier to be successful when you take less risk, so, particularly in the beginning, err on the side of caution. Invest only when you are comfortable with the risk, and adjust your expectations to the corresponding level of return. If you are nervous about an investment, listen to your intuition. There will always be other opportunities to invest.

In the last ten years the world beyond the much-flogged passbook savings accounts has grown enormously. In response to the needs of ordinary investors and to large institutional investors alike, new financial instruments have been introduced yearly. Getting to know these instruments is a formidable task.

For the purposes of this book we are limiting ourselves to the instruments that are quoted in most newspapers. This will provide us with an overview of the majority of investment vehicles now available to the public. They consist of the following:

> stocks (common and preferred)
> bonds (corporate and municipal)
> Government securities (bonds, notes and bills)
> mutual funds
> money-market funds
> options
> futures (commodity and financial)

All of the items on the above list will be referred to collectively as "securities." Thus we are not using the term in its narrower sense as meaning only stocks and bonds.

When you decide to invest there are basically two things you can do with your money. You can buy something or you can loan it out. The most usual form of "buying something" is to buy real estate or to buy stock. When you buy stocks you are buying equity (ownership) in a company. Your return from stocks (dividends) is actually profits from the company that the owners (you among them) are dividing up amongst themselves.

On the other hand, when you buy a bond you are loaning the issuing company money. Your return is the interest payments at a fixed annual rate, and, of course, you will receive the face value back upon maturity.

Dividends from stocks are not usually as high as interest payments from bonds. However, from stocks you have the opportunity for capital gains: that is, you can sell the stock for (it is hoped) a profit. There are also situations where you can sell bonds for a profit, but basically bonds are for long-term investment, not profit taking.

As a rough illustration one might divide up the most common investments in the following way:

Equity	Loans
common stocks	corporate bonds
mutual funds	municipal bonds
money-market funds	Government securities
real estate	certificates of deposit

Note that Government and municipal securities are all debt instruments (since neither the Government nor any of its municipalities are for sale). Options and futures are not in the above table but, as they offer the possibility of acquisition, they would perhaps fall into the category of equity.

How to Get Started

One may become interested in investing at various points in one's life and in various stages of financial array or disarray. This causes concern for some financial advisers who feel that a number of conditions should be met before one begins to invest. Some recommend having six months' salary in reserve and others suggest $10,000. Some even prescribe an examination of your insurance policies and retirement benefits.

Obviously, persons with cash flow problems are not yet in a position to invest. But those with even a small reserve beyond the necessities can begin an investment program as long as they take into consideration one risk in particular: that of timing. For example:

An individual whose sole reserve is $500 might decide to "play it safe" and buy 10 shares (more or less) of the bluest of blue chip companies. However, the primary risk here is not that the shares will suddenly lose their value, but that the investor, with no further reserves, will suddenly need his money back. Should this happen the investor will lose money even if the price of the stock hasn't changed because he will also have to cover the cost of two broker's commissions (one for the purchase and one for the sale).

The point is that timing is an essential part of investing. Not having control of it dramatically increases one's risk for the simple reason that the prices of stocks (and other securities) go up and down. The chance of a stock being up enough *at one specific moment* to cover commissions and a reasonable profit is far less than the chances of a stock being that high within, say, a three-year period. As an investor you want to base your decision to sell a security on the price of that security or other related factors; you don't want to have such a decision dictated to you by your personal financial circumstances.

My own preference for the initial step in investing is to buy shares in a money-market fund. I offer this suggestion for three reasons:

1. Money-market funds offer the highest rates for their relative degree of safety.
2. Such a fund can be used at any time to temporarily park money (such as from the sale of stock) waiting to be invested or reinvested in other securities.
3. One seldom has enough perspective from the beginning to evaluate either stocks or the suggestions of a broker. This step will get you started while giving you time to learn about other types of securities.

Consider the previous example of the spare $500. If the money had been put into a money-market fund it could have been taken out when an emergency arose, without commission or cost, and one would also retain all the interest earned for the time the money was invested.

Mutual funds and money-market funds are discussed in chapters 12 and 13; I will not attempt definitions here. For the moment, the point is only that the money-market fund offers high interest, relative safety, liquidity, and many do not charge for opening an account or for deposits or withdrawals. The major funds are not sold through brokers so you will have to be in touch with them. You will find their advertisements in the Yellow Pages and in the business section of the newspapers. Most have toll-free numbers you can call for information and application forms.

For beginners and experienced investors alike, sources of information are important. Here are some easily accessible places to start.

- The business pages of your local newspaper. Most have good coverage, and there are excellent syndicated columns. Also, don't be afraid to tackle an article on a subject about which you know next-to-nothing. Most of

the time you will find terms defined. After all, they *want* you to understand what they're talking about.

- Television and radio news reports. Listen for news that will affect business: recent trends, a new drug, new regulations, a late freeze, an out-
  break of hostilities, etc. Money can be made by correctly interpreting the
  news.
- Business reports on television (and there are a few on radio), public
  television and the cable channels. A word of warning here. Don't buy
  stock on the basis of tips from television programs. Back the information
  with a bit of research. Check an annual report. Ask your broker.
- Business magazines or newspapers. Try *The Wall Street Journal, Forbes,
  Financial World,* or *Barron's.* Your newsstand will have a selection.
- Ask for information. Every brokerage company, every exchange, every
  mutual fund, every bank has some kind of brochure, booklet, or pamph-
  let explaining their products, services, or securities. This may sound
  simplistic but it is a resource that many people overlook. *The Wall Street
  Journal* will have dozens of places to write for information.

Caution: When requesting material or information don't give
your phone number unless you are seriously interested in that particular service or investment. Particularly in commodities, you can be
plagued to death by telephone salesmen.

- In most financial periodicals you will see advertisements for advisory
  letters. (These are usually monthly letters containing buy and sell recommendations.) Some offers are for a trial sampling of a variety of different
  letters at a modest price. Try a selection while you can get them in an
  introductory offer. Regular subscriptions are often high. You should see
  several before deciding to subscribe. The major full-service brokerages
  also publish investment letters periodically which are free to their customers. Unless you are a very active trader, that, plus the other sources
  listed above, may be enough.

How to Choose a Broker

One of the most anxiety-provoking decisions you have to make as an
investor is choosing a broker. Do you have to have one? I'm afraid so.
While it is possible for individuals to transfer stock among themselves
without a broker it is hardly realistic to think of acquiring very much
stock in that fashion. Any securities bought on an exchange must be

bought by an individual who is also a member of that exchange, and that means a broker. In fact, if your broker is not a member of a particular exchange, say the New York Stock Exchange, and you wish to purchase a security traded on that exchange, then your broker will have to go through another broker who *is* a member.

There are basically two kinds of brokers: full-service brokers and discount brokers. The most important differences between them have to do with the size of the commissions they charge and the services they offer.

Most brokers buy and sell securities for customers' accounts. They also will hold the securities in their customers' accounts for safekeeping (if the customers choose) and provide a monthly status report on those securities. Dividends and revenues from sales will be forwarded to the customer or sometimes held in a money-market account while the funds await reinvestment (although there is a minimum for the money-market account). They will also provide up-to-the-minute quotations for securities you are thinking about buying or selling.

This is about as far as the functions of discount and full-service brokers overlap (although there are some discount brokers who offer a few more services). With a discount broker you call (toll-free, if long distance), give your order, and the broker will follow your instructions. The basic discount broker will not advise you, make recommendations, nor comment on your order in any way. Service is usually extremely fast and your transaction will often be completed before you are off the phone.

With a full-service brokerage the investor has a one-to-one relationship with an individual who is assigned to handle the account (technically, he or she is not a broker but a registered representative or account executive). The broker will have suggestions and recommendations for securities. The suggestions will be from the firm's research department which often has considerable resources. Your investment objectives, your cash needs, your expectations and preferences will usually be taken into consideration. A money-market fund will often be available, and some brokerages even offer credit cards.

One of the most important factors in deciding what kind of broker to choose is the determination of what kind of investor you are going to be. If you rely heavily on an investment letter or if you just want to make up your own mind about investments, then you should take advantage of a discount broker's low fees. Why pay a full-service broker for advice or assistance you don't need? On the other hand, if you want a sounding board for your ideas, if you want advice, and certainly if you want a variety of investment suggestions offered for your selection, then a full-service broker is for you.

Commissions can vary considerably, even among full-service brokers. In general, the fees for discount brokers are anywhere from 40% to 70% of the full-service rates. Ask the brokers you are considering for a commission schedule and do some comparison shopping.

If you are looking for a broker for the first time, arrange appointments with several (don't make the mistake of talking to only one). Be honest about your needs and limitations. Choose the broker with whom you feel the most comfortable, who offers the best services, and who seems most responsive to your needs. As a rule, it is best to select a firm that is a member of the New York Stock Exchange. They are regulated somewhat more closely. Your account will be insured, but should your brokerage fail, your securities could be tied up for weeks, even months.

With a brokerage firm there are a variety of accounts that can be opened. The basic cash account requires payment for all purchases on the average of five business days after the transaction. Options, at least certain kinds of option transactions, require a special options account. Any credit extended to a customer requires what is called a margin account. More will be said about the margin account later but for a beginner a cash account should be adequate.

One word of advice at this point: Don't be alarmed if the broker you interview suggests stock options. There are a few option strategies that constitute a conservative and safe way to increase income from certain stocks in your portfolio. You may want to check these strategies in chapters 14 and 15.

If you have already invested you have probably discovered that the recommendations of your brokerage firm are not infallible. Conceivably, they are right more times than wrong, but even the wisest market researcher on Wall Street (whoever that might be) has made mistakes. However, if you feel you are not getting the return from your investments that you have a right to expect or if you do not feel you are getting adequate service, it is easy enough to switch brokers. Simply select another firm and it will have the necessary forms to switch your account.

A Look at the Exchanges

As a final consideration before proceeding to the quotations, we will take a look at the exchanges. Exchanges do not buy or sell securities nor do they set prices for them (except to make certain regulatory decisions). Exchanges are simply marketplaces where a variety of financial instruments may be traded. For example, both the American Stock Exchange (Amex) and the New York Stock Exchange (NYSE) trade stocks, bonds, and options. The latter also trades stock index futures on its new subsidiary, the New York Futures Exchange.

The largest organized exchange in the United States is the New York Stock Exchange. On the average, 80% of the value of all common stocks publicly traded are traded on the NYSE.

Exchanges serve two main purposes. Historically, the primary function of an exchange is to provide a place where buyers and sellers can meet in order to transact business. In New York, in 1792, twenty-four men decided to meet regularly under a large buttonwood tree near Wall Street for the purpose of trading stock. A year later they moved indoors into the recently completed Tontine Coffee House on Wall Street. That was the beginning of the New York Stock Exchange. The American Stock Exchange also originated as an outdoor market where traders met; from 1850 to 1921 the Outdoor Curb Market (as it was then called) was one of the most colorful tourist attractions in New York City.

The second function of an exchange is to provide support equipment and facilities for trading. The Tontine Coffee House provided little more than shelter from the weather and, presumably, refreshment. Today, the support facilities, particularly communications, are of paramount importance. We will say more about those facilities in a moment.

Trading on an exchange floor is restricted to members of the exchange (that is, those who have a "seat" on the exchange) or their representatives. Each exchange imposes rules on the conduct of its members (the traders) and restrictions on the manner in which trading can take place. These regulations and the more general guidelines of the Securities and Exchange Commission have created fair and orderly markets that have, in turn, earned the confidence of investing institutions and of the public in general.

Only securities that are registered with the exchange may be traded on that exchange. Each exchange has requirements for listed securities having to do with the number of shares in public hands, the number of shareholders, the total value of the shares, and the earning power and stability of the company.

The type of market that has evolved on the exchanges is an auction market. This is not the one-way auction market that one usually thinks of where only buyers compete with one another, but a two-way auction where the buyers compete for the lowest prices they can get and the sellers compete for the highest prices they can get. This kind of market makes for a flexible and yet surprisingly stable pattern of prices.

In the last forty years the volume of trading on security markets has made automation absolutely necessary. On August 18, during the bull market of 1982, daily volume on the NYSE exceeded 100 million shares for the first time in history. Today, such volume is commonplace, and it is impossible for specialists to oversee every trade. Instead, they watch the flow of trades on a computer, intervening as general trends begin to develop. Only large transactions are personally negotiated.

In order to understand how a stock exchange works, we will walk through a typical transaction as it might have been handled on the NYSE twenty-five years ago. The division of labor at that time makes the overall procedure particularly clear. Then we will take a look at how automation has altered the process.

If you gave an order for a NYSE-listed security to a broker, he or the order department of that brokerage would send the order to the floor of the NYSE. If your brokerage firm was a member of the NYSE, the booth maintained by that broker would receive the order. If your brokerage firm was not a member, then it would send the order to the booth of another brokerage firm that was a member and with whom it had an agreement to handle its transactions. The floor broker at the booth would take your order to the trading post where that stock was traded. (Trading posts are roughly round and in the middle of the trading floor; brokers' booths are square and located around the edges of the room.) At the trading post there would be other brokers who had come to that spot in order to buy or sell that particular stock, and the specialist for that stock would also be there.

The specialist is a broker assigned to a stock by the exchange. It is the specialist's job to keep the price of the stocks to which he is assigned as stable as possible. This means buying and selling from his own account when there are more orders to sell than to buy, or vice versa. This is a vital role in price stability. Otherwise an imbalance of buy or sell orders could drive prices wildly in one direction or another.

It was likely that your trade would be between your broker and another broker and not involve the specialist. (Since both brokers would be representing their own clients, what you have, essentially, is one individual buying from another individual.) The floor broker would report back to your brokerage firm's office and you would be notified.

The above scenario was the normal method for trading securities for many years. Now it resembles this procedure only for large orders above 1,200 shares. Substantially larger orders than that (10,000+) are traded on an institutional system, known as ITS, or traded off the floor altogether. At any rate, market orders of *less* than 1,200 shares (which constitute the bulk of individual investor purchases and sales) are now handled by an automated system known as Super DOT. The DOT stands for Designated Order Turnaround.

Through the DOT system, orders are transmitted directly to the trading post. Buy and sell orders are matched and executed electronically as far as possible, and reports of executions are returned directly to the broker's office. Data from all DOT activity is displayed on the specialist's monitor so that he can see at a glance how orders are going, discern any trends, and, in general, monitor all trading activity even though he may not participate directly in those trades.

About 57% of all trades on the NYSE are now processed in this manner. The average turnaround time is fifty-eight seconds.

In the execution of your orders the DOT system and floor traders have other resources besides the New York Stock Exchange. The Intermarket Trading System (ITS) connects the seven major stock markets and makes the quotes of all securities available on all markets where that particular security is traded. Thus if your broker sees on one of the monitor screens that a better price is available on, for instance, the Midwest Stock Exchange, the trade is sent to the specialist for that security on the other exchange.

The DOT system is less personal, much more efficient, and relatively error free. It is also more realistic. There is no reason to take a transaction through a highly labor-intensive and costly procedure for no benefit, and it is quite certain that a single trade of a few hundred shares of any NYSE issue hasn't a ghost of a chance of moving the market. However, as part of a trend, as one of many orders, it may contribute to a price move.

That brings us to the question, what *does* cause the price of stocks to change? The answer is supply and demand. Specifically, it is an *imbalance* of supply and demand: the *continuous* pressure of more buy orders than sell orders or more sell orders than buy orders. High volume will not move prices so long as the orders are fairly evenly split between buy and sell. The absence of orders will not move prices since there is still not an imbalance created. But when a specialist suddenly finds twenty-five orders to buy a particular stock with no offers to sell, he starts moving the price.

Floor Operations

At first sight the trading floor of any exchange looks like a mass of confusion. Let's take a closer look at the NYSE and see if we can sort out some of the components we have been talking about. In the photograph on page xxii we see a section of the main trading floor. In the lower left-hand corner is part of a trading booth (as opposed to a trading post). These booths are located around the edge of the floor and maintained by member firms of the exchange. Here the floor broker with your brokerage firm will receive your order and take it to the trading post where that security is traded.

In the foreground you see trading post eleven (note the "11" above the post among the TV screens). This post is made up of two parts that seem to be connected by the large cooling unit and the "raceway" marked in the photograph. The post is made up of 22 specialist's panels consisting of two vertically stacked TV screens, called "crowd" CRTs (cathode ray tubes) and the counter space below. (You can count the 11 crowd CRTs around each half of the post.) The CRTs, of course, display information about the securities traded at that post location. There is one specialist at each panel and a number of different securities are assigned to him.

The photograph on page xxiii shows a smaller booth without the people and with much of the counter equipment removed. Here we can clearly see the small television screen on long arms protruding from the booth. This is the specialist's monitor screen. It shows, essentially, the same information as the "crowd CRTs" but the arrangement allows the specialist to face away from the booth panel and be prepared to meet traders approaching his position. Note also the instruments that make up the service core of the Intermarket Trading System of which we spoke before.

The photograph on page xxiv shows a closeup from the photograph on page xxii. Here various individuals are identified as well as some of the more important support equipment.

trading post "raceway" contains electrical cables for communication and electrical power. Also contains water pipes for cooling system.

two television screens called "crowd" CRTs for the specialist's position below. They show current prices, volume, and other information pertaining to the securities traded at this position.

cooling unit for electronic instruments

support cable

(Edward C. Topple, NYSE photographer)

part of a trading booth. Here the floor brokers receive orders from their offices and take them to the specialists positions (at the trading posts) where the specified securities are traded.

one half of trading post 11 containing 11 specialists positions called "panels." Each specialist panel has two television screens ("crowd" CRTs) *vertically* stacked above it.

FLOOR OF THE NEW
YORK STOCK EXCHANGE

keyboard for operating
vendor terminal which
can be connected to
whatever additional
information services the
specialist may need, for
instance, options or futures
quotations

service core for the
Intermarket Trading
System (ITS) that links
the NYSE with six
other stock markets

(Edward C. Topple, NYSE photographer)

specialist seat

storage

selector channel switch
for operating the
specialist's monitor
screen

specialist's monitor
screen, will show same
information as "crowd"
CRT and other information

**EMPTY POST ON
FLOOR OF THE NEW
YORK STOCK EXCHANGE**

post number and indicator lights:
1st light (white) calls
    supervisor to phone
2nd light (blue) calls
    for Registered Competi-
    tive Market Maker to
    assist in transaction
3rd light (red) calls for
    Intermarket Trading
    System supervisor

specialist clerk
probably recording
a transaction

printer that prints
ITS transaction
confirmations

(Edward C. Topple, NYSE photographer)

exchange reporter
recording transactions
for ticker tape

mark-sensitive card
reader records
transactions for
ticker tape service

stock specialist in
front of his panel
watching his monitor
screen

CLOSEUP OF
TRADING POST

(courtesy New York Stock Exchange Archives)

EARLY NYSE TRADING POST

At one time trading posts were literally "posts" as can be seen from this 1870s cartoon of trading on the New York Stock Exchange. "U P." stands for Union & Pacific Railroad, the securities of which were traded at this position on the floor. Hand signals, such as those shown here, are still in use today so that traders can make themselves understood over the noise and activity around them.

PART ONE

HOW TO READ
STOCK MARKET
QUOTATIONS

1 New York and American Stock Exchange Quotations

A. Background

Most newspapers carry the financial quotations for stocks, bonds, and mutual funds. To a lesser degree they may also report prices on options, commodities, and money-market instruments. In the following chapters, the listings for each are examined in detail.

We will begin with stock quotations.

Stock is a unit of ownership in a corporation. Corporations sell these units (also called "shares") in order to raise capital. Owners of stock, as part owners of the corporation, are entitled to share in the fortunes of the corporation by, for example, receiving dividends. They also participate in the management of the corporation by voting on major issues and by electing members of the board of directors.

U.S. stock quotations are the most widely disseminated financial quotations in the world. There are three major listings, titled for the markets on which they report.

New York Stock Exchange   also listed in various papers as New York Stock Exchange Issues, NYSE-Composite Transactions, and Combined New York Stock Exchange Trading

American Stock Exchange   also listed as Amex-Composite Transactions

Over-the-Counter   also listed as Nasdaq Over-the-Counter, Over-the-Counter Markets, and OTC

In addition to the listings shown above, there may also be quotations from regional exchanges (such as the Boston, Philadelphia, Midwest, and Pacific exchanges), Canadian, and other foreign exchanges. In this chapter we will limit ourselves to quotations of the two national exchanges, the New York Stock Exchange and the American Stock Exchange, both of which usually appear in the same format.

B. The Quotations

1) In General

The term "quotation" is used throughout this book to mean any kind of report on the activity or state of a security as reflected in its price. Thus the minimum requirement for a quotation is only the name of a security and a price of some kind; this might be the last price at which the security traded or it might be a price which someone is willing to pay (known as a "bid" price). Usually, however, quotations are more extensive. Additional prices might be given, such as the highest and lowest prices over a certain time period; the dividend amount might also be shown as well as the number of shares traded.

Stock quotations vary from paper to paper, but the typical format presents a one-line string of information in the following order. (*The Wall Street Journal* quotations are somewhat more detailed and will be discussed in section 4 and section 9.)

Typical Stock Quotation Format

year's price range	name of the stock	dividend amount	additional information on dividend and price	number shares traded	price range for day	price change from previous day

There are certain types of security analysts known as technicions who base most of their investment decisions on the past price patterns of a security. Usually, however, investors require more information and research before investing or advising others to invest. It is *not* recommended that you invest based on data given in a typical quotation. Additional information is vital, such as the financial condition of the company and the condition of the market sector in which that company operates.

It is from current quotations that you are informed of the present state of a security. Sometimes newspaper quotations are current and sometimes they are not. Saturday and Sunday papers will carry complete quotations from the previous Friday, and since the exchanges are closed on the weekend (i.e., on the day the paper comes out) those quotations will be current.

Weekday papers usually list quotations from the day before, and sometimes an afternoon paper will carry quotations from that morning's transactions (e.g., as of 10:30 AM or as of noon). However, the previous day's quotations are usually satisfactory unless (1) you are a very active trader, (2) you trade in relatively volatile securities such as options or commodity futures or (3) you are going to make a sale or purchase that day and you need an up-to-the-minute quotation. In any of those cases you would call a broker, consult a quote terminal, or check the security on the cable television ticker quotation service.

Most of the time, however, you will probably be reading listings in the print medium. This is by far the most convenient and accessible source of information on securities, and one which it is important to understand thoroughly.

2) 52-Week High and Low

Stock prices are always quoted in points. A point equals $1.00, so a single share of a stock quoted at 12½ points would cost $12.50; a hundred shares would cost $1,250.00.

The stock quotations in the following example are of stocks listed on the New York Stock Exchange. The first two columns in this format give the highest and lowest prices paid for the listed stock during the immediately preceding 52-week period.

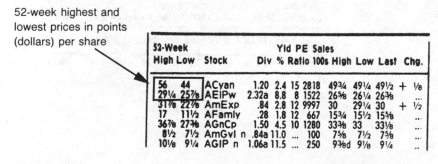

52-week highest and lowest prices in points (dollars) per share

52-Week High Low	Stock	Div	Yld %	PE Ratio	Sales 100s	High	Low	Last	Chg.
56 44	ACyan	1.20	2.4	15	2818	49¾	49¼	49½	+ ⅛
29¼ 25⅞	AEIPw	2.32a	8.8	8	1522	26⅝	26¼	26⅜	...
31⅞ 22⅞	AmExp	.84	2.8	12	9997	30	29¼	30	+ ½
17 11½	AFamly	.28	1.8	12	667	15¾	15½	15⅝	...
36⅞ 27⅜	AGnCp	1.50	4.5	10	1280	33⅜	33	33⅛	...
8½ 7½	AmGvl n	.84a	11.0	...	100	7⅝	7½	7⅝	...
10⅛ 9¼	AGIP n	1.06a	11.5	...	250	9⅜d	9⅛	9¼	..

(The New York Times)

For the first stock shown, American Cyanamid Co., the highest price during the previous 52-week period was $56 per share. The lowest was $44.

Fractions, if any, are usually in (multiples of) eighths of a dollar. Thus, the second stock's high of 29¼ was $29.25, and the low of 25⅞ was $25.875.

Sometimes stocks trading below one or two points are listed in sixteenths or thirty-seconds of a dollar. This is rare for NYSE and Amex listings, but it is somewhat more common in over-the-counter (OTC) quotations. The following table gives the values of sixteenths of a dollar and their multiples.

Fractions of a Dollar

1/16 = $.0625	5/16 = $.3125	9/16 = $.5625	13/16 = $.8125
1/8 = $.125	3/8 = $.375	5/8 = $.625	7/8 = $.875
3/16 = $.1875	7/16 = $.4375	11/16 = $.6875	15/16 = $.9375
1/4 = $.25	1/2 = $.50	3/4 = $.75	

Stocks are usually purchased in round lots.

Round lots are units of 100 shares. Fewer than 100 shares is an *odd lot*. A block of 150 shares, for example, is made up of one round lot and an odd lot of 50. (However, see qualifier "z" on p. 35 for an exception.) There is often an extra transaction charge for the purchase or sale of odd lots on the New York and American Exchanges.

A round lot (100 shares) of the stock listed below—

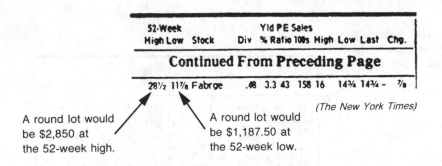

52-Week				Yld	PE	Sales				
High	Low	Stock	Div	%	Ratio	100s	High	Low	Last	Chg.

Continued From Preceding Page

28½	11⅞	Fabrge	.48	3.3	43	158	16	14¾	14¾	– ⅞

(The New York Times)

A round lot would be $2,850 at the 52-week high.

A round lot would be $1,187.50 at the 52-week low.

—would be $2,850.00 if purchased at the previous 52-week high, and $1,187.50 if purchased at the 52-week low. Note that the practice of purchasing in lots of 100 shares makes fractions of a cent rarely a part of an actual purchase price. When there *is* a fraction, it is rounded off to the nearest cent, and half-cents are rounded off to the next-highest cent.

Interpretation: The 52-week high and low are helpful when considering the current price at which a stock is selling. If you are considering buying a stock but the current price is close to the 52-week high, you might wait until it is lower (unless you have good reason to feel that the price will continue to rise or unless you feel that it is nevertheless a good investment). If you are considering selling, it might be a good time to sell (unless, again, you have good reason to think the price of the stock will continue to rise).

On the other hand, should the current price be near the 52-week low, you might get a bargain if you are considering a purchase. (Buying stock when it is at or near its yearly lows, or attempting to time purchases in such a manner, is known as "bottom fishing.") Of course, there might be a reason for the price to be low; for instance if a company were in financial difficulty a low price could be no bargain.

Some investors will not hesitate to buy a stock at an all-time high, and there will always be cases where this is profitable. However, the beginner should be warned that there is a higher degree of risk in buying a stock when it is high, or, indeed, buying stock in general when the market is high.

One must remember that most financial quotations do not include the broker's commission. The sale or purchase of stock usually requires the services of a stockbroker, and there is a fee for either transaction. (The types of brokers and their fees are discussed in the introduction.)

Other points: Stocks that have been trading for less than 52 weeks are called "new issues." In this case, the 52-week high and low are understood to be representative of the stock only as of the inception of trading. New issues are indicated by an "n" after the stock name.

A stock split can also affect the quotation of the 52-week high and low. See the definition of "split" in the glossary.

Sometimes, particularly in daily listings, 52-week highs and lows are omitted.

Name of stock appears in first column when 52-week high and low are omitted. →

Stock	Div.	PE	Sls hds	Daily Hi	Lo	Lst Trn	Net Chg.
SonyCp	.13e	12	1950	15¼	14⅞	15⅛	
SooLin	2.40a	6	1	27¾	27¾	27¾ +	¼
SourcC	2.60		15	21¾	21⅜	21¾ +	⅜
SrcCp pf	2.40		2	16¾	16¾	16¾	
SoAtlFn			44	2¼	2⅛	2¼	
SCrEG	1.92	6	x202	14¾	14⅝	14¾ +	⅛
SoJerIn	2.00	5	3	18⅛	17⅞	18⅛ +	¼
Soudw s	.50	6	12	31⅝	31⅛	31⅝ +	⅝

(St. Louis Post-Dispatch)

The above quotations and most of the quotations in this book are from newspapers that receive their financial data from the Associated Press (AP). The United Press International (UPI) also supplies stock quotations, although mostly smaller newspapers carry them. Recent changes in the UPI financial data system allow newspapers to change the format of the quotations, to select and print only stocks of special or local interest, and to shorten the quotation list to conform to the space available by deleting smaller-priced issues. Frequently newspapers cite the source of their stock quotations (AP or UPI) at the beginning of their listings, as in the example below.

stock quotation from the United Press International (UPI) →

NEW YORK (UPI) — Following are nationwide composite prices for selected stocks listed on the American Stock Exchange.
Wednesday. June 14. 1989

		P-E	Sales (hds)	Last	Net Chg.
Acton		31	60	20¼	
Adams	Resr	5	2	1¾	
Aircoa	2.40	..	72	11¾	+ ¼
Amdahl	.10	11	2430	21⅝	— ⅝
Am Biltr	.15	7	8	x18½	
AMaizeA	.52	11	16	20¼	— ⅛

(The Scrantonian Tribune)

3) Name of the Stock

In the following example, the third column lists the name of the stock, or, more accurately, the company issuing the stock. If there is room, the entire name is given (except for words like "company" or "corporation"). In this example, only the last quotation utilizes the entire company name, Exxon.

52 - Week High	Low	Stock - Div	Yld %	P/E Ratio	Sales 100s	High	Low	Last	Chg.
36¼	20½	ExCel s 1.48	7.0	6	206	21¼	21¼	21¼	......
15	12½	Exclsr 1.89e	14.3	..	5	13¼	13¼	13¼	......
38⅝	29⅜	Exxon s 3	10.0	5	6371	30½	30	30⅛	— ½

(Los Angeles Times)

name of the stock ↗

Most of the time, company names must be abbreviated. When this is the case, obvious abbreviations are used whenever possible. "Un-

Carb," for instance, is Union Carbide, and "IntPapr" is International Paper.

Unfortunately, obvious abbreviations do not exist for all stocks. The following, for instance—

> AcadIns
> CrmK
> ElMeMg

—could be difficult to interpret unless one were already familiar with their names:

> AcadIns = Academy Insurance Group
> CrmK   = Crompton & Knowles
> ElMeMg = Electronic Memories & Magnetics

Note that the abbreviated or shortened form of the name is usually *not* the "ticker" symbol for a stock.

A **ticker symbol** is the abbreviation used for a stock by the exchanges themselves for the purpose of immediate reporting on ticker display boards in other exchanges, ticker-tape machines, and quote terminals throughout the country. These abbreviations are made as short as possible because of the volume of transactions that must be reported. Amex and NYSE ticker symbols are made up of one to three capital letters. OTC stocks utilize four or five capital letters.

Thus there are three labels for every stock:

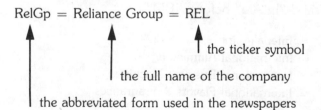

> RelGp = Reliance Group = REL

the ticker symbol

the full name of the company

the abbreviated form used in the newspapers

Interpretation: Ticker symbols are not used in newspapers—at least not as the sole means of identifying stocks—because, in their brevity, they do not resemble closely enough the securities they represent. Longer abbreviations, being closer to the actual names of the companies, are easier to remember and easier for the average investor to find in newspaper listings. *The Wall Street Journal* lists the ticker symbols in the fourth column of its stock listings, but this is *in addition* to the abbreviations given in the third column. (For an example, see section 4, "Ticker Symbols Quoted.")

Other points: The alphabetization of stocks within the listings may seem a problem not worthy of attention, but when you are dealing with highly abbreviated names, it can create additional confusion. Unfortunately, the two news services use different systems, and both can sometimes be found in the same paper.

In the AP system, all capital-letter names appear before upper-and-lowercase names if they are strictly *letters* in the company name and not each the first letter of a word. Thus in this system "CTS" comes before "Cabot" as in the following example:

```
CP Nat  = CP National
CSX     = CSX Corporation
CTS     = CTS Corporation
Cabot   = Cabot Corporation
Cadenc  = Cadence Industries
```

In the UPI system, capital-letter names are not grouped in the beginning but treated like any other words. This makes a company name like CTX Corporation appear close to the end of the Cs while in the first system it would appear close to the beginning.

In addition, one must remember that abbreviations are alphabetized *as if* they were full names. This makes the order of the following abbreviations alphabetically correct. (Note that "Intrlk" comes before "IntAlu," and "IntAlu" before "IBM.")

```
Intrlk  = Interlake, Inc.
IntAlu  = International Aluminum
IBM     = International Business Machines
IntFlav = International Flavors & Fragrances
```

Some types of listings delete stocks that do not trade during the time period covered by the quotation. There may be a lack of buyer interest in a stock or, for a variety of reasons, trading in a particular stock can be suspended. If you are sure of the exchange and abbreviation of a stock but cannot find its quotation in the newspaper, that may be the reason. On Monday *The Wall Street Journal* carries a list of NYSE and

Amex stocks that did not trade during the previous week, under the heading "Closing Bid and Asked of Stocks Not Traded Last Week."

An exception to the above is the so-called "all stocks" listing. In this case the quotations list the last price for every issue no matter if the trade was the same day or weeks earlier.

Qualifiers, usually consisting of just one or two lower-case letters, indicate additional information about the listing. These qualifiers can be found, among other places, immediately following the stock name.

If there are no qualifiers following the stock name, then the listing is for common stock.

No qualifier following the stock name indicates that the listing is for common stock.

52-Week High	52-Week Low		Div.	Yield pct.	P.E. ratio	Sales (hds.)	Week's High	Week's Low	Last	Net chg.
29⅝	15¼	SeaCont	.42	2.2	5	825	21	19	19¼	— ⅝
29⅝	22⅞	Seafst	1.28	4.7	6	572	28¼	27¼	27⅜	— ¾
65¼	51	Seagrm	1.40	2.7	9	x2533	53¼	d 51	51⅜	— 1¼

(Chicago Tribune)

There are two kinds of stock issued by corporations. Everything said about stock up to this point is applicable to common stock, and that is by far the most prevalent type issued. The other type of stock issued is preferred stock. A "pf" following the company name, as in the second stock in the example below, indicates that the listing is for preferred stock.

52-Week High	52-Week Low		Div.	Yield pct.	P.E. ratio	Sales (hds.)	Week's High	Week's Low	Last	Net chg.
13¾	6⅞	Rudick	.56	4.2	7	4	13⅜	13¼	13⅜	+ ⅛
13¾	7	Rudck pf	.56	4.3	..	7	13⅛	13⅛	13⅛	......

(Chicago Tribune)

Qualifier "pf" indicates preferred stock.

Preferred stock is similar to common stock except that the former has a fixed dividend rate. Payment of these dividends takes precedence over the dividends of common stock. Also, they are sometimes cumulative (should the company be unable to meet its obligations). However, preferred dividends *can* be omitted if the company earnings are inadequate. Holders of

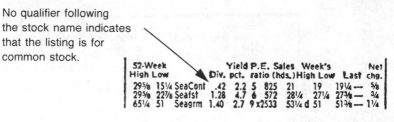

preferred stock do not usually have voting privileges, and it is possible that preferred stock can be recalled and paid off, unlike common stock.

Note in the example above that Rudick (Ruddick Corporation) has issued both common stock and preferred stock. The second listing, in order to make room for the "pf," uses a shorter abbreviation of the company name.

Some companies have more than one issue of preferred stock and distinguish among them with a letter after the "pf." In the following example, White Consolidated Industries lists (in addition to common stock) a preferred "A" and a preferred "C."

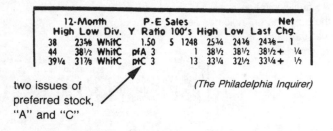

| 12-Month | | | P-E | Sales | | | | Net |
High	Low	Div.	Y Ratio	100's	High	Low	Last	Chg.
38	23⅝	WhitC	1.50	5 1248	25¾	24⅜	24⅜−	1
44	38½	WhitC	pfA 3	1	38½	38½	38½+	¼
39¼	31⅞	WhitC	pfC 3	13	33¼	32½	33¼+	½

two issues of preferred stock, "A" and "C"

(The Philadelphia Inquirer)

It is necessary to distinguish among different preferred stock issues since they usually have different dividend rates or other distinguishing features.

Sometimes different issues of common stock must also be differentiated. One issue, for instance, might have dividend priority over the other. This is the case in the following example where Moog, Inc., class B common stock is listed separately from the class A issue.

| 30⅞ | 12½ | MoogB | .20 | 12 | 251 | 16½ | 14 | 16¼+ | 1½ |
| 31 | 12½ | MoogA | .28 | 12 | 638 | 16¼ | 13¾ | 15⅞+ | 1½ |

two issues of common stock, class B and class A, differentiated by letters

(The Philadelphia Inquirer)

Preferred stock constitutes equity in a company, as does common stock.

Equity is ownership in a company usually by means of common and preferred stock. (Caution: Equity also means the excess value of stock in a company above any indebtedness.)

A "wt" following the stock name indicates warrants, not stock. In the next example, there are two different listings for U.S. Air. The first is for warrants, and the second is for preferred stock.

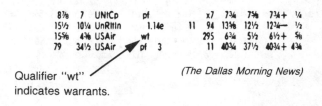

8⅞	7	UNtCp	pf			x7	7¾	7⅝	7¾+	¼
15½	10¼	UnRltln		1.14e	11	94	13⅝	12½	12¾–	½
15⅝	4⅜	USAir	wt			295	6¾	5½	6½+	⅝
79	34½	USAir	pf	3		11	40¾	37½	40¾+	4¾

Qualifier "wt" indicates warrants.

(The Dallas Morning News)

Warrants are long-term guarantees or *rights to purchase* a limited amount of stock at a fixed price from the company that issues the stock. They are often part of a new issue (in some cases actually attached to the stock certificates) and are valid for five to ten years. To obtain the warrant specifications, one must call a broker or consult a stock guide. Warrants may be traded like stock, but they do not in themselves constitute equity in a corporation.

Interpretation: If one owned warrants guaranteeing the right to purchase a particular stock at, for example, $10 a share, and the current price for that stock were $20 per share, then obviously such warrants would be of value. In this example, they would enable one to double one's money (excluding commissions), since, with the warrant, one could purchase the stock for $10 per share and immediately sell it for $20 per share. Or, one could sell the warrants, since they have a market price roughly equal to the "discount" from the market stock price.

4) Ticker Symbols Quoted

The Wall Street Journal has two additional columns of information in its stock quotations. One of these is for the ticker symbols. They immediately follow the name of the security. Unfortunately, ticker symbols are even less help in determining the full name of a stock than the abbreviation. However, with a ticker symbol you can check the security name with your broker. Brokers are usually not familiar with the newspaper abbreviations (abbreviations can be different depending on the sources quoting them, and they can also be changed), but since there is only one ticker symbol per security, it is easy to call up the security name on a quote terminal.

ticker symbol given in *The Wall Street Journal* quotations

	52 Weeks Hi	Lo	Stock	Sym	Div	Yld %	PE	Vol 100s	Hi	Lo	Close	Net Chg
	28⅝	21⅞	Hershey	HSY	.70	2.7	11	498	25½	25	25½	+ ⅜
	65½	43¾	HewlettPk	HWP	.34	.6	16	5311	55½	54½	54⅞	+ ⅛
s	43	28	Hexcel	HXL	.44	1.3	15	55	34½	34⅛	34½	+ ⅜
	19	14⅛	HiShearInd	HSI	.44	2.8	35	5	16	16	16	...
	10⅛	9	HighIncoTr	YLD	1.20a	13.0	...	486	9¼	9⅛	9¼	+ ⅛

(The Wall Street Journal)

5) Dividends

A ***dividend*** is an amount paid to an investor, usually in cash but sometimes in stock and sometimes in both cash and stock. It is distinct from an interest payment in that it is a division of part of the profits of a company among the ownership of the company.

Most dividends are paid regularly every quarter, but they may also be paid biannually, or annually, or even monthly. Some are paid irregularly, the amount and time being decided from year to year.

The third column lists the dividend per share in dollars and cents (fractions of a cent are truncated). This is an annual amount estimated on the basis of the most recent dividend payment unless indicated otherwise by a qualifier.

annual dividend per share in dollars

52-Week High	Low		Div.	Yield pct.	P.E. ratio	Sales (hds.)	Week's High	Low	Last	Net chg.
37⅝	26⅝	Squibb	1.26	4.1	13	3730	31⅛	29½	30⅞	— ¼
14⅞	8¾	StaRite	.20e	1.9	6	83	11	10¼	10⅜	— ⅞
31⅝	15⅝	Staley	.80	4.2	5	1346	20¼	19	19¼	— ¾
34⅞	20½	StBPnt	.84	3.9	8	3159	24⅝ d	20½	21¾	— 3
21⅝	9¼	StdMot s	.56	3.2	8	447	18⅜	16	17⅜	— 1⅛
48½	32⅞	StOilCl	2.40	7.1	5	16860	35¾ d	32⅞	33⅝	— 2¼

(Chicago Tribune)

In the above example, the first stock in the column, Squibb Corporation, shows a dividend of $1.26 per share. For each round lot, this equals $126.00 per year. If the dividends are paid quarterly, an individual owning 100 shares of Squibb would receive a check for $31.50 every three months until the dividend is changed. A blank in the column means there is no cash dividend; there may, however, be a stock dividend.

Some companies are extremely conscientious about paying the same or increased dividends regularly, and some investors buy the stock of such companies for that reason. In cases where all profits are retained by the company (and no dividend is declared), the stockholder's only chance for gain is in the appreciation of the value of the stock (which it is hoped the reinvestment of profits will stimulate).

Some quotations list the dividend without a qualifier only if the dividend is actually a declared rate (presumably with a reasonable expectation of continuing unchanged for the year or longer). See qualifier "d" in the table of qualifiers at the end of the chapter.

Caution: The board of directors decides a company's dividends based on the company's earnings and the company's obligations and future plans. If, for example, a company were experiencing severe earnings problems, the board of directors might decide to lower dividends or terminate them altogether. On the other hand, increases in earnings could mean a raise in the dividend amount.

Numerous qualifiers appear before and after the dividend. See the section on "qualifiers" later in this chapter.

6) Yield

Yield percent is the percent of the current purchase price that the dividend returns annually. It is usually referred to as the "dividend yield."

percent of current purchase price yielded by the dividend

52-week High	52-week Low	Stock	Div.	Yld.	PE	Sales 100s	High	Low	Last	Chg.
27¾	10⅞	Fairchd	.80	6.0	3	608	13½	13⅛	13¼	— ⅛
45¾	26½	Fairc	pf3.60	13.	....	53	28¼	27¾	27⅞	— ⅛
15	10⅛	FamDl	s.34	2.4	10	8	14½	14	14¼	— ¼
15½	9⅜	FrWstF		....	....	6	9⅞	9⅜	9⅝	....
15	6⅜	Farah			8	289	8¾	8⅜	8⅜	— ⅛

(The Washington Post)

In the above quotation, Fairchild Industries closed at 13¼. The yearly dividend was $.80, which divided by $13.25 is .0603773, or (rounded off) a 6% dividend yield. In cases where there is no dividend, there can, of course, be no dividend yield and that column will be blank.

Caution: The dividend yield of common stock changes in the quotations as the price of the stock fluctuates or the dividend changes. However, once you purchase a stock, you lock in the stated dividend yield; and it will not change again unless the dividend does. The "dividend yield" column presents no new information since one can calculate the yield oneself, but it does save the time of performing the calculation for every stock with which one wishes comparisons.

Dividend yield is also helpful in assessing the attractiveness of stocks versus bonds. Since the early 1960s, the average percent return on a medium-term bond (for example, a 15-year bond) has been about 4 percent higher than the average stock dividend. This difference reflects the capital-gain potential of stocks. When the yield gap narrows, stocks appear more favorable; when it widens, bonds are often considered the better investment.

There are many qualifiers that appear in this column. See the section on qualifiers later in this chapter.

7) P-E Ratio

The P-E ratio, short for price-earnings ratio, represents the relationship

of	the price one must pay for one share of stock	to	how much that one share represents in earnings *of the company.*

If a corporation earns $10 million and has issued 5 million shares of stock, then each share can be said to represent $2 of earnings. If the current price for one share of stock is $16, then the ratio between the earnings ($2) and the price ($16) would be 8. Thus the P-E ratio in this example is 8.

What may be initially confusing about the P-E ratio is the word "earnings." Earnings are not dividends. Stockholders may think of their dividends as earnings, but the use of the term in this context refers only to the amount of money earned *by the corporation*. The decision by the board as to whether to grant dividends may depend on the size of the earnings, but that is the only relationship between the two figures. In the above example, in which the corporation earned $2 per share, the board might decide to grant a $.25 dividend, or more, or less, or none at all.

The calculation of the above example in more detail could look something like this:

All income revenue	$80,000,000
− purchases, taxes, and other expenses	− $70,000,000
Earnings (profit)	$10,000,000

$$\text{no. of shares outstanding} \; \overline{\big)\; \dfrac{\text{earnings per share}}{\text{earnings}}} \;=\; 5{,}000{,}000 \;\overline{\big)\; \dfrac{\$2}{\$10{,}000{,}000}}$$

$$\text{earnings per share} \; \overline{\big)\; \dfrac{\text{P-E ratio}}{\text{price of the stock}}} \;=\; \$2 \;\overline{\big)\; \dfrac{8 \;=\; \text{P-E ratio}}{\$16}}$$

In other words, the price-earnings ratio determines the relationship of

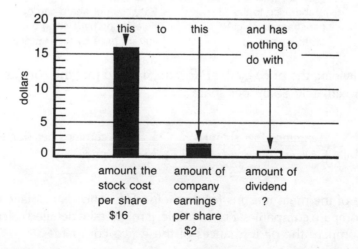

Again, what the board of directors decides to declare as a dividend is an entirely different matter. In this case, it would probably be a good deal less than $2 since it is *from* the earnings that dividends are paid. A company with a deficit will, by definition, have no earnings, and such a company will therefore have no P-E ratio and will probably not pay dividends.

The P-E ratio is an attempt to evaluate the shares of a company. Obviously it would be significant if a company earned a profit of, for example, $10 million, but one could not meaningfully relate such a fact to a specific company's shares until one knew how many shares there were. A share would be worth more if there were 5 million dividing up the earnings than if there were 500 million. In the present example, 5 million shares outstanding would represent $2 per share in earnings. If there were 500 million, then each share would represent 2¢. This presumably would affect the price of the stock.

One can determine the earnings per share from the P-E ratio and the current price. In the following example, the P-E ratio for International Business Machines is 11. This means that the current price of each share ($62.625) is 11 times the estimated earnings per share (probably with some rounding off).

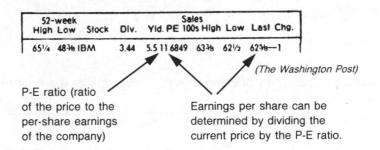

52-week High Low	Stock	Div.	Yld.	PE	Sales 100s	High	Low	Last	Chg.
65¼ 48⅞	IBM	3.44	5.5	11	6849	63⅜	62½	62⅜	—1

(The Washington Post)

P-E ratio (ratio of the price to the per-share earnings of the company)

Earnings per share can be determined by dividing the current price by the P-E ratio.

By dividing the price by the P-E ratio, we find that the company earns approximately $5.69 per share.

$$P\text{-}E\ ratio \overline{)\ \dfrac{earnings\ (per\ share)}{current\ price}} \qquad 11\ \overline{)\ \dfrac{\$\ 5.693\ \text{earnings per share}}{\$62.625\ \text{price}}}$$

One of the main reasons for providing P-E ratios is to make it easier to compare companies. For example, it might take detailed calculations to compare the performances of these two companies:

Company One
   a) earned $2 million last year
   b) has 8 million shares outstanding
   c) is priced at $3 per share

Company Two
   a) earned $45 million last year
   b) has 30 million shares outstanding
   c) is priced at $13.50 per share

However, if you knew that the P-E ratio was 12 for the first and 9 for the second, then you would know that your investment dollars would represent more earnings if placed in the second company. Specifically, for every dollar invested in Company One, that company would be earning $.0833; for every dollar invested in Company Two, that company would be earning $.1111. The P-E ratio should not, of course, be the sole measure of a stock, but it may be an important clue to future price performance.

The price of a stock is usually based more on what someone thinks the company *will* do, rather than on what the shares, in some concrete sense, are actually worth. However, the purpose of the P-E ratio is to attempt, at least, some kind of uniform evaluation.

Interpretation: It is difficult to categorically define a high P-E ratio, because the average tends to vary from industry to industry. For some, 15 is high; for others, 30. When a stock has a high P-E ratio in comparison to other companies in the same field, it reflects optimism, whether justified or not, in the stock's potential. The company may be bringing out new products; it may be a take-over candidate. But for whatever reason, the (relatively) higher the P-E ratio, the more speculative the stock becomes.

A low P-E ratio could mean that the stock is undervalued or, conversely, that it is not expected to appreciate soon. A low P-E ratio does not necessarily mean that the price of a stock is destined to rise; however, many consider it a sign of strength. A *drop* in P-E ratio definitely means strength if the drop is a result of increased earnings.

8) Sales in Hundreds

"Sales in hundreds," usually called "volume," records the number of shares traded in hundreds (i.e., in numbers of round lots); odd-lot transactions are not included. The following example shows that 280,200 shares of W.R. Grace & Company were traded. Since the quotation is from a Sunday paper, this is the total sales figure for the previous week. A daily paper would quote only shares traded during the previous day.

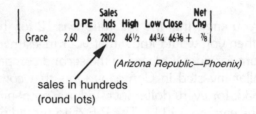

	D	PE	Sales hds	High	Low	Close	Net Chg
Grace	2.60	6	2802	46½	44¾	46⅜	+ ⅞

(Arizona Republic—Phoenix)

sales in hundreds
(round lots)

For those securities that trade in lots of other than 100 shares (10 shares for NYSE issues and 10, 25, or 50 shares for Amex issues), the sales are recorded in full (the actual number) and the entry flagged with the qualifier "z." (See "z" on p. 34.)

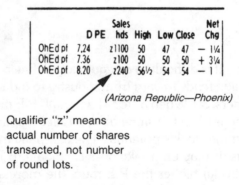

	D	PE	Sales hds	High	Low	Close	Net Chg
OhEd pf	7.24		z1100	50	47	47	− 1¼
OhEd pf	7.36		z100	50	50	50	+ 3¼
OhEd pf	8.20		z240	56½	54	54	− 1

(Arizona Republic—Phoenix)

Qualifier "z" means
actual number of shares
transacted, not number
of round lots.

Every trade is comprised of both a sale and a purchase. Without one, there cannot be the other. Should there not be a purchase order on the exchange floor when your broker sends in a sell order, then a specialist in that stock (who is assigned by the exchange) will purchase your shares for his own account at or near the current market price. This works in reverse if you are buying. In such a way liquidity (ease of purchase and sale) is maintained on the exchanges.

Interpretation: A sudden increase in the number of shares being traded might indicate a variety of things: good news, bad news, rumor of either, or the recommendation of the stock by a widely read advisory letter.

Many analysts attempt to predict future movement of stock based on whether volume increases when the price rises or when it falls (or whether it decreases under either condition). If the price of a stock does not seem to be sensitive to large volume changes, it could mean that there is an inordinately large number of shares outstanding.

Shares outstanding are the total number of shares issued of a particular stock that are owned by the public or by the board of directors.

9) High—Low—Close (or Last)

The "high," "low," and "close" are the stock's prices for the previous day's trading (or for the previous week's trading if quoted in a Sunday or weekly paper). These prices provide a rough profile of the stock's activity during the time period covered.

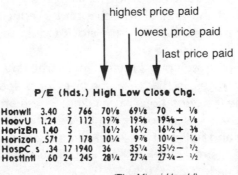

		P/E	(hds.)	High	Low	Close	Chg.
Honwll	3.40	5	766	70⅛	69⅛	70	+ ⅛
HoovU	1.24	7	112	19⅞	19⅝	19⅝	− ⅛
HorizBn	1.40	5	1	16½	16½	16½	+ ⅜
Horizon	.57t	7	178	10¼	9⅞	10⅛	− ¼
HospC s	.34	17	1940	36	35¼	35½	− ½
Hostintl	.60	24	245	28¼	27¾	27¾	− ½

(The Miami Herald)

For the first stock listed above, Honeywell, Inc., the highest price paid was 70⅛, the lowest was 69⅛, and the closing price was 70. During the course of the day's trading, the price fluctuated an entire point.

The *closing price* is the last price paid for a stock, whether the transaction took place hours before the final bell (on a light day of trading) or moments before closing. In a paper that quotes weekly prices, the closing price is the last price paid on the last day that the security traded.

Many times the closing price reported is not from either of the national exchanges. There are a large number of stocks simultaneously listed on one national exchange and on one or more of the regional exchanges. When NYSE or Amex issues trade on regional exchanges, the transactions are reported in the "composite" quotations of the relevant national exchange. (Virtually all quotations for NYSE and Amex are composite and include all trades of round lots no matter what the exchange.) Since the Pacific Exchange closes a half-hour later than the New York exchanges, it is frequently the case that the closing price of such issues is from a transaction on the Pacific Exchange.

It is a misconception that a stock always opens the next day at the price it closed the previous day. Sometimes news breaks after the market closes that will affect the price of the stock. In that case, the exchange specialist in that particular stock will confer with floor officials and directors of the exchange and raise or lower the price before the market opens, so as to stabilize the trading of that stock as quickly as possible. This process can also take place while the market is open, in which case trading in that particular stock may be halted.

Another situation in which a stock sometimes opens at a different price is the day it trades ex-dividend. (*See* the "x" qualifier in the table of qualifiers at the end of the chapter.) Frequently it opens lower, because any new purchaser of the stock would receive one less quarterly dividend.

Some evening editions provide the same-day quotations for the national exchanges. In that case, the last prices specified are indicated as of the time the quotations were taken. These are not closing prices, since the exchange is still open, but they are the latest prices the paper could obtain and still meet press deadlines. Sometimes these prices are labeled "last" instead of "close." In the following example, the last price column is labled "Ticker 1:30."

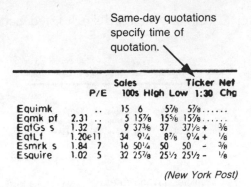

Same-day quotations
specify time of
quotation.

		Sales			Ticker	Net
	P/E	100s	High	Low	1:30	Chg
Equimk	..	15	6	5⅞	5⅞	......
Eqmk pf	2.31	..	5	15⅞	15⅝	15⅞ ......
EqtGs s	1.32	7	9	37¾	37	37⅛ + ⅜
EqtLf	1.20e11		34	9¼	8⅞	9¼ + ⅛
Esmrk s	1.84	7	16	50¼	50	50 − ⅜
Esquire	1.02	5	32	25⅞	25½	25½ − ⅛

(New York Post)

For NYSE and Amex, the stock market is an auction market. Traders (floor brokers) on the exchange floor negotiate prices with other traders or with an exchange specialist who handles a particular stock. The individual buying stock (through a broker) can usually find out within an eighth of a point what the transaction will cost. On the other hand, if the instruction is to buy "at the market," the transaction will be effected immediately at the best possible price.

At the market, sometimes called a "market order," means that the transaction (purchase or sale) will be executed immediately at the best asked or bid price that can be negotiated. This is the most common mode of transaction.

One can instruct the broker (who instructs the trader) not to pay above a certain price. This is known as a limit order.

Buy limit is an instruction not to pay more than a specified amount (the limit) for a particular stock. The buyer should specify the duration of time for which the order is good. Some brokerages impose their own time restraints for limit orders.

Buy limits can have the unfortunate effect of missing a purchase should the price of the stock not fall enough before turning up again.

Conversely, one can instruct a broker not to sell below a certain price. This is a *sell limit* order.

Two important qualifiers that sometimes appear in the day's (or week's) "high" and "low" columns are "u" and "d." A "u" (for "up") in the "high" column indicates that the high for that day (or for that week, if a weekly quotation) is a new 52-week high. In the following example, Procter & Gamble, the third stock listed, set a new high of 83¼.

Stock	Div	PE	Sales Hds	High	Low	Last	Net Ch
PrimeC		18	2666	24⅛	22¾	22⅞ −	⅝
PrimMt	.10r	10	119	16⅜	16	16⅜ +	¼
ProctG	4.20	10	1234	u83¼	81⅝	81⅝ −	⅛

(San Francisco Chronicle)

Qualifier "u" indicates
that a new 52-week high
has been reached.

A "d" (for "down") in the day's (or week's) "low" column indicates that the low for that day (or week, if a weekly paper) is a new 52-week low. In the following example, Crane Company, the fourth stock listed, shows a new low of 32.

Stock	Div	PE	Sales Hds	High	Low	Last	Net Ch
Cowles	1.00	18	7	29½	29½	29½	
CoxBds	.26	18	73	35	34⅝	34⅝ +	½
Craig		22	13	6⅞	6¾	6¾ −	⅛
Crane	1.60a	6	25	32⅜	d32	32 −	¼

(San Francisco Chronicle)

Qualifier "d" indicates
that a new 52-week low
has been reached.

The Wall Street Journal uses arrows in the left margin of the quotations to indicate new 52-week highs and lows.

In *WSJ* quotations an arrow pointing up indicates a new 52-week high.

An arrow pointing down indicates a new 52-week low.

| 52 Weeks | | | | | Yld | | Vol | | | | Net |
Hi	Lo	Stock	Sym	Div	%	PE	100s	Hi	Lo	Close	Chg
73½	61¾	Citicorp pf		6.00e	9.3	...	64	64⅜	63¾	64¼ −	⅛
↑101⅞	96	Citicorp pfB		7.70e	7.5	...	30	102	102	102 +	¼
53¾	35	CityTrBcp	CYT	1.12	2.6	8	58	44¼	43⅜	43½ −	½
↓ 3	¾	Clabir	CLG	...	...		41	¾	¹¹/₁₆	¾	...
8	2⅝	ClairStrs	CLE	.10	1.3	...	1002	7¾	7½	7⅝ −	⅛

(The Wall Street Journal)

Reasons for the rise and fall of stock prices are many and complex. However, most of them eventually resolve themselves to a single issue: supply and demand. If many people want to buy a particular stock, the price goes up; if many people want to sell, the price goes down.

Lack of buyer interest in itself is not enough to move stock prices. Issues that do not trade for an entire week will not necessarily show price movement. It is the continuous presence of sell orders when there are no buyers, and vice versa, that causes the prices of stocks to rise and fall.

10) Net Change

The last column usually indicates the net change. This is the amount of change (plus or minus) between the current closing price and the closing price of the previous trading day.

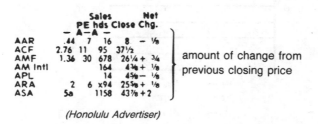

(Honolulu Advertiser)

For daily quotations, it is the difference between the current closing price and the day before. For weekly quotations, it is the change between the closing price on the last day of the present week's trading and the closing price on the last day of the previous week's trading.

In the above daily quote, the closing price for AAR Corporation was down ⅛ from the closing price the day before; the second stock was unchanged; the third, AMF, Inc., was up ¾ of a point.

If a last price (e.g., from a 1:30 ticker) is given instead of a closing price, the net change is still as of the previous day's close (and not the previous day's 1:30 ticker).

Caution: The net change has a limited meaning. It is a rough guide, at best, to the progress of a stock, and there are circumstances in which it can be misleading. Consider the example below. A stock could have been trading during one week (week "A") between 10 and 15 points, and it is possible that it could have closed low that week at 10. (The closing price is marked on the chart by a short, thick horizontal line.) The following week (week "B"), the high and low range could have been from 9 to 10.5, and the stock could have closed at 10.5.

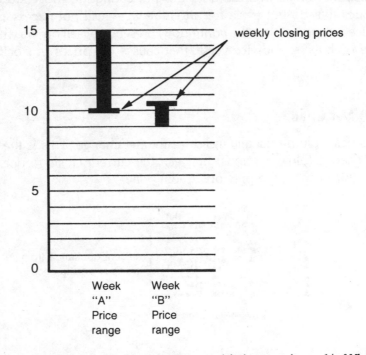

The net change at the end of week "B" would show only + ½. While the stock has recovered from the low of 9, and while it did close ½ point above the previous week's close, it has still not regained the enormous ground lost during week "A." Thus the net change should not be taken as an adequate representation of the previous week's trading.

C. Highlighting Price and Volume

As an additional help to readers, *The Wall Street Journal* indicates out-of-the-ordinary movement in the price and volume of NYSE, Amex, and some over-the-counter issues. All stocks showing a 5% or more increase in price (from their previous closing prices) are indicated by boldface type, and those showing the greatest volume changes are indicated by underlining.

In *WSJ* quotations boldface type indicates a 5% minimum increase in price.

In *WSJ* quotations underlining indicates securities with the greatest volume increase.

52 Weeks Hi	52 Weeks Lo	Stock	Sym	Div	Yld %	PE	Vol 100s	Hi	Lo	Close	Net Chg
40¾	35	MesaRoyTr	MTR	1.31e	3.3	35	17	39½	39¼	39½	+ ⅛
3⅜	**1⅜**	**MesabiTr**	**MSB**		**...**	**...**	**35**	**2⅝**	**2½**	**2⅝**	**+ ⅛**
7⅜	5¼	Mestek	MCC		...	9	97	6¾	6¾	6¾	...
15⅞	7½	MetroFin	MFC	.44b	2.8	8	143	15¾	15⅝	15⅝	...
7½	4½	MexicoFd	MXF	.34e	5.8	...	2956	6⅛	5¾	5⅞	+ ⅛
34⅝	22	MichEngy	MCG	1.52	4.9	181	6	30¾	30½	30¾	+ ¼

(The Wall Street Journal)

The volume-change underlining is shown only for forty securities on the NYSE, twenty on the AMEX, and forty on the National Market System (over-the-counter). It is also reserved for stocks selling at more than $5 per share and with an average daily volume of over 5,000 shares for the last 65 days; thus less substantial stocks and so-called penny stocks are excluded.

Do not mistake an up or down arrow (as discussed in section 9) for an indication of a new 52-week high or low. A stock can move up or down 5% or more without setting any new 52-week highs or lows.

D. Additional Information

The most comprehensive coverage for the largest number of stocks will be found in *Barron's,* a weekly periodical published by Dow Jones & Company. The treatment of dividends and earnings is the distinguishing feature of these quotations. The following is a sample from the quotations of NYSE-Composite Transactions.

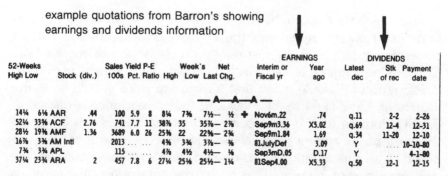

example quotations from Barron's showing earnings and dividends information

52-Weeks High	52-Weeks Low	Stock	(div.)	Sales 100s	Yield Pct.	P-E Ratio	Week's High	Week's Low	Last	Net Chg.	EARNINGS Interim or Fiscal yr	EARNINGS Year ago	DIVIDENDS Latest dec	DIVIDENDS Stk of rec	DIVIDENDS Payment date
		—A—A—A—													
14¼	6⅛	AAR	.44	100	5.9	8	8¼	7⅜	7½	– ½ ✚	Nov6m.22	.74	q.11	2-2	2-26
52¼	33⅝	ACF	2.76	741	7.7	11	38⅞	35	35⅞	– 2⅞	Sep9m3.36	X5.02	q.69	12-4	12-31
28½	19⅜	AMF	1.36	3689	6.0	26	25⅜	22	22⅝	– 2¾	Sep9m1.84	1.69	q.34	11-20	12-10
16⅞	3⅜	AM Intl		2013	...	...	4⅜	3¾	3⅞	– ⅜	81JulyDef	3.09	Y	....	10-10-80
7¾	3¾	APL		115	...	...	4⅞	4½	4½	– ⅛	Sep3mD.05	D.17	Y	....	4-1-80
37¼	23¾	ARA	2	457	7.8	6	27¼	25⅛	25½	– 1¼	81Sep4.00	X5.33	q.50	12-1	12-15

(Barron's)

Briefly, the figures in the "Earnings" and "Dividends" columns are interpreted as follows:

first line—AAR Corporation has just declared a dividend ("+" before "earnings" column). Six-month earnings as of November (Nov6m) were $.22 per share. Last year, at this time, per-share earnings were $.74. The current dividend will be a quarterly dividend (q) of $.11, which will go to stockholders of record (Stk of rec) on February 2. The payment will be made on February 26.

> **Stockholders of record** are parties registered on the books of a corporation as shareholders (also applies to shareholders with shares held in street name).

> **In street name.** Stock certificates that are held for an investor by a brokerage firm are said to be "in street name." The name of the brokerage (that at one time probably had an office on "the Street" —Wall Street) is recorded in the books of the issuing company. Dividends (and sometimes annual reports) are sent to the brokerage, which then forwards them to the investor.

second line—ACF Industries had nine-month earnings of $3.36 as of September. This compares with $5.02 a year ago, but the later figure included a nonrecurring profit (x—also called "extraordinary item"); it could have been, for instance, the sale of a factory. The quarterly (q) dividend was $.69, and it went to stockholders of record on December 4. Payment was on December 31.

fourth line—AM International showed a deficit (Def) in July 1981. This compares to a profit of $3.09 a year ago. Their most recent dividend was paid (Y) on October 10, 1980.

You may have noticed that the P-E ratios given in *Barron's* quotations don't always agree with the earnings/statements and current prices. For example, in the first quotation above, the six-month AAR Corporation earnings is slated as $.22. That would annualize to $.44. A P-E ratio of 8 would mean that the current price should be in the vicinity of $3.52 ($.44 × 8). However, the current price is quoted at 7½. The reason for the discrepancy is that the P-E ratio is based on the ratio of the current price to the last 52-weeks earnings. It is not based on an annualization of the quoted earnings if those earnings are only for a part of the year. Thus in the present example the earnings used to calculate the P-E ratio was the last six-month's figure which was quoted at $.22, and the immediately prior six-month's figure (making a 52-week total) which is not shown anywhere in the quotation. However, it would have had to have been in the neighborhood of $.70 for the P-E ratio to work out to 8. This seems reasonable since the six-month earnings for the first six-month segment of the previous year, shown in the second earnings column, is $.74. (In this particular quotation format earnings are given for a specific segment of the present fiscal year and that same segment, for comparison, in the prior fiscal year.)

Many newspapers are particularly conscientious about comprehensive coverage of companies within (or with offices located in) their area. The following is an example from the *San Francisco Sunday Examiner & Chronicle.* Besides helpful percentages, information on earnings is given. The format is clear, and the spacious layout makes the quotations easy to read. The qualifiers are few and easy to interpret.

example of an exceptionally complete quotation format for companies with headquarters or offices in the area served by the paper

▌Regional stock closeup

Company	Mkt	Price							Volume		Earnings and Dividends					P/E Ratio	
			Pct. Change						Last Week's		Earnings per Share			Indi-cated			
		Last Week's Close	Last		Year to Date	5-Year		Shares Traded	Pct. of Shares Out-standing	Last 12 Months		5-Year Annual Growth Rate	Div-idend Yield	5-Year Av-erage	Cur-rent
			Week	4 Wks		High	Low			Amount	Change				
		$	%	%	%	$	$	(000)	%	$	%	%	%	–	–
Adv Micro Dev	N	17.88	−2.1	3.6	−48.2	44.50	2.72	127	.81	.83 S	−51.5	32	.0	12.4	21.5
Ahmanson H F	N	15.00	−7.0	−4.8	−23.1	28.25	9.63	249	1.05	−.05 N	−100.0	−19	8.0	5.4	NE
Alexander Baldwin	O	24.25	−1.5	5.4	−24.2	40.75	12.63	32	.35	3.88 N	−42.9	28	7.4	6.7	6.3
Amdahl Corp	A	27.75	−7.1	−.9	−17.8	71.50	11.13	125	.73	1.33 N	232.5	−14	1.4	22.0	20.9
Am Bldg Maint	N	20.25	3.8	12.5	29.6	22.00	8.75	11	.52	2.67 N	11.3	11	4.2	6.9	7.6
Am Microsystems	O	40.50	3.5	72.3	38.5	40.63	6.00	306	7.41	1.67 N	83.5	37	.0	23.0	24.3
Amfac Corp	N	26.00	2.0	.0	−2.8	35.88	13.00	49	.36	3.85 N	−11.9	29	5.5	7.7	6.8
Ametek Inc	N	31.75	−8	12.4	1.2	35.38	9.63	56	.51	2.39 N	18.9	10	3.8	9.9	13.3
Andersn Jacob	A	13.38	8.1	4.9	−40.6	25.50	1.75	30	1.38	.80 F	−16.7	21	.0	11.2	16.7
Arcata Corp	N	36.00	7.5	6.7	26.3	39.00	9.75	170	2.56	3.36 Q	.3	11	3.6	6.2	10.7
Bancal TriState	N	25.50	−6.4	−12.8	.0	43.00	12.38	11	.24	2.41 N	−39.6	19	4.7	9.5	10.6

N = NYSE
A = Amex
O = OTC

(San Francisco Sunday Examiner & Chronicle)

N = nine months
S = semiannually
Q = quarterly
F = fiscal

E. Qualifiers

A large number of alphabetic qualifiers appear throughout stock quotations. The particular qualifiers and their definitions depend on the news service supplying the quotations to the newspaper. The majority of examples in this chapter have been taken from newspapers who receive their financial quotations from The Associated Press. The other major news agency supplying such quotations in this country is United Press International. Some of the qualifiers they use are the same as the Associated Press, some are not.

Because The Associated Press supplies the majority of papers, the AP definitions are listed first. When UPI definitions are the same, or when there is no UPI definition, no further comment is made. When there is a separate UPI definition, or when the UPI definition is the sole definition, it is marked in brackets: "[UPI . . .]."

Newspapers usually provide a table of symbols. However, the definitions are often unclear because of their brevity. For instance, the definition "when distributed" is probably understood only by persons with some previous investing experience. The following explanations are thus intended to supplement newspaper definitions by providing additional commentary and reasonable detail.

Most newspapers use the same qualifiers for over-the-counter quotations as for the quotations from the national exchanges. However, you should verify this in your own newspaper before assuming that the following definitions are also applicable to the over-the-counter quotations. *The Wall Street Journal,* for example, uses UPI quotations for OTC stocks and AP for the NYSE and Amex listings.

QUALIFIERS FOR STOCK QUOTATIONS

Qualifier	Definition
a	The amount in the "dividend" column includes one or more amounts in addition to the usual dividend.
b	The amount indicated in the "dividend" column is the annual cash dividend and there was a stock dividend.
c	The amount indicated in the "dividend" column completely liquidates the stock (as in the final dividend from income shares of a dual-purpose fund or the final payment from a bankrupt company).
cld	"Called," meaning a company is calling in (and paying off or perhaps substituting new stock for) a particular issue of preferred stock.

d
or
↓   The price indicated (usually in the "low" column) is a new 52-week low. For an example, *see* section 9, "High—Low—Close (or Last)." Sometimes this applies to the closing price only.

e   The amount indicated in the "dividend" column was declared or paid within the preceding 12 months but there is no regular rate.

g   Following the stock name, it means dividends and earnings are in Canadian currency. Trading, however, is in U.S. dollars. No yield or P-E ratio is shown. Dividends may be subject to Canadian withholding for U.S. citizens.

h   A temporary exception to NASD qualifications has been made for this security.

i   The dividend indicated was declared or paid after an earlier stock dividend or split.

j   The dividend amount indicated has been paid so far this year, but the current dividend has been omitted or deferred, or no action was taken on dividends at the last board meeting.

k   The dividend indicated has been declared or paid so far this year on a cumulative issue of preferred stock with dividends in arrears.

    A *block* is a large number of shares, usually over 10,000.

n   This is a new stock issued within the last 52 weeks. The listed 52-week high and low are as of the inception of trading.

Yearly High Low	Ann. Div.	P.E. Ratio	Sales (hds.)	Week's High Low	Net Last Chg
20⅜ 13	Fairfd n	.24	7	303	19⅜ 17½	17¾+ ¼

An "n" indicates
new issue.

(Ft. Worth Star Telegram)

Because of its effect on the 52-week high and low price, the "n" is retained in the quotation for 52 weeks.

nd "Next day" delivery of stock certificates. Settlement (payment) is also required on that day.

pf Preferred stock.

pp The holder still owes one (in some quotations, more than one) installment on the purchase price.

r   The amount indicated was declared or paid in dividends during the preceding 12 months, plus a stock dividend.

rt The quotation is for "rights," not stock.

>*Rights* are like warrants, except they are shorter-term. Some stocks, particularly new issues, first appear in units that can include rights. After the rights are exercised or expire, the stock will trade without them. Rights can be traded separately from stocks.

s Following the stock name, it means that either a stock split or a stock dividend within the last 52 weeks has increased the number of shares outstanding by 25% or more. In *The Wall Street Journal* quotations, it appears in the left-hand margin.

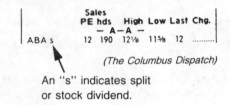

An "s" indicates split
or stock dividend.

>A *split* is a division of shares into a larger number. For instance, a two-for-one split of a stock selling at $10 per share would mean that the stockholders, by virtue of the split, would own twice as many shares at $5 per share. However, a split is usually interpreted as a sign of strength and often stimulates market interest, which results in higher relative prices for the new stock.

When there is a stock split, the 52-week high and low are changed to correspond to the new price. For example, in a two-for-one split, the 52-week high and low would both be halved in order to be in line with the new price of the stock. A *reverse split* results in fewer shares than before. Because of its effect on the 52-week high and low, the "s" is retained in the quotation for 52 weeks.

t This amount was paid in stock dividends during the preceding 12 months. Value given is of the stock on the ex-dividend or ex-distribution date. (*See* "x-dis.")

u
or
↑ The amount indicated (usually in the "high" column) is a new 52-week high. Sometimes this applies to the closing price only.

v Trading of this issue has been halted on the primary market on which it is listed.

vj
or
vi (The correct symbol is "vj.") Appearing before the company name, it means that the company is in bankruptcy or receivership, or that it is being reorganized under the Bankruptcy Act and/or the securities are in control of such companies.

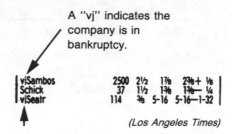

A "vj" indicates the
company is in
bankruptcy.

viSambos	2500	2½	1⅞	2⅜+ ⅛
Schick	37	1½	1⅜	1⅜— ¼
viSeatr	114	⅜	5-16	5-16—1-32

(Los Angeles Times)

Bankruptcy does not necessarily mean a company ceases to exist or that the stockholders lose their entire investment. After emerging from bankruptcy, the stock of some companies has appreciated considerably. However, if the company *is* liquidated, then common stockholders will be paid, proportionate to the number of shares they hold, only after major creditors, bondholders, and preferred stockholders. (*See* "bankruptcy" in the glossary.) "Vj" is constituted of two letter (and letters that do not usually appear as adjacencies) as a fail-safe in order to guarantee against a typographical error mistakenly indicating that a company is bankrupt. In some newspapers the tail of the "j" does not print, causing it to look like an "i."

wd "When distributed." The stock has been legally issued but the certificates are not yet available. For example, they may not have been printed. If the security trades at this time, the purchaser will not receive the certificates until they are made available and are distributed.

wi Short for "when, as, and if issued." The stock is trading before it has cleared all legal requirements for issuance. Should the stock not be issued, all trades will be canceled.

wt The quotation is for warrants, not stock.

ww "With warrants." Sometimes new issues of stock appear in units that include a number of warrants. These may be detached and traded separately or remain with the stock certificates as they are specified here. You must determine from your broker or a stock guide the length of time for which the warrants are still valid.

x "Ex-dividend" or "ex-rights," meaning the security traded the day *after* dividends or rights were awarded. Often appears in the "sales" or "volume" column. In the *WSJ* it appears in the left-hand margin.

    Ex-dividend, "without dividend," means the immediately prior dividend was paid to the previous owner on the previous day and the purchaser of stock from this issue will not receive a dividend until the next payment is declared.

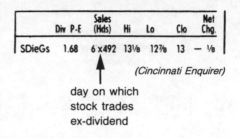

(Cincinnati Enquirer)

day on which
stock trades
ex-dividend

x-dis   "Ex-distribution," indicating the day after the distribution of stock dividends was made.

       Ex-distribution, "without distribution," means the immediately prior stock dividend was declared to the previous owner on the previous day and the purchaser of this stock will not receive it.

xr   "Ex-rights," indicating that the stock is now trading without the rights formerly attached to it.

xw   "Ex-warrants," indicating that the stock is now trading without the warrants formerly attached to it. *See* "ww."

y   Ex-dividend (*see* "x") and sales in full—i.e., the actual number of shares traded is shown.

z   "Sales in full," meaning the actual number of shares is quoted, not the number of round lots. This is not done because of odd lot transactions; it is done to accommodate those stocks that normally trade in lots of other than 100 shares (i.e., 10-, 25-, or 50-share lots).

F. Summary Diagram

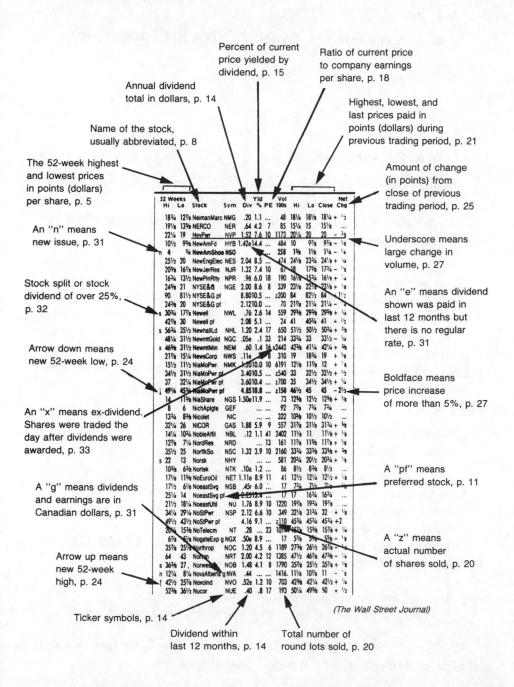

Percent of current price yielded by dividend, p. 15

Ratio of current price to company earnings per share, p. 18

Annual dividend total in dollars, p. 14

Highest, lowest, and last prices paid in points (dollars) during previous trading period, p. 21

Name of the stock, usually abbreviated, p. 8

The 52-week highest and lowest prices in points (dollars) per share, p. 5

Amount of change (in points) from close of previous trading period, p. 25

An "n" means new issue, p. 31

Underscore means large change in volume, p. 27

Stock split or stock dividend of over 25%, p. 32

An "e" means dividend shown was paid in last 12 months but there is no regular rate, p. 31

Arrow down means new 52-week low, p. 24

Boldface means price increase of more than 5%, p. 27

An "x" means ex-dividend. Shares were traded the day after dividends were awarded, p. 33

A "pf" means preferred stock, p. 11

A "g" means dividends and earnings are in Canadian dollars, p. 31

A "z" means actual number of shares sold, p. 20

Arrow up means new 52-week high, p. 24

Ticker symbols, p. 14

Dividend within last 12 months, p. 14

Total number of round lots sold, p. 20

(The Wall Street Journal)

2 Over-the-Counter Stock Quotations

A. Background

Over-the-counter stocks (abbreviated OTC) are stocks *not* listed on either national exchange. These stocks are traded by telephone, one broker to another, which is different from the exchanges, where transactions are executed on an exchange floor by specialists.

At one time newspaper quotations for over-the-counter stocks were of necessity less comprehensive than quotations for stocks on the national exchanges. While this is still true in some listings, those quotations for what is called the National Market now cover over-the-counter as thoroughly as exchange issues. Individual papers, of course, may omit some of the components, like yield, P-E ration, or the 52-week high and low, but many major papers have adopted this new comprehensive format. The quotations usually appear under some version of the following headings:

NASDAQ National Market
National Market Issues

National Market quotations can be interpreted the same as quotations for exchange issues; however, many papers carry one or more lists that are not in the National Market format. The remainder of this chapter will be devoted to those quotations.

Traditionally, over-the-counter quotations have differed from exchange quotations in two important ways:

1. Less information is given.
2. Daily quotations list two prices, called "bid" and "asked" prices.

"Bid" and "asked" prices are both current prices but they are not necessarily the amounts of actual transactions.

Bid price is the price a dealer is willing to *pay* for a stock. Bid prices quoted in the newspaper are always the highest available.

Asked price is the price at which a dealer is willing to *sell* a stock. Asked prices quoted in the newspaper are always the lowest available.

There are far more companies whose stock is traded over the counter than companies on the national and regional exchanges combined. Stocks of most banks and insurance companies are traded OTC, as are most U.S., municipal, and corporate bonds. Corporate bonds listed in newspapers are usually those traded on New York and American stock exchanges. OTC corporate bonds are not usually listed.

"Over-the-counter" does not so much describe a type of security as it does a method of trading. In fact, there are circumstances where stock listed on an exchange can trade over the counter, thus becoming, for the purposes of the transaction, an over-the-counter security.

At one time, NASDAQ companies were typically smaller and less well known than companies on the national exchanges; however, this is no longer true. At present, there are over 1,600 NASDAQ companies eligible for the Amex and over 600 eligible for the NYSE, but they have not chosen to be so listed. One of the reasons for preferring the NASDAQ market has to do with the price competition (between multiple market makers) that is made possible by the NASDAQ system.

OTC stock quotations that are in addition to the National Market list appear in newspapers under many headings:

Over-the-Counter Quotations
Over-the-Counter Market
NASDAQ Bid and Asked Quotations
NASDAQ Over-the-Counter
OTC

Many papers also carry an additional OTC list entitled:

Additional OTC Quotes

or

NASDAQ Supplementary OTC

And some papers also carry separate quotations on the stock of companies either based in the region or having extensive operations there.

The agency that initially reports the OTC stock price data from the market makers is NASDAQ (National Association of Securities Dealers Automated Quotations Service). Wholly owned by the National Association of Securities Dealers, it is the regulatory agency for the over-the-counter market.

Minimum criteria for listing stocks on the NASDAQ system require SEC registration, at least two market makers, assets of $2 million, and a capital surplus of $1 million. Those companies that meet the highest qualifications appear in the National Market list. The newest and smallest are found in the "pink sheets" among other quotations distributed to brokers daily by the National Quotations Bureau. From these sheets, your broker can find either price quotations or the names of firms that "make a market" in particular stocks and from whom one can get bid and asked prices.

> *Making a market* means that a brokerage is buying and selling stock of a particular company for the brokerage's own account (the OTC equivalent of the specialist). In the NASDAQ system, this involves entering the bid and asked prices (the prices at which the brokerage will buy or sell the stock) into the NASDAQ computer, where it is immediately accessible to all brokerages and traders throughout the United States. Any number of brokerages may make a market in the same stock.

B. The Quotations

1) Format of Daily Quotations

There are varieties of formats in which the daily OTC listings may appear. Only those items unique to OTC quotations will be discussed in detail. OTC quotations such as the two that follow are printed in the same format as the national exchanges and should be interpreted as set forth in chapter 1.

Associated Press NASDAQ National Market quotations in the same format as their NYSE and Amex quotations

52-Week High	52-Week Low	Stock	Div	Yld %	PE Ratio	Sales 100s	High	Low	Last	Chg.
37¼	29¾	BoatBn	2.00	6.3	16	305	32⅛	31⅞	31⅞	...
18	14¼	BobEvn	.26	1.6	15	773	16¼	16	16	...
13¼	8¾	Bogert		...	...	80	9½	9½	9½	+ ½
22½	14¼	Bohema	.20b	1.0	...	126	19¾	19	19¼	+ ¼
4¾	¾	Bombay		...	...	50	1	1	1	+ ⅛

52-Week High	52-Week Low	Stock	Div	Yld %	PE Ratio	Sales 100s	High	Low	Last	Chg.
45	34	CnsTom	.34a	.7	69	4u	46	40½	46	+ 4¾
34	24¼	CnstlBc	1.24	3.6	10	98u	34½	34	34½	+ ½
1 13/16	¾	Consul		...	...	512u	1⅞	1¾	1¾	− 1/16
6	4¼	ConsFn	.12	2.5	16	3	4¾	4¾	4¾	− ¼
21¼	16¼	ConWat	1.04	5.9	11	101	18	17½	17¾	...

(The New York Times)

The Wall Street Journal NASDAQ National Market in the same format as NYSE and Amex quotations

	52 Weeks Hi	52 Weeks Lo	Stock	Sym	Div	Yld %	PE	Vol 100s	Hi	Lo	Close	Net Chg
	10⅝	1½	Pancretec	PNCR		...	...	92	10⅛	9⅞	10	- ⅛
	8¾	3¾	Pantera	PANT		...	...	685	4⅜	4⅛	4⅜	...
	7¾	6	ParisBusnFm	PBFI	.23e	3.2	...	6	7¼	7¼	7¼	+ ½
	29¾	24½	ParkComm	PARC		...	19	233	26¾	26	26¾	+ ¼
	7¾	5⅛	ParkOhio	PKOH		...	...	71	6⅛	6	6	...

	52 Weeks Hi	52 Weeks Lo	Stock	Sym	Div	Yld %	PE	Vol 100s	Hi	Lo	Close	Net Chg
	35	26¾	RoadwySvc	ROAD	1.10	3.3	17	2574	33¼	32	33¼	+1
s	16⅝	10¾	RoanokeElec	RESC	.40a	2.6	8	353	16	15¼	15⅝	- ⅜
	18¼	7¾	RobnsMyrs	ROBN		...	12	7	17	17	17	...
s	23¼	15¾	RobtHalf	RHII		...	19	179	18¼	17¾	17¾	- ½
	2⅜	1 3/16	RobesnInd	RBSN		...	...	2	2 3/16	2 3/16	2 3/16	+ ⅛

(The Wall Street Journal)

In most OTC daily quotations, the name of the stock is listed first. Extensive quotations usually include the dividend, volume, prices, and net change.

daily OTC quotations that include dividend, volume, prices, and net change

		Sales	High	Low	Last	Chg
AB Fort		1115	17¾	17½	17⅝	— ⅛
AFG		302	10¼	10	10	— ¼
AGM	.40	0	10¼	10¼	10¼	....
AMCbl s		679	7⅛	6¼	7⅛	+ ⅜
ASK Cpt		662	14½	14	14	— ⅜
AVM Cp		42	4	3¾	4	+ ⅛
Abitibi g	1.60	5	17½	17¼	17½	....
AcadIns		851	14⅝	14¼	14¼	— ⅜
AcLosRes		150	5⅝	5	5⅛	— ½
Accelrtn	.05e	187	2⅝	2⅜	2½	— ⅛
Accuray	.10e	344	7¼	7⅛	7¼	+ ⅛
AcetoCh	t	20	15¾	15¾	15¾	....
ACMAT		50	5¾	5½	5½	— ¼
AcmeEl	.32	124	10½	9¼	10½	+1

(The Columbus Dispatch)

Prices in columns labeled "high," "low," and "last," as in the example above, are always the high, low, and last *bid* prices (except for those quotations in the national exchange format, in which case the prices are transaction prices). Often dividend, yield, and volume are dropped, and brief quotations give only the bid and asked prices.

Stock	**Bid**	**Ask**
AB Fort	18¼	18½
AFG	8¾	9½
AGM	10¼	11
AMCbl s	7	7¼
ASK Cpt	13	13⅛
AVM Cp	4¼	4½
Abitibi g	18	18¾
Acadlns	13⅝	13⅞
AcLosRes	4⅛	4⅜

abbreviated daily OTC quotations that include only bid and asked prices

(The Dallas Morning News)

Some include only the last bid price and the net change.

	Net
	Bid chg.
VaNBsh	17⅝ — ¼
VisTech	11½ + ¾
Vitram	4⅛ — ⅛
Voltln s	15¼ — 3
VIntCap	7¾ + ⅝
Voyager	11⅝ — ⅛
VulP s g	5¼ — ¼
Vyquest	5¾ .....
WD40 Co	34¼ + ¾
Wacoal	15¾ — ¼
Walbro	6½ — ¼
Waldbm	15½ ......

(Chicago Tribune)

The stock names are abbreviated in the same manner as in the listings of the national exchanges. As with the NYSE and Amex, abbreviations and methods of alphabetizing can vary. Also, like NYSE and Amex stocks, these abbreviations are not the ticker symbols. For OTC stocks, the "ticker" symbols are constituted of four or five capital letters. (NYSE and Amex stocks use one to three capital letters.) The fifth letter of an OTC ticker symbol (if it has one) is not an integral part of the symbol but a qualifier appended by NASDAQ. The meaning of these qualifiers is given in section D at the end of this chapter.

The dividends in OTC quotations are yearly figures listed in dollars and cents. As with exchange issues, dividends are usually paid quarterly. Sales are shown in hundreds. Note that for OTC stocks there is no extra charge for purchase of odd lots, as there is on the national exchanges.

2) Bid and Asked Prices

As mentioned before, a unique feature of OTC quotations is the "bid" and "asked" prices.

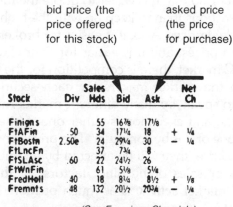

bid price (the price offered for this stock)

asked price (the price for purchase)

Stock	Div	Sales Hds	Bid	Ask	Net Ch	
Finigns		55	16⅞	17⅛		
FtAFin	.50	34	17¼	18	+	¼
FtBostn	2.50e	24	29¼	30	−	¼
FtLncFn		37	7¾	8		
FtSLAsc	.60	22	24½	26		
FtWnFin		61	5⅛	5¼		
FredHoll	.40	18	8¼	8½	+	⅛
Fremnts	.48	132	20½	20¾	−	¼

(San Francisco Chronicle)

Bid and asked prices should *not* be confused with the high and low prices of the NYSE and Amex listings. The reason both bid and asked prices are quoted reflects certain differences between the OTC market system and the exchanges.

Further explanations: The exchanges are auction markets. On an exchange floor, a broker with an order from a client may approach another broker, known as a specialist, who is the floor broker making a market in a particular stock. The first broker will inquire about price, and the specialist will give *two* prices (for example, 19¼ and 19½). It is understood that he will pay the first price and that he will sell at the second. These are bid and asked prices.

The first broker may take one or the other of the prices, depending on his instructions, or he may try to negotiate another price, either with the specialist or with other brokers who have come to this spot in order to make transactions in the same stock. In certain cases, the specialist may even send for other brokers whom he knows to have an interest in buying or selling the stock of this particular company. Of course, an auction will not actually take place for every trade, but the mechanism for this type of transaction does exist.

There are numerous such transactions in the course of the day, and both bid and asked prices may change many times (although not usually by much), so that it is easier to quote the range (high and low) of actual transactions than to keep up with the highs and lows of *both* the bid and asked prices. Also, it is easier for brokerages to work from last transaction prices, and it is easier for their clients to understand.

On the OTC market, there is competition for the best bid and asked prices among the market makers for each security. The prices are "posted," so to speak, by many different market makers on the NAS-DAQ computer, and execution is either one-to-one, broker-to-broker, on the telephone or it is by computer. The prices posted are firm offers although, of course, they will be affected by an imbalance in demand for purchases or sales or by other factors. At the present level of volume, OTC market activity is as much or more liquid than the exchange markets.

There is another difference between the two types of markets that is important to many companies listed by NASDAQ. On an exchange, the transaction for each stock is often in the hands of one person, the specialist for that particular issue. (An exception to this is the Pacific Exchange, where there are two trading floors and consequently two specialists for each stock.) Many companies are more comfortable in the NASDAQ market, where any number of market makers can compete with one another for the best bid and asked prices. The efficiency of the communications system and the built-in competitiveness of the market maker's system have made the NASDAQ market an attractive alternative to the exchanges.

When one inquires of a broker about an OTC stock, the broker can obtain the highest bid and lowest asked price from his computer terminal or from the pink sheets, or by calling a market maker. The difference between the bid and asked prices, called the "spread," is the profit the market maker hopes to gain in the many transactions—purchases *and* sales—of this stock. (The amount of the spread is a function of volume: The higher the volume, the narrower the spread.) The entire process is extremely efficient because of the NASDAQ quotation system, and often a transaction can be completed while the investor is still on the phone.

Lower-priced stocks are often included in the NASDAQ supplementary list entitled "Additional OTC Quotes" or "NASDAQ Supplementary OTC." Here one can find the stock of many companies that list below $3 a share. Prices below 2 points are often shown in sixteenths; and below 1 point, in thirty-seconds. These fractions can sometimes be inconvenient to translate into dollar amounts. For the decimal (and dollar) value of eighths, sixteenths, and thirty-seconds, see Appendix 1.

Another name for extremely low-priced stock is "penny stock."

Penny stock. The term is properly applied only to stock prices so low that they are quoted in cents (small fractions can be very awkward). It is often used to mean any relatively low-priced stock.

Although NASDAQ does not report prices in dollars and cents, sometimes stocks on regional and foreign exchanges are quoted in dollars and cents.

One of the leading publications of price quotations for penny stocks is *The National OTC Stock Exchange* (which is a weekly newspaper, not an exchange). The following is an example of their quotations. They are clear and self-explanatory, and the prices are in dollars and cents.

Example of "penny stock" quotations. Prices in dollars and cents.

Symbol	Company	This Week	% Change	SIX-MONTH High	Low	Prospectus Date
AMSI	Adv. Monitoring Sys.	9.88	-8.1	11.25	5.63	05/06/80
TNET	Amer. Telenet	0.09	0.0	0.19	0.09	03/13/80
	Amer. Thermal Res.	3.00	20.0	7.50	1.62	—
	Amer. Wind Turbine	0.04	0.0	0.08	0.02	—
AAPL	Apple Computer	20.88	0.6	33.00	15.25	—
AQUA	Aquaculture Prod.	0.06	0.0	0.19	0.06	09/23/80
ATTC	Atro-Trol Tech.	9.25	0.0	26.00	9.25	01/24/79
BSLT	BSL Tech.	1.50	0.0	3.75	1.50	12/02/80
BNCO	Bion Corp.	0.38	-14.3	0.94	0.38	08/03/81
	Brunton Co.	0.10	25.0	0.10	0.05	—
	Casino Gaming Sys.	0.13	0.0	1.25	0.13	—
CENT	Centuri	7.38	1.7	8.50	4.00	—
CESI	Cogenic	1.94	- 24.0	1.94	0.81	05/21/81

(The National OTC Stock Exchange, formerly The Denver Stock Exchange)

A prospectus is a document describing a new issue for prospective buyers. The prospectus date, in the last column of the above example, is the date when the company officially went public (i.e., offered shares to the public). Prospectus dates are not given for longer-established companies.

The most comprehensive weekly listings of OTC stocks are contained in *Barron's.* Although a "yield" is not given (it can be calculated from the dividend and the current price), nor a weekly high and low, it does list a 52-week high and low along with information concerning the company's earnings.

comprehensive weekly OTC quotation including 52-week high and low bid prices

and a report on the company's earnings

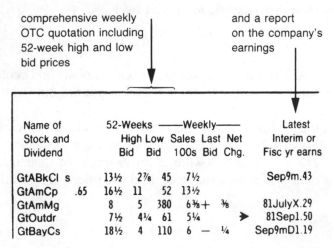

Name of Stock and Dividend		52-Weeks High Low Bid Bid	——Weekly—— Sales Last Net 100s Bid Chg.			Latest Interim or Fisc yr earns
GtABkCl s		13½ 2⅞	45	7½		Sep9m.43
GtAmCp	.65	16½ 11	52	13½		
GtAmMg		8 5	380	6⅜+	⅜	81JulyX.29
GtOutdr		7½ 4¼	61	5¼		81Sep1.50
GtBayCs		18½ 4	110	6 —	¼	Sep9mD1.19

(Barron's)

The following information is provided in the column labeled "Latest Interim or Fisc. yr earns":

a) the month of the report from which the data was taken
b) the number of months the report covers ("m" is for months) or the year if it is a report for the entire year
c) the amount of earnings per share in dollars and cents, sometimes preceded by a qualifier

An interpretation of each of the above earnings quotations from the top is as follows:

Sep9m.43   = The September nine-month (m) earnings per share are $.43.

. . . .   = earnings information is not available.

81JulyX.29   = The earnings for the entire 1981 fiscal year, over in July, are $.29 per share, but this figure includes a nonrecurring profit (x), such as from the sale of corporate property.

81Sep1.50   = The earnings for the entire 1981 fiscal year, over in September, are $1.50 per share. The arrow means this figure includes earnings from a new source.

Sep9mD1.19 = The September nine-month (m) earnings figure shows a deficit (D) of $1.19 per share.

C. Qualifiers

Most newspapers use the same qualifiers for OTC stocks as for quotations from the national exchanges. In that case (which should be verified by the reader), there is usually only one table explaining the symbol for both, and the definitions at the end of chapter 1 should be consulted.

D. The Fifth Letter of OTC Ticker Symbols

OTC stocks are easily distinguished from exchange issues by their ticker symbols, which contain four or five letters (exchange issues contain one to three). The fifth letter, if present, is a qualifier appended by NASDAQ. The following table gives the meaning, in brief, for these letters.

A = class A, common or preferred stock

B = class B, common or preferred stock

C = the security has been temporarily exempted from listing qualifications by NAS-DAQ

D = new issue, within last 52 weeks

E = the National Association of Securities Dealers has found the company to be delinquent in filing necessary documents with the SEC

F = foreign security

G = the company's first convertible bond

H = the company's second convertible bond

I = the company's third convertible bond

J = voting issue

K = non-voting issue

L = miscellaneous

M = fourth preferred stock issued by this company

N = third preferred stock issued by this company

O = second preferred stock issued by this company

P = first preferred stock issued by this company

Q = in bankruptcy

R = rights

S = shares of beneficial interest

T = issue, usually units, which contains warrants or rights

U = units

V = when issued and when distributed

W = warrants

Y = American Depositary Receipts (ADRs) of a foreign security

Z = miscellaneous

3 Regional and Canadian Exchange Quotations

A. Background

No U.S. newspaper carries a comprehensive list of securities from any of the regional stock exchanges. However, this does not constitute the benign oversight that it might at first appear. The majority of stocks on regional exchanges are dually listed—that is, they are also listed on one (but not both) of the national exchanges. A regional transaction in any of these securities is reported to, and becomes a part of, the "composite" quotations of the respective national exchange.

The computer linkage system that joins the regional exchanges and reports their transactions to the national exchanges is the Intermarket Trading System (ITS).

Regional exchanges linked by ITS to both Amex and NYSE.

Boston Stock Exchange
Cincinnati Stock Exchange
Philadelphia Stock Exchange
Midwest Stock Exchange (Chicago)
Pacific Stock Exchange (Los Angeles and San Francisco)

There are several advantages to a stock being listed on more than one exchange. The specialists on each floor will be in competition, and your broker will thus have a choice of exchanges on which to look for the best price. You may not know from your broker on what exchange your order was actually executed, but over 50% of the volume of dually listed stocks actually takes place on markets outside New York.

The linking together of regional exchanges through the ITS and other systems is one of several initial steps that may result in the formation of a single national exchange system. An early example of the joining together of exchanges is the Pacific Exchange. With two trading floors 400 miles apart (one in San Francisco and one in Los Angeles), they are so efficiently joined by numerous communication lines that they indeed function as a single exchange.

Quotations from Canadian stock exchanges are often reported in U.S. newspapers. The Canadian exchanges are as follows:

Canadian Stock Exchanges

Alberta Stock Exchange
Montreal Stock Exchange
Toronto Stock Exchange
Vancouver Stock Exchange
Winnipeg Stock Exchange

The Toronto Exchange is the largest in Canada, and in dollar volume it is the third-largest in North America (NYSE being first and Amex second). Canadian stocks may be purchased directly through U.S. brokerages at the same commission charged for U.S. stocks.

Most newspapers do not list more than one U.S. regional exchange, if any. A Canadian exchange listing will usually be for Toronto. *The New York Times* and *The Wall Street Journal* carry all the regional exchanges daily except Cincinnati, and they also list the Toronto and Montreal exchanges.

B. The Quotations

1. Regional U.S. Exchanges

Quotations for regional exchanges more closely resemble brief national exchange listings than OTC quotations. Unless otherwise stated, the prices are of actual transactions, not bid and asked prices.

regional stock exchange, extensive quotation

Exclusive Midwest stocks

			Sales hds	High	Low	Last	Chg.
AtheyPd		.70b	1	11½	11½	11½	— ⅜
BallyPP			77	5⅜	5	5⅛	— ⅛
FstMich		1.20e	10	18	18	18	.....
GreifBr	s	.24	112	18½	17⅞	18⅛	+ ⅛

(Chicago Tribune)

Sometimes quotations from regional exchanges list bid and asked prices. These are always the *closing* bid and asked prices.

regional exchange
quotations listing
bid and asked
closing prices

Philadelphia Exchange

Stocks	Bid	Ask
U.S. Air...............................	12⅜	12⅞
B.F.Saul...............................	7	7¾
Balt. Gas & Elec Pfd C	25	27
Balt. Gas & Elec Pfd D..	32	36
Balt. Gas & Elec Pfd E....	45	49
Balt. Gas & Elec Pfd F.. ...	68	98
Balt. Gas & Elec Pfd G......	52	56
Balt. Gas & Elec Pfd H........	44½	48½
Balt. Gas & Elec. Pfd I	47	51
Balt. Gas & Elec Pfd J.........	55	59
Consolidated Oil Gas	—	—
DC Trading&Development....	1½	1⅝

(The Washington Post)

In the above example, the most active stocks are listed, and dually listed issues are not deleted. Several of the above corporations trade on the NYSE.

Quotations in *Barron's* give the most comprehensive information about stocks on regional exchanges. The "earnings" column is interpreted in the same manner as described for OTC stocks in chapter 2.

Barron's gives
earnings information
and yearly high and
low prices for regional
stock exchange
listings.

Name of Stock and Dividend	Latest Interim or Fisc yr earns	High	Low	Prev. Wk's Close	Last Wk's Close	Net Chge
BOSTON						
AldenElec.18e	Sep6m.30	4.37	2.12	2.75	3.12	+ .37
Atlan-Tol	Jan.36	10.62	8.37	8.75	8.37	− .38
CapeCodBk	Sep9m4.80	41	36	40	41	+ 1
CascoNthn 1.40	Mar3m.80	15¾	14½	15¼	15¾	+ ½
Cstl Carib		7.00	4.75	6.12	6.19	⊢ .07
ColumChase.06	Feb6m.06	6.00	4.00	5.75	5.25	− .5C
DataArchit		11.00	7.25	10.25	9.00	−1.25
DietrExp		2.44	1.50	1.87	1.81	− .06
EstUtahMn		2.37	1.75	2.12	1.94	− .18
EdgcbSt.40		6.25	4.87	5.75	5.75	
Exolon.80a	Sep9m.75	15¾	11¾	12	12	
Lamston 1.50	Jan3.00	17½	11¾	15¾	17½	+ 1¾

(Barron's)

2. Canadian Stock Quotations

Canadian quotations within an individual paper are usually in the same format as regional U.S. quotations. Prices are in Canadian dollars unless otherwise marked. The newspaper instructions should be checked carefully. In the following example, a "$" means the quotation is in Canadian dollars (points) and the absence of a "$" means the quotation is in Canadian cents. Thus the high for the last stock listed is $28.00 Canadian, and the high for the next-to-last stock is $.85 Canadian.

Toronto Stocks

TORONTO (UPI)—Toronto stocks.
Quotations in Canadian funds.
Quotations in cents unless marked $

	Volume	High	Low	Close	Chge
Abti Prce	960	$21½	20	20	—2⅛
Agnico E	4500	$7⅜	7⅛	7¼	
Agra Ind A	200	$8⅜	8⅜	8⅜	
Alta Nat	300	$24¼	24	24¼	+ ¼
Algo Cent	2100	$17½	17½	17½	+ ¼
Andres W A	800	$12¾	12⅝	12¾	
Argus C pr	437	440	440	440	
BP Can	13937	$22¾	22¼	22½	— ⅝
Banister C	7100	$7	7	7	
Bank Mtl	110107	$21⅞	21⅝	21⅞	— ⅛
Bank N S	6629	$23¾	23½	23⅝	+ ⅛
Bell Canad	131017	$17⅞	17⅝	17⅞	+ ⅛
Bralor Res	6450	$11¼	10¾	11	— ¼
Bramalea	58400	$7	6¾	7	— ¼
Brenda M	100	$9¼	9¼	9¼	— ⅜
BCFP	4157	$11⅜	11⅛	11¼	
BC Phone	4300	$14¾	14⅝	14⅝	
Brunswk	3025	$12	11⅞	12	
CAE	5050	$8½	8⅛	8¼	— ¼
Cad Frv	311826	$9¼	9	9	— ¼
Camflo	6525	$16	15¼	15¾	— ½
Camreco	100	85	85	85	
C Nor West	10200	$28	27¼	27¼	— ¾

Canadian quotations marked "$" are in Canadian dollars; all others are Canadian cents.

(The Tampa Tribune)

Canadian quotations in most papers are less extensive than the above example. The following lists only closing prices. Here, the three-digit prices are Canadian cents; all others are Canadian dollars.

Closing prices of selected issues on foreign exchanges last week are listed below. Montreal and Toronto exchange prices are in Canadian dollars except for the issues quoted in three figures, which are Canadian cents.

TORONTO

850	AMCA Int	20
1375	Abti Prce	22
7855	Agnico E	7¼
325	Greyhnd	21
10	Hard Crp A	186
2200	Hawker	11⅜
1106	Hayes D	7¼

Canadian closing prices only. Three-digit figures are Canadian cents; all others are Canadian dollars.

(The Washington Post)

Because of our close political ties with Canada, and its physical proximity to the U.S., Canadian stocks do not require American Depository Receipts as do stocks in most other foreign countries. However, the buyer should be aware that earnings (dividends or interest) from Canadian securities are subject to a 15% Canadian withholding tax. (There are exceptions—should you hold controlling interest in a corporation.) Capital gains are not, however, provided the transaction takes place on a U.S. exchange.

4 Foreign Stock Quotations

A. Background

Many foreign companies have stocks that trade on established U.S. exchanges. For example, a few listed on the NYSE are:

Alcan Aluminium Ltd. (Canada)
EMI Ltd. (Great Britain)
Honda Motor Company Ltd. (Japan)
KLM Royal Dutch Airlines (Netherlands)
Norlin Corporation (Panama)

Since these companies are listed on a U.S. exchange, their quotations, in dollars and cents, are no different from those of other stocks. Anyone thus has easy access access to (these) foreign quotations. However, few newspapers carry quotations from foreign exchanges. Such quotations would be in the currency of the country in which the exchange is located.

B. The Quotations

1. In Foreign Currency

The New York Times daily quotations carries one of the most extensive lists, under the heading "Other U.S. and Foreign Stock Exchanges." A sample from the Frankfurt and Tokyo exchanges is shown below. Only closing prices are given and they are quoted in the currency of the respective countries.

quotations from
foreign exchanges
in foreign
currencies

FRANKFURT
(in German marks)

AEG	43.30	Mannesmn	146.70
Allianz Ver	430.50	Metallges	263.00
BASF	132.80	Munch Rvrs	515.00
Bayer	115.10	RWE	169.00
Bayer Verns	273.50	Schering	275.70
BMW	189.70	Siemens	199.20
Commrzbnk	129.80	Suedzucker	257.00
Daiml Benz	279.00	Thyssen Hu	72.30
Deutsch Bk	267.00	Thyssen Ind	55.00
Dresdnr Bk	132.10	Veba	126.70
Hoechst AG	116.30	Volkswagen	130.60
Karstadt	186.00		

TOKYO
(in Japanese yen)

Asahi Chem	333	Mitsui	340
Bnk of Tokyo	296	Mitsumi	350
Banyu	680	Nippon Oil	1,030
Canon Cam	865	Nippon Stl	169
C. Itoh	331	Nippon Elec	798

(The New York Times)

The Wall Street Journal carries two listings of foreign securities. One, under the heading "Foreign Securities," is in U.S. dollars (actually, ADRs—to be discussed later). The other, under the heading "Foreign Markets," is in the currencies of the respective countries and lists a current closing price and a closing price for the previous trading day.

foreign quotations
in foreign currency
showing two closing
prices

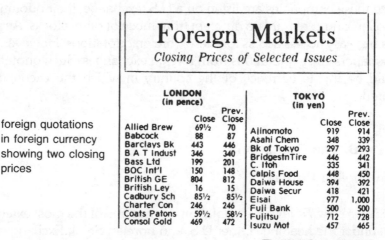

Foreign Markets
Closing Prices of Selected Issues

LONDON (in pence)			TOKYO (in yen)		
	Close	Prev. Close		Close	Prev. Close
Allied Brew	69½	70	Ajinomoto	919	914
Babcock	88	87	Asahi Chem	348	339
Barclays Bk	443	446	Bk of Tokyo	297	293
B A T Indust	346	340	BridgestnTire	446	442
Bass Ltd	199	201	C. Itoh	335	341
BOC Int'l	150	148	Calpis Food	448	450
British GE	804	812	Daiwa House	394	392
British Lev	16	15	Daiwa Secur	418	421
Cadbury Sch	85½	85½	Eisai	977	1,000
Charter Con	246	246	Fuji Bank	500	500
Coats Patons	59½	58½	Fujitsu	712	728
Consol Gold	469	472	Isuzu Mot	457	465

(The Wall Street Journal)

To determine an approximate price for foreign securities in U.S. dollars, one must multiply the price by the applicable exchange rate.

Exchange rates are included in most newspapers, and in *The Wall Street Journal* they appear in the following format:

large volume interbank currency-exchange rate

Foreign Exchange

The New York foreign exchange selling rates below apply to trading among banks in amounts of $1 million and more, as quoted at 3 p.m. Eastern time by Bankers Trust Co. Retail transactions provide fewer units of foreign currency per dollar.

	U.S. $ equiv.		Currency per U.S. $	
Country	Thurs.	Wed.	Thurs.	Wed.
Argentina (Peso)				
Financial	.000095	.000095	10,500.00	10,500.00
Australia (Dollar) ...	1.1250	1.1278	.8889	.8867
Austria (Schilling) ..	.0631	.0635	15.84	15.74
Belgium (Franc)				
Commercial rate ..	.026008	.02610	38.45	38.325
Financial rate	.023529	.02366	42.50	42.265
Brazil (Cruzeiro)	.00816	.00816	122.59	122.59
Britain (Pound)	1.9205	1.9225	.5207	.5201
30-Day Forward ...	1.9180	1.9195	.5214	.5209
90-Day Forward ...	1.9140	1.9147	.5225	.5223
180-Day Forward ...	1.9132	1.9138	.5227	.5225

number of U.S. dollars per unit of foreign currency

number of units of foreign currency per one U.S. dollar

(The Wall Street Journal)

Most exchange rates published in newspapers are interbank rates, such as the ones shown above. These rates are usually unavailable to individuals and not applicable to brokerage transactions of less than $1 million. The exact rate for stock transactions varies according to the circumstances, but, as a rule of thumb, 2% can be added to the interbank rate.

In the above example, from a Friday edition, the column labeled "Thursday" gives the most current rate. For the British pound, we see that the exchange rate is $1.9205. (The 30-, 90-, and 180-day forward are rates for interbank futures and are not relevant to current exchange rates.) Two percent of $1.9205 is $.0384, giving us an estimated exchange rate of $1.9589.

The London Exchange quotation shown above lists Allied Brew closing at 69½ pence. There are 100 new pence in the British pound. Multiplying the price of the stock in foreign currency by the approximate U.S. equivalent of £ we get an approximate per-share price of the stock in U.S. dollars.

.695 pence (price of stock)
× 1.9589 U.S.$ (approx. exchange value of £1)
$ 1.3614 U.S.$ (price of stock in U.S. $)

2. American Depository Receipts

Most foreign stocks quoted in U.S. papers are available in this country by means of American Depository Receipts (ADRs).

> An ***ADR*** is a certificate printed in this country by a U.S. bank indicating that a foreign stock certificate is deposited in your name in a foreign branch of a U.S. bank.

When purchasing an ADR stock, you receive, or your broker holds for you, one or more ADR certificates. ADRs are a convenience to investors, but they also are a necessity. Most countries have laws prohibiting the removal of stock certificates from the country. The stock, however, is still as liquid as if the certificate were in the United States. Payment for ADR stock, and dividends received, are in U.S. dollars. Most are subject to foreign withholding tax, and capital-gains tax is applicable only in the country in which the trade takes place, probably the United States.

The following example shows the bid and asked prices for selected stock from the Tokyo Stock Exchange available through American Depository Receipts.

Japanese Adrs
(From Nomura Securities Int'l. Inc.)
Tky. Dow-Jones 7,602.69 (—44.74)
Volume 350,000,000

Shares		
Canon	21½	21⅝
Daiei	54⅛	54¼
Fujitsu	29¾	30¾
Hitachi	59⅛	59¼
Ito-Yokado	17¾	18¼
Japan Air Lns.	106½	107¼
Kirin Brew.	20¼	20½
Komatsu Mfg.	38¾	39¾
Makita Elec.	19½	19⅞
Marui	42¾	43¾
Mitsui & Co.	33¼	33⅝
Nippon Elec.	87⅞	88⅛
Nippon Optcl.	28¾	29¾
Nissan Motor	36⅛	36½
Nomura Sec.	24¼	25¼
Ricoh	29¾	30¾
Sekisui Pref.	34¾	35¾
Sharp	36½	37½
Shiseido	38¾	39½
TDK Electr.	32	32¼

bid and asked prices of Japanese stocks available through ADRs

(The Honolulu Advertiser)

5 "Ticker" Quotations

A. Background

Ticker quotations are trade-by-trade continuous transaction reports that specify the name, price, and usually the volume of the security traded.

Ticker quotations are associated in most people's minds with stocks, but there are ticker quotations for bonds, options, and futures as well. In this chapter, we will concern ourselves only with ticker quotations broadcast on cable TV. These are the Consolidated Tape networks A and B, which report only on stocks and a small number of bonds. Although there are other networks available, these two are the most well known and the most likely to be seen on display boards in brokerage offices throughout the United States.

The two networks of the Consolidated Tape report all transactions from the following exchanges:

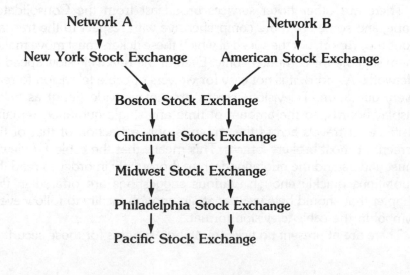

Network A   Network B

New York Stock Exchange   American Stock Exchange

Boston Stock Exchange

Cincinnati Stock Exchange

Midwest Stock Exchange

Philadelphia Stock Exchange

Pacific Stock Exchange

Stocks cannot trade on an exchange unless they are registered on that specific exchange, and, as mentioned in an earlier chapter, stocks may be registered on only one national exchange but on any number of regional exchanges. Thus Network A reports transactions on the New York Stock Exchange and on all transactions of NYSE issues that occur on the above regional exchanges. Network B does the same for all Amex transactions and for transactions of Amex issues on regional exchanges.

The quotations reported on the two networks are first broadcast to the seven exchanges themselves; after a 15-minute delay, they are broadcast to ticker machines, display boards, and cable-access television across the United States and internationally. One of the benefits of exchange membership is the 15-minute "edge" on transaction prices that this system provides.

Ticker quotations should not be confused with the securities quotations available on quote terminals: an entirely different service and in an entirely different format. A quote terminal provides a summary of detailed information, on demand, for any specific stock requested. Such information might include high and low transaction prices for the year, the daily opening transaction price, current bid and asked prices, a P-E ratio, dividend information, etc. The ticker quotation system with which we are concerned transmits less information per issue, but it is comprehensive with respect to recording all transactions (with a single exception, to be discussed later). Ticker quotations are a constantly changing report on all trades on all relevant exchanges, and as such constitute a kind of pulse of the market.

There are other ticker services broadcast from the Consolidated Tape, and some are more comprehensive with respect to the transactions they report, but the speed at which these tickers must move makes them suitable for computers only. Even at the relatively slow speed of Networks A and B, it is not easy for viewers of cable television to read every quotation. Television screens are not as wide (long) as ticker display boards, so the amount of time any single quotation remains visible as it travels across the screen is only a fraction of that of the screens at most brokers' offices. This means that the cable-TV viewer must understand the quotation format thoroughly in order to read the quotations quickly enough. Various suggestions are offered in this chapter that should help viewers attain enough facility to follow every symbol in the cable-television format.

There are at present no ticker quotation systems for those securities that are exclusively traded over the counter. Each listed OTC stock does have, however, an alphabetic symbol (similar to those used by tickers) that is used to obtain current quotation data from quote terminals.

Before proceeding to the ticker symbols themselves it should be mentioned that the term "quotation" is being used in its broadest sense to indicate any kind of price report on a security. Strictly speaking, ticker quotations are referred to as "transactions" since they are reporting a price at which stock actually changes hands. The term "quotation" is often reserved for the reporting of bid and asked prices. The distinction between the two is called to your attention in case you encounter either term used in that fashion.

B. The Quotations

1. The Top Line

The general format of the old ticker-tape-machine printout has been preserved in modern ticker quotations. The top line usually indicates the name of the security; the bottom line, the volume and the price. (See also the explanation for photo 7.)

(Consolidated Tape: Network A)

Ticker symbols for stocks on the NYSE and Amex are made up of one to three capital latters. The top line of the above tape segment reads as follows:

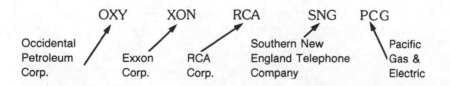

As discussed earlier, ticker symbols are sometimes not easy to remember. (The above are easier than most.) Knowing the ticker symbols in advance for the stocks whose quotations you are watching for on the ticker is, of course, essential.

Preferred issues are indicated by a "Pr" following the stock symbol. Do not mistake the "P" in "Pr" for a letter of the symbol. In the following example, "CHG" is the stock symbol and "Pr" indicates "preferred."

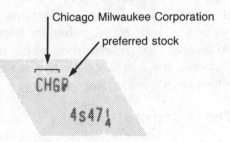

(Consolidated Tape: Network A)

In the next example, a two-letter symbol, "PC," is followed by "Pr."

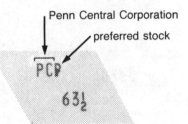

(Consolidated Tape: Network A)

Identifying letters follow the "Pr" if necessary.

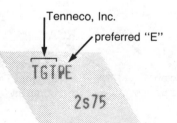

(Consolidated Tape: Network A)

INSIDE A
TICKER MACHINE

This view of the inside of an early ticker machine shows the two print wheels. The use of separate wheels for alphabetic and numeric characters gave the ticker tape its characteristic format (letters across the top, numbers across the bottom). This format is still used today even though it is no longer a necessity. The upper wheel, made of felt, provided ink. The paper tape ran beneath the two print wheels.

Convertible securities (which in the case of stock are always preferred issues) are indicated with a ".CV."

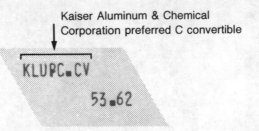

Kaiser Aluminum & Chemical
Corporation preferred C convertible

KLUPC.CV
53.62

(Consolidated Tape: Network A)

Classes of common stock (A, B, C, etc.) are indicated by a period followed by the appropriate letter.

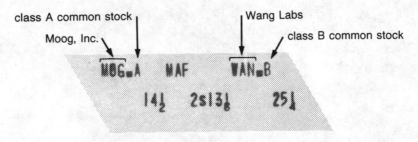

class A common stock

Moog, Inc.

Wang Labs

class B common stock

MOG.A   MAF   WAN.B
14½ 2s13⅛   25¼

(Consolidated Tape: Network B)

Two indications that appear in the top line in small letters are for rights ("rt") and "when issued" ("wi"). For example:

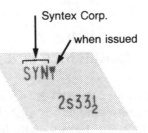

Syntex Corp.

when issued

SYNwi
2s33½

(Consolidated Tape: Network A)

"When *distributed*," however, appears in large letters following a period.

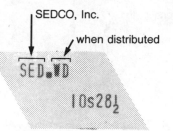

(Consolidated Tape: Network A)

Warrants are indicated by a "WS" following a period.

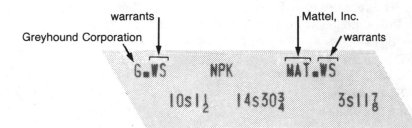

(Consolidated Tape: Network A)

Some warrants have an additional code letter such as this one (an added "O"), which was added at the request of the issuing corporation.

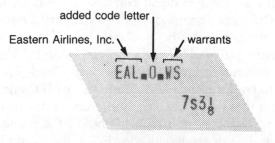

(Consolidated Tape: Network A)

"XD" is used to indicate the day on which a stock goes ex-dividend.

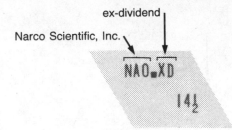

(Consolidated Tape: Network A)

In summary, here are the stock symbol qualifiers that might appear with the stock symbol on the top line:

Stock Symbol Qualifiers for Ticker Quotations

∎A, ∎B = class A, class B, etc.
Pr, PrC = preferred stock, preferred "C" stock
^r_t = rights
∎WD = when distributed
^w_i = when issued
∎WS = warrants
∎XD = ex dividend

As mentioned earlier, there are occasional bond quotations on Network B. For the bond qualifiers, see p. 103.

Few investors have ready access to ticker machines, but almost everyone has access to cable television, where stock-market ticker quotations are a regular feature. The screen is usually divided into three horizontal sections—the top being Network B (Amex); the bottom, Network A (NYSE); and the middle for news, financial data, and other material. (See photo 6.)

If you are learning to read ticker symbols on cable TV, it is suggested that you first concentrate on the top line only. Check for letters that might be easy to confuse, such as "U" and "V" or "D" and "O." Look for any qualifiers that might be used; preferred, ex-dividend, and class A, B, etc., are the most common. Note in photo 6 the shape of the "Pr" on network A and compare it with the "Pr" in the examples on page 60. After you are comfortable with the shape of the letters and their speed, you can begin adding the second line to your field of concentration.

2. The Bottom Line

a) *Volume*

The numbers on the second line usually begin slightly to the right of where the letters on the top line end. In normal operating mode, both volume and price are indicated. Volume is first, indicating the number of round lots transacted, followed by a small "s" for "share." The last number is the price.

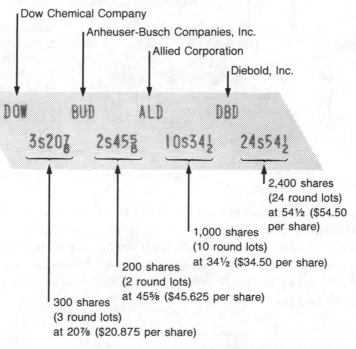

(Consolidated Tape: Network A)

If no volume indication precedes the price, it can mean either that the tape is in an operating mode where it is not printing the entire transaction or that the transaction was for only 100 shares (one round lot). Concerning the former, when the volume of transactions becomes so great that the ticker is in danger of falling as much as a minute behind, the ticker begins to abbreviate quotations in an effort to catch up. One way of doing this is to abbreviate the price and omit the volume. Whenever price and volume are affected in this way, an announcement appears on the tape. This mode of operation will be detailed under "Abbreviated Forms of Quotations" on p. 70. Meanwhile, in the examples below, volume is clearly not being omitted, because the three quotations in question are preceded and followed by quotations that do state the volume. It is therefore safe to assume that each of the middle three quotations below are for 100 shares of stock, one round lot.

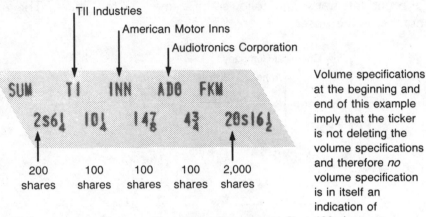

TII Industries

American Motor Inns

Audiotronics Corporation

SUM   TI   INN   ADO   FKM

2s6⅛   10⅛   14⅞   4¾   20s16½

200   100   100   100   2,000
shares   shares   shares   shares shares

(Consolidated Tape: Network B)

Volume specifications at the beginning and end of this example imply that the ticker is not deleting the volume specifications and therefore *no* volume specification is in itself an indication of 100 shares.

There is one other circumstance where volume is deleted, and that is when only closing prices are being given. Again, this is easy to spot since none of the quotations will have volume (because, strictly speaking, they are not transaction reports) and all the quotations will be in alphabetical order. There will be an announcement to the effect that only closing prices are being given.

Closing price quotations; no volume is given and the ticker symbols are grouped alphabetically.

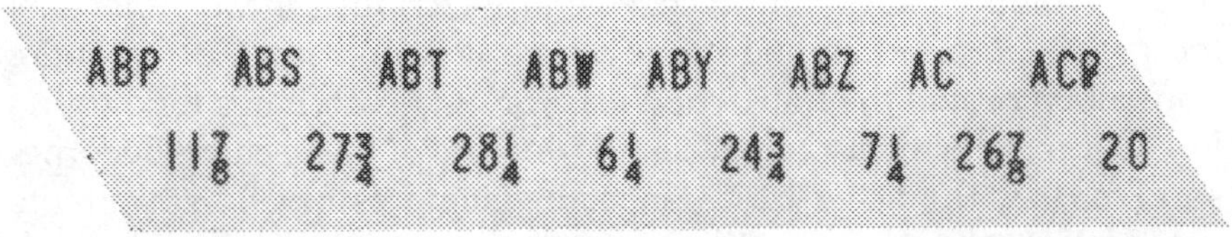

ABP   ABS   ABT   ABW   ABY   ABZ   AC   ACP

11⅞   27¾   28⅛   6¼   24¾   7¼   26⅞   20

(Consolidated Tape: Network A)

When the volume of a transaction is particularly large—10,000 shares or more—the volume is stated in full rather than in round lots.

(Note in the following examples that a square period is used instead of a comma.)

Block transactions,
10,000 shares or over,
specify volume in
actual number of
shares traded.

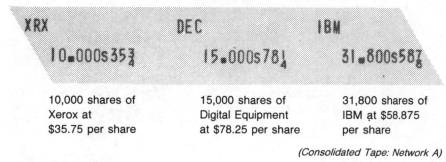

10,000 shares of   15,000 shares of   31,800 shares of
Xerox at   Digital Equipment   IBM at $58.875
$35.75 per share   at $78.25 per share   per share

(Consolidated Tape: Network A)

b) *Lots of Other Than 100 Shares*

There are some stocks that, because of their price or infrequency of transaction, will trade in less than 100 shares per round lot. The symbol for these transactions is "$\frac{s}{s}$." On the NYSE, these lots are always made up of 10 shares.

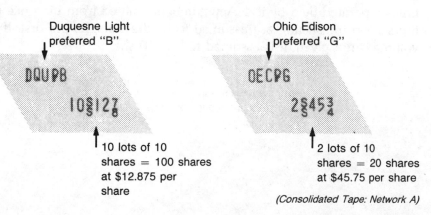

Duquesne Light   Ohio Edison
↓ preferred "B"   ↓ preferred "G"

10 lots of 10   2 lots of 10
shares = 100 shares   shares = 20 shares
at $12.875 per   at $45.75 per share
share

(Consolidated Tape: Network A)

However, on the Amex, "$\frac{s}{s}$" can mean lots of 10, 25, or 50 shares. The only way one can determine how many shares designated "$\frac{s}{s}$" constitute a round lot on the Amex is to consult a stock guide. If the security is traded in lots of other than 100, it will state the number in parentheses after the exchange abbreviation. In the following example, the first stock trades in lots of 50 shares while the second trades in lots of 10.

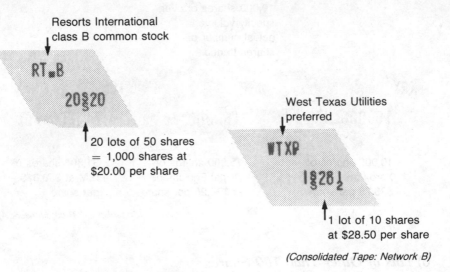

Resorts International
class B common stock

20 lots of 50 shares
= 1,000 shares at
$20.00 per share

West Texas Utilities
preferred

1 lot of 10 shares
at $28.50 per share

(Consolidated Tape: Network B)

c) *Two Transactions Combined*

When there are two separate transactions in the same security, they are often combined in the same quotation. The transactions are sometimes separated by a period. Any numbers omitted from the price in the second transaction are assumed to be the same as the first. If a volume is not given, it is assumed to be 100 shares.

two transactions with
complete volume and complete
price quotations

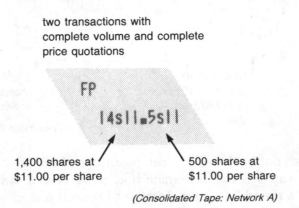

1,400 shares at
$11.00 per share

500 shares at
$11.00 per share

(Consolidated Tape: Network A)

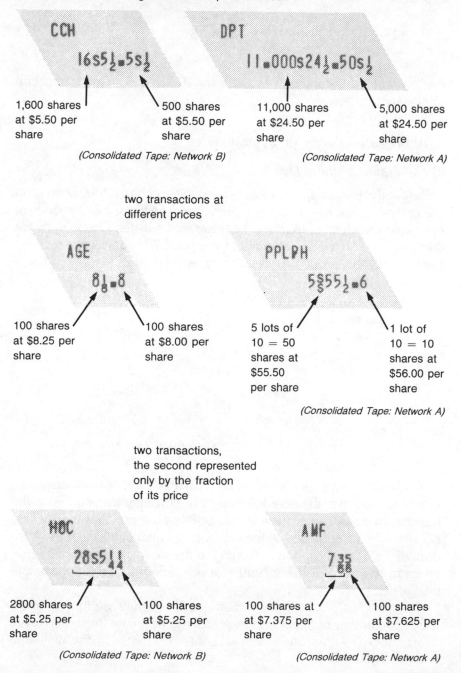

two transactions with
digits of second price omitted

CCH

16s5½.5s½

1,600 shares
at $5.50 per
share

500 shares
at $5.50 per
share

(Consolidated Tape: Network B)

DPT

11.000s24½.50s½

11,000 shares
at $24.50 per
share

5,000 shares
at $24.50 per
share

(Consolidated Tape: Network A)

two transactions at
different prices

AGE

8⅛.8

100 shares
at $8.25 per
share

100 shares
at $8.00 per
share

PPLPH

5⅜55½.6

5 lots of
10 = 50
shares at
$55.50
per share

1 lot of
10 = 10
shares at
$56.00 per
share

(Consolidated Tape: Network A)

two transactions,
the second represented
only by the fraction
of its price

HOC

28s5¼¼

2800 shares
at $5.25 per
share

100 shares
at $5.25 per
share

(Consolidated Tape: Network B)

AMF

7 ⅜⅝

100 shares at
at $7.375 per
share

100 shares
at $7.625 per
share

(Consolidated Tape: Network A)

The combination of two transactions can be confusing at first. The two clues to watch for are:

a)   a period separating the two prices
b)   repetition of the fraction

And assume the second transaction is for 100 shares unless it is specifically stated otherwise.

3. Abbreviated Forms of Quotations

a) *Digits and Volume Deleted*

Before the ticker falls a minute behind the combined transactions on the exchange floor and on the regional exchanges, various modes of operation are effected to move the ticker along faster. One is to delete the volume and the initial digits of the price. The announcement on the tape for this mode of quotation is as follows:

announcement of
abbreviated quotation
mode

DIGITS.&.VOL.DELETED

...   ■■

(Consolidated Tape: Network A)

Traders and investors are expected to know the approximate range in which securities they are following are currently trading. Since the majority of transactions are within ½ point of the previous transaction, no one need be confused by the deletion of initial digits from the price quotations. The discussion pertaining to the example below, of course, refers to the price of the securities at the time that the tape example was generated.

If one begins watching the quotations while they are in this mode, the large number of apparent low prices will be a sure indication (even if one doesn't know the securities) that the tape is in the digit-and-volume-delete mode.

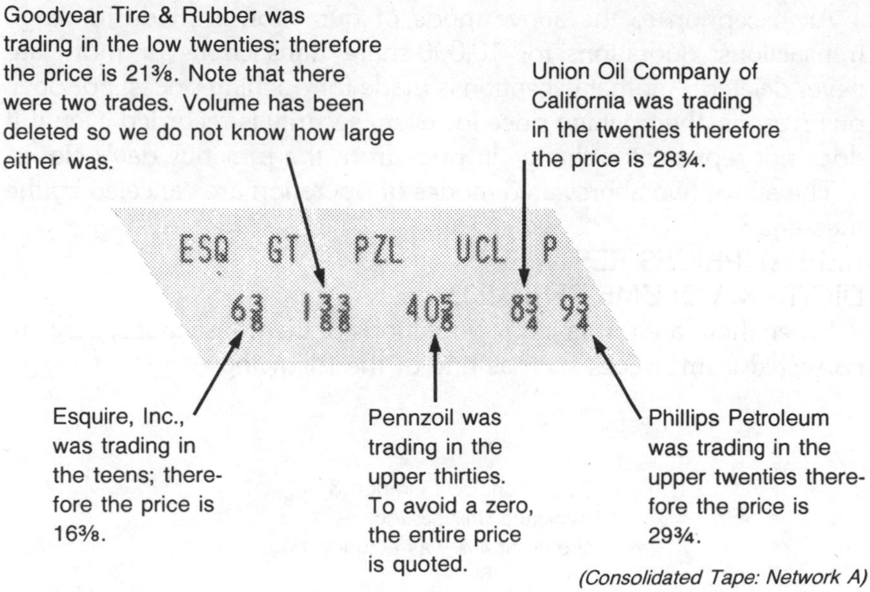
Goodyear Tire & Rubber was trading in the low twenties; therefore the price is 21⅜. Note that there were two trades. Volume has been deleted so we do not know how large either was.
Union Oil Company of California was trading in the twenties therefore the price is 28¾.
ESQ GT PZL UCL P
6⅜ 1⅜⅜ 40⅝ 8¾ 9¾
Esquire, Inc., was trading in the teens; therefore the price is 16⅜.
Pennzoil was trading in the upper thirties. To avoid a zero, the entire price is quoted.
Phillips Petroleum was trading in the upper twenties therefore the price is 29¾.

(Consolidated Tape: Network A)

There are two circumstances where digits and volume are never deleted: One is for sales over 10,000 shares (which are always reported in full), and the other is when the quotation is the first for that security during the day. (Opening transactions are always reported in full.)

b) ***Repeat Prices Omitted***

Another abbreviated mode of quotation is the deletion of transaction prices if there is no price change,—that is, if it takes place at the same price as the immediately preceding transaction in that security. This mode begins when the ticker falls a minute behind.

The notice for this mode of operation is as follows:

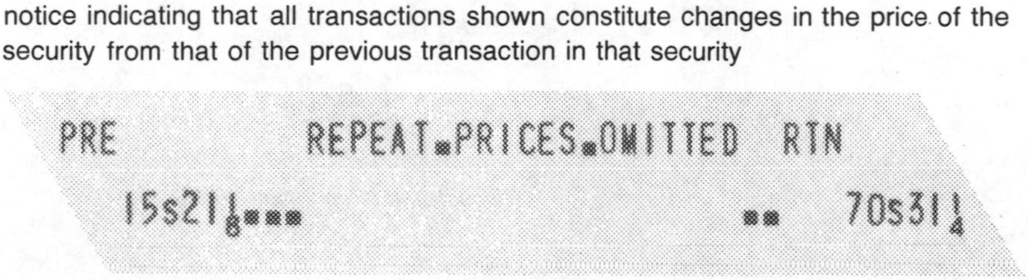
notice indicating that all transactions shown constitute changes in the price of the security from that of the previous transaction in that security
PRE REPEAT.PRICES.OMITTED RTN
15s21⅛... .. 70s31¼

(Consolidated Tape: Network A)

(Notice that words in ticker-style messages are separated by a period.)

An exception to the above mode of quotation is made for large transactions; quotations for 10,000-share transactions or more are never deleted. Another exception is made for opening prices. For obvious reasons, the opening price for every security is recorded even if it does not represent a change in price from the previous day's close.

The above two abbreviated modes of operation are canceled by the messages:

REPEAT PRICES RESUMED

DIGITS & VOLUME RESUMED

When there are errors in the quotations of the transactions, they are corrected in messages such as one of the following:

Correction: Last Orange &
Rockland Utilities, Inc.
quoted at 4⅞ was actually 4¾.

CORR.LAST.ORU WAS.

..   4⅞   4¾..

(Consolidated Tape: Network A)

Cancel 19 transactions back the
General Telephone & Electronics
transaction of 1,300 shares
at 29½.

CXL. SLS.BK.GTE

..   19   13s29½..

(Consolidated Tape: Network A)

If the transaction itself was an error, the following message cancels it.

Error: last GCA Corporation
at 2⅝ (disregard)

(Consolidated Tape: Network A)

And an outright cancellation of the transaction is indicated this way:

Correction: Two transactions back, the
Brock Hotel transaction of 14,000
shares at 3 was actually 10,000
shares at 3.

CORR. SLS.BK.BHC   WAS.
    2   14.000s3   10.000s3..

(Consolidated Tape: Network A)

c) *Trading Delayed or Halted*

When the trading of a stock is halted, for any of a variety of reasons, notices appear such as the following:

Trading halted in Hipotronics,
Inc., last transaction was 15½.

TRD.HLT.HIP.ODR.INF.LST
...   15½..

(Consolidated Tape: Network B)

When trading is resumed, it is announced as follows:

TRD.RESUMED.HIP

(Consolidated Tape: Network B)

Sometimes the opening of trading in a security will be delayed pending distribution of news.

Opening delayed for Thorofare Market, news
pending; last trade was 3⅜.

.OPG.DLY.TMI.NEWS.PND.LST

$3\frac{3}{8}$

(Consolidated Tape: Network B)

If the news item has already been distributed, the message reads:

Opening delay of Browning-Ferris
Industries on the NYSE; news has
been distributed; last trade was 30½.

.OPG.DLY.BFI&N.DISS.OF.NEWS.LAST

$30\frac{1}{2}$

(Consolidated Tape: Network A)

In the above example, "&N" indicates that trading was halted only on the NYSE, not any of the regional exchanges. (BFI is also registered on the Midwest and Pacific exchanges.)

d) *Bonds and Treasury Bills on the Amex*

Bonds are traded on both the NYSE and Amex. There is a separate bond ticker for the NYSE (which carries the heaviest volume of bonds of the two exchanges); the Amex includes bonds within its stock quotations. An example is as follows:

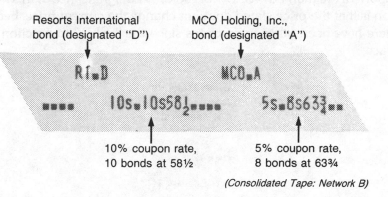

Resorts International
bond (designated "D")

MCO Holding, Inc.,
bond (designated "A")

10% coupon rate,
10 bonds at 58½

5% coupon rate,
8 bonds at 63¾

(Consolidated Tape: Network B)

Treasury bills are traded on the Amex (but not on the NYSE), and quotations are in the following format:

Treasury bill due 6/10/82,
10 bills at 11.81%

(Consolidated Tape: Network B)

e) *Miscellaneous*

Sixteenths: Sixteenths are not available on the ticket printing mechanism. They are therefore indicated with a ".16."

Consolidated Oil & Gas Warrants,
1,000 warrants at 9/16

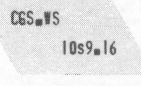

(Consolidated Tape: Network B)

Out-of-sequence reports: Transaction reports that are out of sequence (i.e., they occurred at some point in the past and were not reported) are marked "■SLD" for "sold." The significance of this indication is that the price stated does not change the current price, because there have been other transactions since the "■SLD" transaction took place.

General Motors sold
(sometime in the past)
500 shares at 40⅜.

GM■SLD

5s40⅜

(Consolidated Tape: Network A)

A late reported opening transaction quotation appears as follows:

Thorofare Market opened (late); first
trade was 1,000 shares at 3½

TMI■OPD

10s3½

(Consolidated Tape: Network B)

Index reports: Various indexes are regularly reported in announcements such as the following:

At 1:30 P.M., the NYSE market is up 1¢ (average per share);
the NYSE Index stands at 63.52, up .02.

P■M■■■NYSE■MKT■UP CTS■■NYSE■IDX   UP

1■30   I   63■52 0■02■■

(Consolidated Tape: Network A)

At closing, reports such as the above are broken down into their various components (i.e., industrials, utilities, etc.).

Closing: Both Network A and Network B print a list of stocks that pay dividends on that day. The list is entitled "Ex Dividend Tomorrow." This means that a purchase the next day will not entitle the purchaser to the current dividend. (Actually, it means that a purchase the next day would not allow sufficient time for the purchaser to become a stockholder of record by the day dividends are distributed—usually four days away.

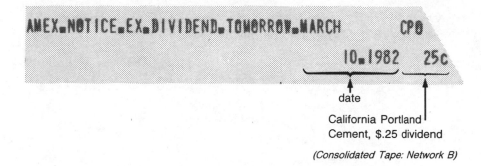

date

California Portland
Cement, $.25 dividend

(Consolidated Tape: Network B)

The Amex, as in the above example, uses "c" for cents. The New York Exchange spells out "cents" and omits it when the figure is in dollars. For the last quotation below, note that there are no "cents" indicated, so the dividend is $2.8125.

When cents are
not specified, the
dividend is in
dollars.

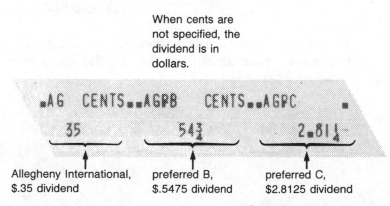

Allegheny International,   preferred B,   preferred C,
$.35 dividend $.5475 dividend $2.8125 dividend

(Consolidated Tape: Network A)

Final transaction prices for NYSE issues are reported on Network A as follows:

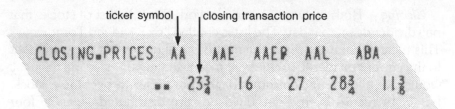

ticker symbol ┐   ┌ closing transaction price

CLOSING.PRICES AA │ AAE AAEP AAL ABA

.. 23¾ 16   27   28¾ 11⅞

(Consolidated Tape: Network A)

On the NYSE, a final report is given on the 15 most active stocks. Note that 1,528,900 is the volume.

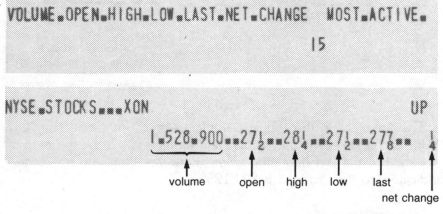

VOLUME.OPEN.HIGH.LOW.LAST.NET.CHANGE MOST.ACTIVE.

15

NYSE.STOCKS...XON   UP

1.528.900..27½..28¼..27½..27⅞.. ¼

volume   open   high   low   last

net change

(Consolidated Tape: Network A)

The closing bid and asked prices are given for stocks that did not trade. The prices are separated by a period, and the asked price is abbreviated wherever possible.

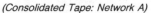

BID.ASK.PRICES.OF.STOCKS.NOT.TRADED AAEP

.. 27.⅞

bid price   asked price

(Consolidated Tape: Network A)

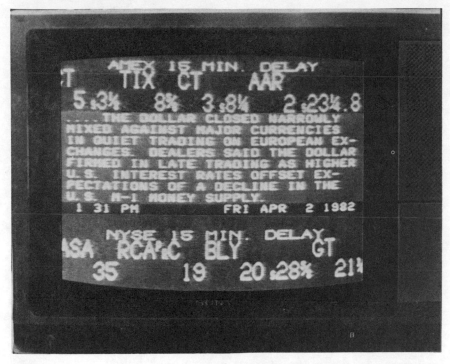

*(courtesy Manhattan Cable TV and Reuters NEWS-VIEW.
Photo: Perry McLamb)*

CABLE TV
TICKER QUOTATIONS

The most generally available access to ticker quotations is via cable TV. Network B, Amex quotations, is shown across the top of the screen, and Network A, NYSE quotations, is shown across the bottom. One of the benefits of exchange membership is exclusive access to ticker quotations for fifteen minutes thus the broadcast is delayed, as indicated on the screen. Other financial news is usually shown in the middle of the screen. In the NYSE quotations, note the format of "Pr"; it is somewhat different from the printed ticker symbol.

Other market statistics are given on Network A, such as volume from the regional exchanges.

On the Amex, the closing report includes the open, high, low, and last trade for each stock as well as the volume and the closing bid and asked prices.

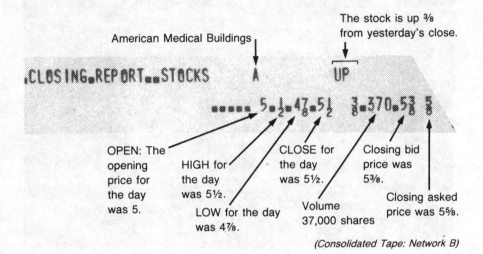

(Consolidated Tape: Network B)

6 How to Read Quote Terminals

A. Background

Quote terminals have become increasingly available to the public in brokerages, in offices, and even in such unlikely places as railroad stations. Scaled-down models of quote terminals are being marketed for home use, and financial quotations can also be accessed through home computers.

Many quote machines are more than passive information retrieval systems. They are, for instance, used by market makers to enter bid and ask prices for NASDAQ securities. However, the concern of this chapter is only with obtaining stock quotations and other relevant information about securities.

There are several manufacturers of quote terminals, such as Quotron and Bunker Ramo, and their models, of course, vary. Arrangements of the keyboards vary, and the information on the screen can be formatted to the user's specifications. Given the variety of hardware and software it is only practical to generalize information and procedures here from a few examples.

To obtain information on most models simply follow these steps:

1. Punch in the ticker symbol for the stock desired. (Do not use the shift key for capital letters.)
2. Punch in a qualifier, if necessary (e.g., the "Pr" key for preferred). Other qualifiers may require a period such as ".WS" for warrants or ".A" for class A.
3. Punch a transfer key such as one of the following, depending on the model:
    a) price
    b) send

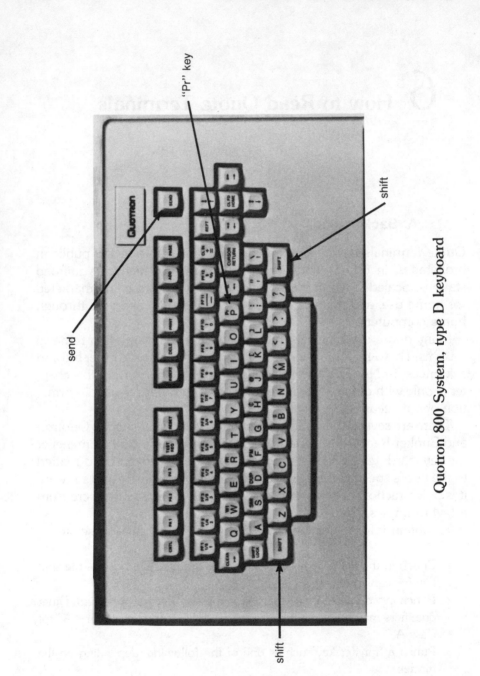

Quotron 800 System, type D keyboard

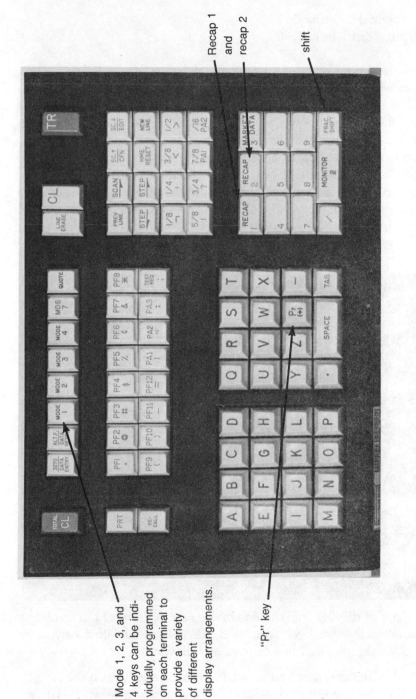

Recap 1 and recap 2

shift

Mode 1, 2, 3, and 4 keys can be individually programmed on each terminal to provide a variety of different display arrangements.

"Pr" key

Bunker Ramo Market Decision System 7 keyboard

c) mode 1 or mode 2

d) recap 1 or recap 2

Note that, as on computer terminals, all letters are capital. However, in cases where a shift key is needed (sometimes "Pr" requires a shift) one depresses first the shift key and then the "Pr" key. There is no need to hold the shift key down, as on a typewriter; the keys need only to be depressed sequentially.

Two standard keyboards are shown in the examples that follow. Two sample displays are also shown. The content and format of the information on the screen will vary depending on how the terminals have been programmed. However, note that there is some consistency in the symbols used (e.g., L = last, H = high, B = bid, A = ask, etc.).

Sample Quotron Display

In this type of display *only the line at the very bottom of the screen* is the quotation that has been requested (IBM). Marked with an arrow in the above example, that line is read as follows:

IBM = ticker symbol punched; N = last trade was on the NYSE; −55⅞ = the last trade was at 55⅞ which was down (−) from the previous trade; B 55¾ = current bid price; A 56 = current ask price; O 56¼ = the opening price for the day; H 56⅜ = high for the day; L 55⅞ = low for the day; V 184,500 = volume; the arrow (≥) at the end of the line means that more information is available, such as the time of the last trade.

All the material above the bottom line has been programmed for constant display and will appear no matter what quote has been requested. That material is read as follows:

line 1:

```
DC 5·17½  NME 5·19  HUM 6·33¾  CPL 8·19⅝  GLM 5·23⅝  DMP 6·1
```

This is a block ticker that shows only transactions above a specified volume. In this particular example only trades of 500 shares or more on either the NYSE or Amex tickers will appear.

lines 2, 3, and 4:

```
CPL 8·19⅝  PEP 2900·33½  USHRD 3·24¼  GLM 5·23⅝  AL 4·25⅞
NES 23¾ BHW SLD 20¾  AEP SLD 3·17  IBM 55⅞  SOC 9·36⅞⅞
SLF 5½ 7·¼
```

This is the NYSE ticker (Network A).

lines 5, 6, and 7:

```
P M  357 27  UP 2.47 . . . . . .  DJI 4⅞  DMP 6·17¾  UAS 9·6⅞
TNUI ND 16¼ 83· 20·100 . .  TOP N 3·16⅞  CLN 1700·24¼
DYN 2·8¾  VSH 8⅝  HO 3·25½ . .
```

This is the Amex ticker (Network B).

line 8:

```
        IBM 2·55⅞ 6·⅞  IBM 40 000 · 55⅞  F 19⅞  IBM 55⅞
```

This is a selective ticker. It reports only transactions for which it has been programmed. These will vary depending on the securities the person using this terminal wishes to follow.

lines 9, 10, and 11:

```
INDU − 09  COMP + 84   IBM −55⅞ .   WU −23¾+⅛  T −56¼+⅜·
VOLU 20.309 UVOL 10.562 EAL +8+¼   WUJD +4+¼  S +16¾+⅜
TRIN 1 12   DVOL 6.493  XRX −47½+½· QUOT −37−½  X −28−1
```

This is a selective monitor. Various statistics and averages are continually updated depending on what the user has requested.

Sample Bunker Ramo Display

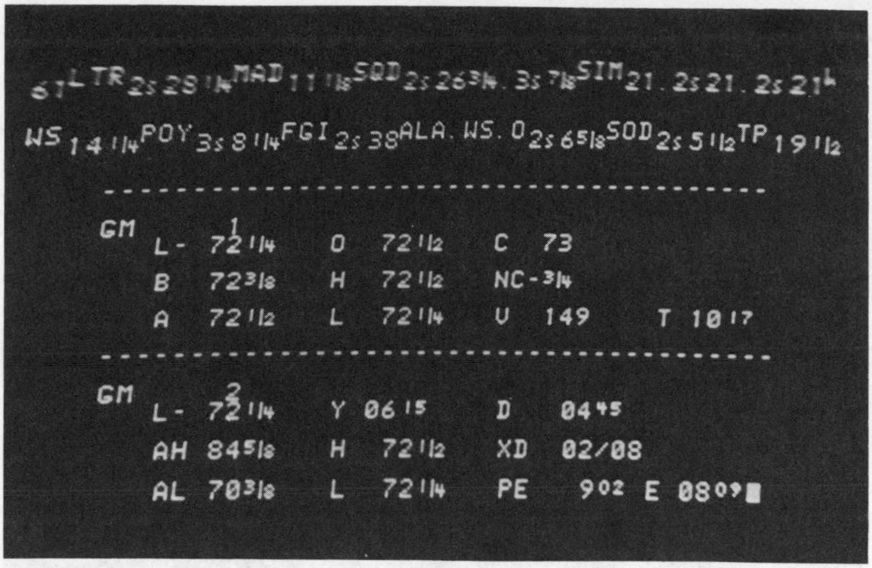

Use of one of the "mode" keys (mode 1, mode 2, etc.) will result in a screen display divided into three parts as shown above. (The segments are separated by a dotted line.) The content of the three segments can vary depending on how the terminal is programmed. The above example is read as follows:

TOP SEGMENT:

Line 1 is the NYSE ticker (Network A).
Line 2 is the Amex ticker (Network B).

MIDDLE SEGMENT:

```
-------------------------------------------
GM     1
    L- 72 1|4    O  72 1|2   C  73
    B  72 3|8    H  72 1|2   NC-3|4
    A  72 1|2    L  72 1|4   V  149     T 10 17
```

This is called the "current recap" and it shows current information on the security requested. If one punched the "recap 1" key (instead of a "mode" key) this segment would be the only display on the screen.

GM = ticker symbol punched. 1 = "recap 1" display (which can be obtained by punching the "recap 1" key).

first column symbols (to the right of "GM")

L−72¼ = last trade (minus indicates it was lower than the previous trade). Sometimes a letter appears here indicating the exchange, if it is other than NYSE or Amex.

B 72⅜ = current bid price

A 72½ = current ask price

second column symbols

O 72½ = opening price for the day

H 72½ = high for the day

L 72¼ = low for the day

third column symbols

C 73 = closing price of the previous day

NC − ¾ = net change from previous day

V 149 = volume (in round lots)

fourth column symbols

T 10:17 = time of the last trade

- - - - - - - - - - - - - - - - - - - -

BOTTOM SEGMENT:

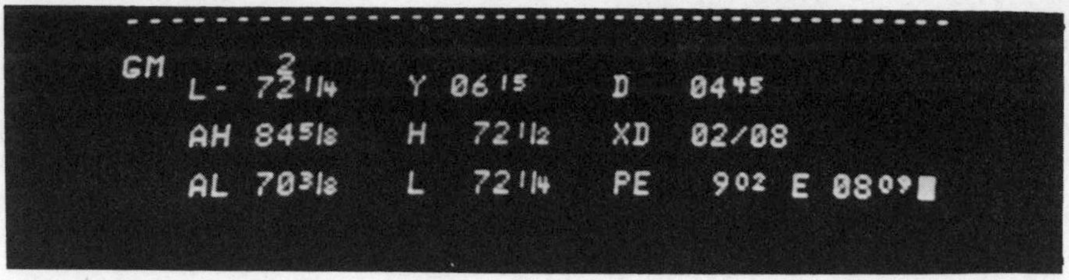
GM 2
L- 72 1/4 Y 06 15 D 04 45
AH 84 5/8 H 72 1/2 XD 02/08
AL 70 3/8 L 72 1/4 PE 9 02 E 08 09

This is called the "statistical recap" and it shows updated statistics on the security requested. If one punched the "recap 2" key (instead of a "mode" key) this segment would be the only display on the screen.

GM = ticker symbol punched. 2 = "recap 2" display (which can be obtained by punching the "recap 2" key).

first column symbols (to the right of "GM")
L−72¼ = last trade (minus indicates it was lower than the previous trade).
AH 84⅝ = annual high
AL 70⅜ = annual low

second column symbols
Y 6.15 = yield % from dividends
H 72½ = high for the day
L 72¼ = low for the day

third column symbols
D 4.45 = annual dividend in dollars
XD 2/8 = ex-dividend date
PE 9.02 = P-E ratio

fourth column symbols
E 8.09 = latest per-share earnings annualized

PART TWO

HOW TO READ
BOND
QUOTATIONS

(Edward C. Topple, NYSE photographer)

**THE BOND ROOM
OF THE NEW
YORK STOCK EXCHANGE**

7 Corporate Bonds on the NYSE and Amex

A. Background

Bonds are long-term debt obligations. When you buy a corporate bond, you are not buying a small part of a company, as with stock; you are lending a company money. In return, the company obligates itself to pay a specified rate of interest and to return the face value of the bond upon maturity.

A great variety of bonds are available. They are issued by (that is, the borrowers are):

Corporations
Municipalities (states, counties, cities, school districts, etc.)
Government Agencies (Government National Mortgage Association [GNMA], Federal Farm Credit, etc.)
Governments (U.S. and foreign governments)

If you are considering the purchase of bonds, you should discuss your investment objectives with a broker or banker to determine the bond type most suited to your needs. Bonds may be obtained through stockbrokers and commercial banks; however, the latter handle only transactions of municipal and government issues.

In this chapter, we will consider corporate bonds. As is the case with other loans, bond obligations must be met by corporations whether they produce earnings in a given year or not. Should a corporation default, interest payments are usually cumulative. (However, for an exception see "income bond" in the glossary.)

A bond is known as a "fixed-income security" because its interest rate (also known as coupon rate) does not vary. Bonds are considered a safer investment than stocks because they have prior claim to the assets of a company in case of bankruptcy. Also, the interest payments of bonds take priority over the payment of stock and preferred-stock dividends. However, corporations often have several issues of bonds, and the claims of some issues may take priority over others. Those with the highest priorities are referred to as senior debt obligations.

In general, there are two major categories of corporate bonds:

1. *Unsecured bonds,* called "debentures" (pronounced "de-ben'-churs"), which are backed only by the general credit of the corporation.
2. *Secured bonds.* The major types are:
   a) *Mortgage bonds,* backed by the mortgage of real property.
   b) *Equipment trust certificates,* backed by the mortgage of equipment, such as railroad cars or airplanes.
   c) *Collateral trust bonds,* backed by securities, on deposit, of another company.

In evaluating a bond, the financial condition of the corporation is generally more important than whether the bond is secured or unsecured.

Other types of bonds, somewhat less common, are floating-rate bonds, for which the interest rates vary with the rate of Treasury bills or some other security; income bonds, for which the interest depends, to an extent, on the earnings of the corporation; and zero-interest bonds which do not pay interest until maturity. You may want to check each of these in the glossary.

Convertible bonds are a kind of hybred between stocks and bonds, and they are the only type differentiated in the quotations. They are discussed later under "Current Yield."

The face value of most quoted corporate bonds is $1,000. Known as the "par value," this is the amount on which the rate of interest is calculated (thus a 9½% bond would pay $95 per year) no matter what you paid for the bond. Par value is also the amount that will be returned to the owner at maturity.

The majority of bonds are unlisted and traded over the counter. Even so, there are over 3,000 separate issues traded on the New York Stock Exchange.

The NYSE bond room is a trading room separate from the rest of the exchange. The computer and communications systems rival those of the stock floor, and a separate bond ticker is also maintained. Some bond transactions are processed by computer and some are traded by open outcry in a central trading ring on the bond room floor. It is an NYSE rule that orders of 9 or less bonds must go to the floor to be traded, thus giving the small investor maximum benefit from the exchange system.

Bond quotations never appear in the same listings as stock. They are quoted separately under a variety of headings, including:

New York (or American) **Exchange Bonds**
New York Stock Exchange Bonds (or Amex Bonds)
Listed Bonds—N.Y. Exchange (or American Exchange)

B. The Quotations

1) 12-Month High and Low

Some weekly bond quotations begin with the 12-month high and low, similar to stock quotations, as shown in the following weekly quotations from bonds listed on the NYSE:

price range of previous 12 months (not given in all quotations) in percent of par value

12-month High	Low	Bonds	Cur. Yld	Sls In $1,000	High	Low	Last	Net Chg.
		A	**B**	**C**	**D**			
63½	35	AMInt 9⅞95	22.9	117	43	38½	41	......
67⅛	50	APL 10¾97	19.4	16	56⅞	55⅜	55⅜	- ⅞
56½	42	ARA 4⅝s96	cv	13	47¾	47¾	47¾	- ¼
72⅛	54⅞	AbbtL 6¼93	11.0	4	56⅞	56⅞	56⅞	+ 1⅜
72	51¼	AetnLf 8⅛07	14.7	85	59⅞	55⅛	55⅛	- 2⅞
102½	97	AlaBn 16.95s99	16.8	13	101⅛	100	101	+ 1
66	52	AlaP 9s2000	16.4	20	56⅞	55	55	- ½
64¾	50⅝	AlaP 8½s01	16.1	43	52⅞	51⅛	52⅞	+ 1⅛
61	46½	AlaP 7¾s02	16.0	34	49¼	47½	48½	+ ½

(The New York Times)

Bond prices are quoted in percent of par, so that the 12-month high for the first bond listed above at 63½ is $635.00 (63½% of $1,000) and the low of 35 is $350.00.

Some people have the mistaken idea that the prices of bonds do not fluctuate. A glance at the 12-month high and low demonstrates otherwise. However, the *circumstances* under which bond prices fluctuate are generally different from the circumstances under which stock prices rise and fall. Bond prices are affected by:

1. the general level of interest rates (which interacts with the coupon rate)
2. the bond rating (by Moody's or Standard & Poor's)
3. the amount of time until maturity
4. supply and demand
5. stock price (for convertibles)

Interpretation: Each bond has a fixed interest rate. The relationship of that rate to current interest rates is one of the most important factors in determining the price of a bond. For example, if you were to buy a long-term bond ($1,000 face value) that paid 5% (i.e., $50 a year) but the current interest rates were 10%, then you would expect to pay approximately $500 for that bond (ignoring, for the time being, yield to maturity), which is one-half the face value. This would mean that the yield on your cash outlay (a $50 annual yield on $500) would be 10% a year, thus bringing the (effective) interest that the bond paid into line with current rates.

When a bond sells below par, as in the above example, it is known as a *discount bond.* When it sells above par, it is a *premium bond.* Even the prices of new bonds, when they are first issued, are adjusted by this process, and only occasionally do they sell exactly at par.

The second factor in the price of a bond is its rating. There are two standard rating companies: Moody's Investment Service and Standard & Poor's. Their rating levels are roughly equivalent, and their decisions with respect to the ratings of individual corporations are usually similar.

BOND RATINGS

Standard & Poor's	Moody's	
AAA	Aaa	highest quality
AA+	Aa1	high quality
AA	Aa2	
AA−	Aa3	
A+	A1	upper medium quality
A	A2	
A−	A3	
BBB+	Baa1	medium quality
BBB	Baa2	
BBB−	Baa3	

BB+	Ba1	speculative
BB	Ba2	
BB−	Ba3	
B+	B1	very speculative
B	B2	
B−	B3	
CCC	Caa	poor quality, may be in default
CC	Ca	highly speculative
C	C	poorest quality
D		in default

The above definitions are only approximations. For precise definitions, see Appendix 2, "Definitions of Ratings by Moody's and Standard & Poor's." The purpose of the ratings is to give an evaluation of the financial condition of the company and its ability to meet the obligations of the bond. The lower the rating, the higher the interest rate necessary, since for higher risk one expects to receive a higher return. The highest-rated bonds thus pay the lowest interest, but they offer maximum safety.

The factor of supply and demand, which is paramount to the price of stock, does not play quite as direct a role in the price of bonds. An increase in demand for a bond will tend to push its price upward, but such a demand is almost always the result of other determinants, such as interest rates. An increase in earnings, which would cause a rise in the price of a company's stock, would ordinarily not affect the price of its bonds, since the coupon rate of the bond does not change.

Another factor in the price of bonds is the maturity date. In the earlier example of the 5% bond (for which one paid $500), if it matured the following year it would not be available for $500. That would mean a more than 100% gain (including interest) in two years when, at maturity, the company redeemed the bond for $1,000. Obviously, the price of discounted bonds must take the date of maturity into consideration. It is also the case that longer-term bonds react more strongly to interest-rate changes than shorter-term bonds, since over a long span of time a small interest-rate difference can add up significantly.

There is an additional influence on the price of convertible bonds, and that is the price of the common stock of the corporation. If a convertible bond (par $1,000) could be redeemed for 100 shares of common stock and the stock were at 15, then the bond would be worth at least $1,500 if converted (the value of 100 shares). However, should the price of the common stock drop below $10, there would be some downside protection. In that case, the price of the bond would tend to fall in line with other bonds of a similar coupon rate, rating, and maturity year, since, obviously, the coupon rate would remain the same.

2) Corporation Name

As with stocks, the corporation names are usually abbreviated. Unfortunately, the abbreviation for a particular bond is often not the same one used in the stock quotations. For instance, in the example below, the last company, Baker International, is abbreviated "BakInt." In the NYSE stock quotations, the abbreviation is "BkrIntl."

12-mo. High	Low		Yield	Sales $ (thous)	Weekly High	Low	Close	Net Ch.
95½	67	BPNA 10s00	14.9	1	67	67	67	— 3
84½	61	BPNA 9¼01	15.2	10	61	61	61	— 2⅞
96	79	Bache 14s00	14.7	814	96	93⅛	95⅛	+ 1⅝
87	66⅛	BakInt 7.55s87	11.0	8	68⅜	68⅜	68⅜	+ 2¼

name of the company (abbreviated) issuing the bond

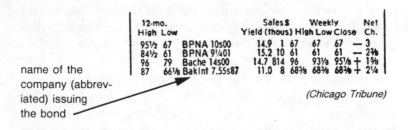

(Chicago Tribune)

Even though a bond is traded on an exchange, it will not be listed if it does not trade that day.

Bonds of a company that has changed its name due to a merger or acquisition may continue to be listed under the original name until maturity or until the bonds are called. In the case of a merger, the bonds of the original company are often converted into common stock of the successor company or new bonds may be issued.

3) Coupon Rate and Maturity Year

The ***coupon rate*** is the fixed interest rate on the par value of the bond, usually $1,000 for corporate bonds. The coupon rate never varies except in the case of floating-rate notes and income bonds.

The term "coupon rate" comes from the coupons that are attached to the bond certificate. These coupons must be clipped and sent (directly, or through a bank or broker) to the issuing corporation in order for payment of interest to be made. The issuing company does not keep a record of who owns its bonds, so such bonds are considered to be owned by the person who has them in his possession. Obviously, bonds in this form, called "bearer form," must be kept in a safe place. If bearer bonds are held by a broker, the brokerage will usually clip and send in the coupons for the client's account. When bearer bonds are held by a brokerage, the buyer should keep the confirmation or delivery ticket from the broker as proof of ownership.

The coupon rate and maturity year are a part of the name of the bond and appear immediately after the corporation abbreviation.

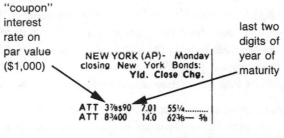

(Chicago Tribune)

The 12-month high and low are frequently omitted in daily quotations, as in the above example, so that the name of the bond appears in the left-hand column. The first bond shown is an American Telephone & Telegraph issue listed "3⅞ s 90" which is referred to as the "AT&T, 3⅞'s of '90." The 3⅞ is the coupon rate; the "s" is used probably because of the way the name is spoken, and the 90 is the year, 1990.

The use of "s" is not always necessary; its primary function is to separate the coupon rate from the year of maturity, but there is no need when a fraction appears in the coupon rate. In the second quotation, also for an AT&T bond, the coupon rate is 8¾%, the year of maturity is 2000, and there is no "s."

Some bonds have the coupon rate quoted in decimals. In the example below, the coupon rates for the last two Ford Motor Credit bonds are 8.85% and 9.7%.

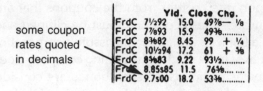

some coupon rates quoted in decimals

		Yld.	Close	Chg.
FrdC	7½92	15.0	49⅞	− ⅛
FrdC	7⅞93	15.9	49⅜	....
FrdC	8⅜82	8.45	99	+ ¼
FrdC	10½94	17.2	61	+ ⅝
FrdC	8⅝83	9.22	93½	....
FrdC	8.85s85	11.5	76⅝	....
FrdC	9.7s00	18.2	53⅜	....

(The Washington Post)

Interest is usually paid twice a year. Thus a bond with a coupon rate of 8% would pay $40 every six months. Payment dates are the first, fifteenth, or thirtieth of the month. If a bond pays on January 15, it will also pay on July 15; if February 15, then also August 15, etc. There are some bonds, however, that pay interest quarterly, and even monthly.

With respect to interest payments, bonds come in two varieties, registered form and bearer form.

Registered bonds are registered by the issuer in the name of the owner, and interest payments and final redemption are mailed automatically. Most newly issued corporate bonds are registered or are at least available in both registered and coupon form. Some bonds are registered with respect to principal but not interest so they would have coupons like a bearer bond.

Bearer bonds, as mentioned earlier, have coupons attached to the bond certificates. These must be detached and sent to the issuer in order for the interest payment to be mailed.

For corporate bonds, there is a general preference for the registered form. For municipal bonds, bearer form has been preferred but as of 1983 new issues of municipals will only be in registered form.

Sometimes capital letters follow the maturity year when it is necessary to distinguish bonds that would otherwise appear identical (except for price). The following two Gulf & Western bonds are an example:

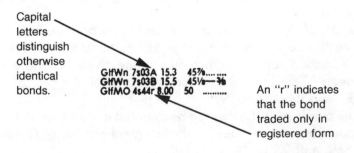

Capital letters distinguish otherwise identical bonds.

GlfWn	7s03A	15.3	45⅞	....
GlfWn	7s03B	15.5	45⅛	− ⅜
GlfMO	4s44r	8.00	50	....

An "r" indicates that the bond traded only in registered form

(The Miami Herald)

In the third quotation of the example above, a lowercase "r" follows the maturity year. This indicates that the registered form of the bond traded on that day. In this case the "Gulf Mobile & Ohio 4% due in '44" was originally issued in both bearer and registered form, and one can assume that both forms are still available. Other qualifiers, usually lowercase, may follow the maturity year. Check the section on qualifiers later in this chapter.

4) Current Yield

Current yield is the percent of the current price that will be paid in the form of annual interest.

The current yield tells a prospective buyer the annual percent of yield on the investment that will be locked in if the bond is purchased at the current price (the closing price shown in that particular quotation).

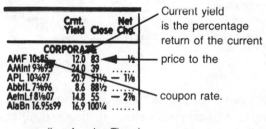

(Los Angeles Times)

In the example above, the current yield for AMF bonds, the first quotation, is 12%. Since we know from the "10s85" that the coupon rate is 10%, we know the dividend will be $100. The current price is $830 (as shown in the next-to-last column), and $100 is approximately 12% of $830. (Actually, it's slightly more since .12 times 830 is 99.6.)

Obviously, after purchase, the current yield percent is locked in and becomes the annual percentage of interest return the investor will receive until maturity. When the bond matures, the investor receives the last interest payment plus the par value of the bond. In the above case, that would constitute a $170 capital gain.

Since the coupon rate and the current price are provided in each bond quotation, one can calculate the current yield for oneself by dividing the annual interest amount by the price paid. For this reason many newspapers save space by omitting the current yield in their bond quotations. It is a convenience, however, for comparing bonds. Otherwise the calculations have to be made for every bond one wishes to consider.

If a "cv" appears in the current-yield column, it indicates a convertible bond. This is the only major bond type designated in the quotations.

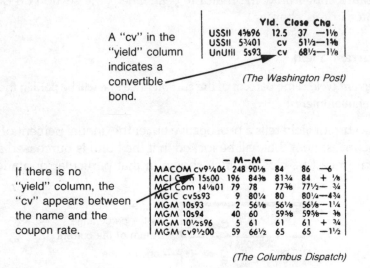

A "cv" in the "yield" column indicates a convertible bond.

	Yld.	Close	Chg.
USSII 4⅜96	12.5	37	—1½
USSII 5¾01	cv	51½	—1⅜
UnUtil 5s93	cv	68½	—1⅛

(The Washington Post)

If there is no "yield" column, the "cv" appears between the name and the coupon rate.

— M—M —					
MACOM cv9¼06	248	90⅛	84	86	—6
MCI Com 15s00	196	84⅜	81¾	84	+ ⅛
MCI Com 14⅛01	79	78	77⅜	77½	— ¾
MGIC cv5s93	9	80¼	80	80¼	—4¾
MGM 10s93	2	56⅛	56⅛	56⅛	—1¼
MGM 10s94	40	60	59⅜	59⅜	— ⅜
MGM 10½s96	5	61	61	61	+ ¾
MGM cv9½00	59	66½	65	65	—1½

(The Columbus Dispatch)

The convertible privilege allows the investor to convert the bond into a specified amount of common stock in the issuing company at any time (sometimes it is after or before a specified date). As mentioned before, this feature causes the price of the bond to track somewhat the price of the underlying stock.

Another yield often cited for bonds is the yield to maturity. Although not usually part of newspaper corporate-bond quotations, it will be mentioned by your broker and you will see it in newspaper articles. Yield to maturity gives a more accurate picture of the total yield of a bond, primarily because it takes into account the capital gain or loss from the return of par at maturity.

Yield to maturity is an percentage figure used to compare bonds to one another that takes into account:

1. the price paid for the bond relative to its face value
2. the time left until maturity
3. the coupon rate

The calculation of yield to maturity is complex because it attempts to arrive at a single percentage figure to represent money, part of which is received over a long period of time and part of which is received at one time (maturity).

One cannot simply annualize the capital gain (or loss) because, for example, receiving $1,000 at the end of a 10-year period is different from receiving $100 a year for 10 years. In the latter case the money has more economic potential since one could reinvest the first $100 for a 9-year period by the time the last $100 was received; one could reinvest the second $100 for an 8-year period, etc.

The yield to maturity attempts to realistically represent the potential of a bond. It is also a convenience in that it is used to compare bonds to one another that are of different prices, yields, and amounts of time till maturity.

5) Volume

In daily and weekly quotations, the volume listed is the exact number of bonds sold. (The term "sales in $1,000" refers to the par value of each bond.) If there are no transactions, a bond is not listed.

Volume listed
is exact number
of bonds traded.

	Sales $1000	High	Low	Last	Chg
K mart cv6s99	242	61½	61	61⅛	— ⅜
Kaisr cv9s05	5	71	71	71	....
KaneMil 9½s90	10	68	68	68	....
KaufBrd 12¼99	18	71½	71½	71½	...

(The Columbus Dispatch)

As always, volume is a clue to marketability. If you are purchasing bonds to hold to maturity, then this is not an issue. Most listed bonds trade in sufficient volume to maintain liquidity, but you should be aware that a small number of bonds in an issue that is seldom traded can be difficult to buy or sell.

6) High—Low—Close (or Last) Change

The format of these prices is the same as for stock quotations. However, the prices are in percent of par value.

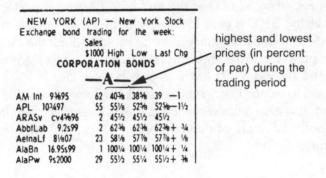

NEW YORK (AP) — New York Stock Exchange bond trading for the week:

	Sales $1000	High	Low	Last	Chg
CORPORATION BONDS					
—A—					
AM Int 9⅜95	62	40⅜	38⅝	39	−1
APL 10¾97	55	55⅛	52⅝	52⅝	−1½
ARASv cv4⅝96	2	45½	45½	45½	
AbbtLab 9.2s99	2	62⅜	62⅜	62⅜	+ ¾
AetnaLf 8⅛07	23	58⅛	57⅞	57⅞	+ ⅛
AlaBn 16.95s99	1	100¼	100¼	100¼	+ ¼
AlaPw 9s2000	29	55½	55¼	55½	+ ⅜

highest and lowest prices (in percent of par) during the trading period

(The Dallas Morning News)

The most current price is the closing price. As with stock, one cannot be sure of the price of a bond until one's broker has completed the transaction. Also, accrued interest must be added to bond prices—that is, all interest that has accumulated since the last interest payment must also be paid to the seller of the bond. This charge sometimes comes as a surprise to the new purchaser of corporate bonds. The first interest payment, however, will be a full payment so that the initial accumulated interest charge is recovered.

"Last" or "close" is most current price; does not include accrued interest.

AMEX BONDS

	($1000)	High	Low	Close	Chg.
ArrowEl 12s98	2	64½	64½	64½	.....
BergnBrn cv9⅞01	10	101	101	101	−2
Condec 10s97	25	57	57	57	+1½
ConsOG 9s88	3	66	66	66	− ½
ConsOG 9¼92	1	67½	67½	67½	...
ConTel cv5¼86	4	78¼	78¼	78¼	− ¾
CrysOilcv 11⅜00	117	87	86½	86½	−1
DamOil 13.20s00	2	67	67	67	−3½
Digicon 10½01	12	91	90	90	−3
DorchGs cv8½05	30	73	72½	72½	− ½
DuroT cv5¾92	1	80	80	80	.....
EAC cv6½85	19	86½	85½	85½	−1⅜

(Houston Chronicle)

"Change" or "net change" is the change from the previous closing price. Note that since the quotation is in percent of par, +1 means +$10 (for a $1,000 bond), not +$100 as it does for a round lot of stock. In the last quotation below, −1⅞ is therefore −$18.75.

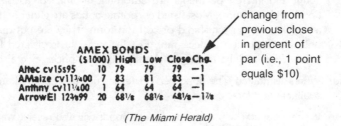

change from previous close in percent of par (i.e., 1 point equals $10)

AMEX BONDS

	($1000)	High	Low	Close	Chg.
Altec cv15s95	10	79	79	79	−1
AMaize cv11¾00	7	83	81	83	−1
Anthny cv11¼00	1	64	64	64	−1
ArrowEl 12¾s99	20	68⅛	68⅛	68⅛	−1⅞

(The Miami Herald)

C. Qualifiers

A large number of alphabetic qualifiers can appear within bond quotations. Do not mistake for qualifiers the capital letters, mentioned earlier, used only to distinguish bond issues from the same corporation.

Qualifiers sometimes vary from paper to paper. The newspaper definitions should always by checked particularly for quotations of local issues. Although they will not be as thorough as the following definitions, one should verify that, in fact, a letter or symbol is being used in the same way as defined below.

QUALIFIERS FOR BOND QUOTATIONS

Qualifier	Definition
ct or cf	Certificate. This bond has matured but the certificate is still of value and still being traded.
cv	Convertible bond. See definition on p. 100
f	Flat, meaning the bond is traded without the accrued interest (i.e., it won't be added to the price). Once an interest payment has been missed the bond trades flat. After an extended period in which interest payments are met it is possible to restore a bond to normal trading.

Bond sells flat (without accrued interest).

62   22   Mego   12⅞94f   155 25   22½ 23 − 1¾ |

(The Dallas Morning News)

m   Matured. These bonds have already matured; they are no longer drawing interest, and their negotiability has been impaired. They should be redeemed.

nc non-accrual bond; there is no obligation to pay back interest owed.

r   Registered. The bondholder's name is registered with the company or its agent and interest payments are automatically mailed (as opposed to bonds with coupons). Most listed corporate bonds are either registered or available in either registered or coupon form. They are not marked "r" unless a distinction is necessary. For instance, the registered form and bearer form may be trading at slightly different prices. See also p. 98.

wd When distributed. The bond certificate has not been printed and will be available at a later date.

ww With warrants. The purchaser of these bonds will also receive warrants for the purchase of a specified amount of common stock of the issuing company at a specified price. The warrants are usually attached to the bond certificate.

x   Ex-interest. This is the day on which a new purchaser of a bond that normally trades flat will not qualify for the current interest payment.

xw Ex-warrants. The purchaser of the bond will not receive warrants. This indication is used for bonds that once had warrants but presumably now they have expired, been sold, or they have been exercised by a previous owner.

vj (Sometimes appears, incorrectly, to be a "vi") the company is in bankruptcy or receivership or is being reorganized under the Bankruptcy Act. Claims of the bondholders are prior to those of common or preferred stockholders in case of liquidation. However, when corporations have more than one bond issue, some may take precedence over others.

D. What the Quotations Don't Tell You

When considering the purchase of bonds, you should find out a number of things about the specific bonds from your broker or from a Standard & Poor's bond guide.

Rating: Know the current rating of the bond (ratings change), and understand the risks of each rating level. Although not a part of the regular bond quotations, ratings appear in the announcements of new issues and the announcements of rating changes.

announcement of new bond issues containing Moody's rating

New Bond Issues

FRIDAY, FEBRUARY 5

Issues	Moody's Rating	Current Bid&Asked	Chng	Yield
UTILITY BONDS				
So.west Bell 16⅛s21	Aaa	95⅛-95⅝	+⅜	16.90
Fla Power Corp 15¾s11	A+	93-93½	+¼	16.84
CORPORATE BONDS				
Shell 14¼s11	Aaa	90-90½	+1	15.76
Genl Foods 7s11	Aa	45½-46	+⅛	*15.44
Tenneco 14½s06	A	87½-88	...	16.50
INTERMEDIATE NOTES				
Du Pont 14s14	Aa	93¼-93¾	+⅜	15.29
Security Pac 0s86	Aa	50-50⅝	...	14.78
Union Carb 14½s91	Aa	95⅛-95⅝	+⅜	15.37
World Bank 15⅛s91	Aaa	97-97½	+⅜	15.62
World Bank 15s88	Aaa	97¼-97¾	+⅜	15.53
INTERNATIONAL ISSUES				
Ontario 17s11	Aaa	101¼-101¾	+⅜	16.70
Brit Col Hydro 15½s11	Aaa	94-94½	+⅜	16.40
Hydro Que 16⅝s92	Aa	100½-101	+⅛	16.41

* Original issue discount

Source: First Boston Corp.

(The New York Times)

announcement of bond rating changes

BOND RATING CHANGES

	FROM	TO
Moody's		
UPGRADE	FROM	TO
Youngstown Sheet & Tube Co. all outstg. lst mtg. bonds	B	Ba
DOWNGRADE	FROM	TO
Dow Chemical Co. all outstg. debs.	Aa	A
Dow Chemical Overseas Capital N.V. 9⅝% gtd. Eurobonds, 1994	Aa	A
Richardson-Merrell, Inc. 8.85% s.f. debs., 1999	Aa	A
Richardson-Merrell Overseas Finance N.V. 8¾% gtd. debs., 1985	Aa	A
Standard & Poor's		
UPGRADE	FROM	TO
E.F. Hutton Group Inc. 12% s.f. debs., 2005	A–	A
E.F. Hutton Group Inc. 9½% conv. sub. debs., 2005	BBB+	A–

(Barron's)

A few newspapers, however, include bond ratings such as in this example from *The Tampa Tribune*.

Bond ratings, such as these are rarely included in bond quotations

	Rating	Yld	Vol. (hds)	Last	Net Chg.
BnkAm 7⅞03	AAA	15.	30	53¼—	1¼
BkamR 9½00	A	10.	25	94	+1
Bnk NY 12s06	....	12.	22	99⅝+	⅝
Baxter 4¾s01	BBB	3.3	11	145	—4½
BectonD 5s89	A	6.2	22	80½—	½
BellC 14½s91	AA	15.	16	96	+1⅜
Bell Cda 9s08	AA	16.	5	56½	......
BellCda 8¾06	AA	16.	45	55	......
BITel 11⅞s20	AAA	16.	25	73½—	1¼
BITPa 9⅝s14	AAA	16.	44	61	— ½

(The Tampa Tribune)

For a definition of the bond ratings by Moody's and Standard & Poor's, see Appendix 2.

Type of Bond: whether a debenture, mortgage bond, etc. You may want to familiarize yourself with the following types of bonds listed in the glossary:

a) convertible bond
b) floating-rate or variable-rate bond
c) income bond
d) sinking-fund bond
e) serial bond
f) zero interest bond

It would also be helpful to know whether the bond is a junior or senior debt obligation.

Senior debt obligations are bonds whose claims to the assets of the corporation rank above all others. Bonds with subordinate claims are *junior debt obligations*.

Call Provision: "Calling" a bond means redeeming it before maturity. Many bonds have such a provision and it is a common way for corporations to retire debt early, particularly if the interest rates of the debt obligations are relatively high. The call provision should state the earliest year in which the bond can be called and the price at which it can be redeemed (sometimes above par). Redemption is at the option of the issuer and often through a sinking fund.

A *sinking fund* is a fund established by the corporation for the purpose of buying back bonds before maturity. All bonds subject to this kind of redemption are designated Sinking Fund debentures (abbr. SF Deb.). There is usually a time limit before which the bond is not eligible for redemption. Many consider the call provision a nuisance since bonds are usually intended as long-term investments. However, if a discounted bond is called, a substantial capital gain can be realized. If, on the other hand, during a period of low interest rates, the market price of a bond should approach or exceed the call price, then one would not want the bond to be called.

Months of Interest: Obviously, you should find out what months to expect interest payments. Also, not all bonds pay twice a year; some pay quarterly and some every month.

Terms of Conversion: If a convertible bond, you should know how many shares the bond can be converted into and within what time period.

8 Tax-Exempt Municipal Bonds

A. Background

Tax-exempt bonds, also called municipal bonds, are debt obligations issued by states and their political subdivisions and by certain agencies and authorities within the states. Interest (but *not* capital gains) from these bonds is exempt from federal income tax and also from the income and property taxes of some states.

"Political subdivisions" include cities, towns, and counties. "Agencies and authorities" include a huge array of municipal bodies that issue debt obligations in order to build or support projects for the benefit of the citizens of the state or municipality. Such projects include public utilities, port facilities, college dormitories, airports, sewers, turnpikes, etc. Usually the facility to be built will eventually generate income.

Municipal bonds should not be confused with U.S. government securities. Interest from the latter is not exempt from U.S. income tax, although it might be exempt from state and local taxes.

Relatively few papers print quotations for municipal bonds. Those that do list them under headings such as:

Public Authority Bond Issues
Tax-Exempt Authority Bonds
Tax-Exempt Bonds

The distinguishing feature of municipal bonds is that, due to a Supreme Court decision in 1895, the interest is exempt from federal income tax. It is also exempt from income and personal-property tax in *some* states but not all. Some states exempt the interest only from their *own* bonds for their own residents. (*See* "State Taxation of Municipal Bonds," p. 115.) Municipal bonds are thus subject to the following taxes:

1. Long and short-term capital-gains tax on the sale of municipal bonds.
2. State income and property taxes unless specifically exempted. (The regulations change from state to state; *see* p. 115.)
3. Inheritance tax.

Many people may not report the inheritance of municipal bonds, thinking they are not taxable. This error is difficult for the IRS to correct since bearer form makes ownership difficult to trace. Perhaps for this reason new issues of municipal, as of Jan. 1, 1983, are only available in registered form.

The higher one's tax bracket, the greater the advantage of the exemption of municipal bonds. Obviously a person in the 50% tax bracket with an 8% return on a municipal bond would be receiving the equivalent of twice that amount from a taxable bond. Because of their tax exemption, municipal bonds are not issued to yield as much as corporate bonds. In general, municipal bonds yield about 30% less than their corporation equivalents. Under most circumstances, an investor should be above the 35% tax bracket in order to realize significant tax advantages. To compare municipal yields with those of taxable bonds, see "Figuring Comparable Yields in Taxable Securities," p. 114.

There are many types of municipal bonds; some of the major types are:

1. *general obligation bonds* (called GOs). These are the most secure. They are backed by the full faith and credit of the municipality, which, by definition, includes its power of taxation.
2. *special tax bonds*. These are backed by limited taxes such as a sales tax on a specific product.
3. *revenue bonds*. These are backed by the income from the facility being financed.

Among the notes (*short-term* debt obligations) of municipalities are BANs (bond-anticipation notes), TANs (tax-anticipation notes), and RANs (revenue-anticipation notes). These offer tax-exempt income for the short term, usually a year or less, and are issued in denominations of $25,000. They are not usually quoted in the newspapers except for the announcement of a new issue. They are rated by Moody's MIG (Municipal Investment Grade) ratings; see "Short Term Loan Ratings" in Appendix 2. Also in this group are project notes (PNs), which are issued by local housing authorities or urban-renewal agencies in minimum denominations of $5,000. They are backed by the full faith and credit of the Department of Housing and Urban Development (HUD).

Most municipal bonds are not quoted in the newspaper. Those that *are* are usually revenue bonds (described above) issued by public authorities. They are also likely to be *term* bonds.

> *Term bonds* describes an issue of bonds or a segment of an issue in which every bond matures on the same date and has the same coupon rate.

The term bonds quoted in newspapers are usually in $5,000 denominations. Coupon form is considered the most desirable, although some are available in registered form. Some are also sinking-fund bonds (*see* p. 107).

Although *serial* bonds, as opposed to term bonds, are not as frequently quoted in the newspapers, one should be aware that they are a common form of municipal bond.

> *Serial bonds* are bonds of the same issue that mature in different years and have different coupon rates. The investor thus has a wide choice of maturities and interest rates within a single issue. Prices are different for each date and are expressed in yield-to-maturity percentages. These must be translated into dollars and cents by means of special bond tables.

B. The Quotations

Daily quotations are in the same format as brief quotations for corporate bonds. Sometimes the entire year of maturity is given rather than just the last two digits. The first quote in the example below is for a Battery Park 6⅜ bond due in 2014.

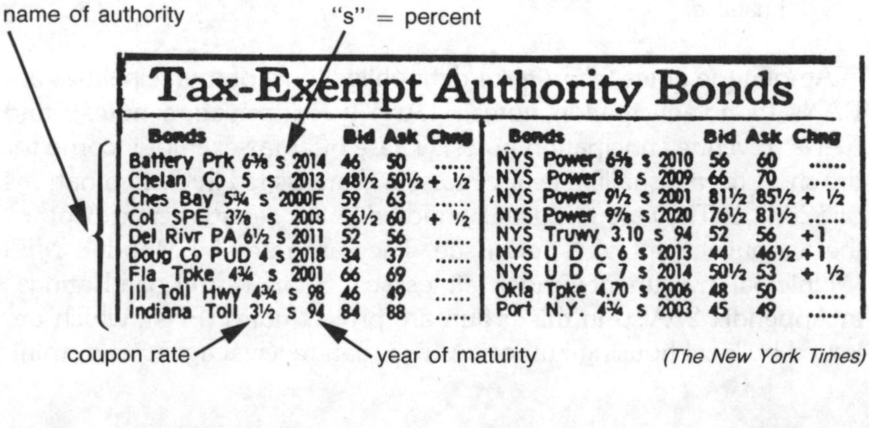

name of authority   "s" = percent

Tax-Exempt Authority Bonds

Bonds	Bid	Ask	Chng	Bonds	Bid	Ask	Chng
Battery Prk 6⅜ s 2014	46	50	......	NYS Power 6⅜ s 2010	56	60	......
Chelan Co 5 s 2013	48½	50½	+ ½	NYS Power 8 s 2009	66	70	......
Ches Bay 5¾ s 2000F	59	63	......	NYS Power 9½ s 2001	81½	85½	+ ½
Col SPE 3⅞ s 2003	56½	60	+ ½	NYS Power 9⅞ s 2020	76½	81½	......
Del Rivr PA 6½ s 2011	52	56	......	NYS Truwy 3.10 s 94	52	56	+1
Doug Co PUD 4 s 2018	34	37	......	NYS U D C 6 s 2013	44	46½	+1
Fla Tpke 4¾ s 2001	66	69	......	NYS U D C 7 s 2014	50½	53	+ ½
Ill Toll Hwy 4¾ s 98	46	49	......	Okla Tpke 4.70 s 2006	48	50	......
Indiana Toll 3½ s 94	84	88	......	Port N.Y. 4¾ s 2003	45	49	......

coupon rate   year of maturity   *(The New York Times)*

Price quotations for term bonds are in percent of par, which makes them easy to translate into dollars and cents (that is, easier than for serial bonds). In the following example, the third NYS Power bond, maturing in 2001, has an asked price of 85½. That would be $855 per $1,000 par; so for a $5,000 bond, the price would be $4,275 (5 × $855). Accrued interest must also be added to both bid and asked prices.

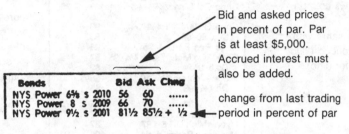

Bid and asked prices in percent of par. Par is at least $5,000. Accrued interest must also be added.

change from last trading period in percent of par

(The New York Times)

As with corporate bonds, the "change" is also quoted in percent of par. Thus if the above quotation were for a $5,000 bond, a change of +½ would indicate an increase in price of $25. (½ = $5 × 5 = $25).

Current yield is not given in most quotations, but it can be calculated easily. For the last quotation in the above example, the coupon rate of 9½% yields $95 per $1,000 bond; so that for a $5,000 bond the cash return is $475. This is an 11.11% yield on the current price, $4,275.

$$\frac{475}{4,275} = .1111 = 11.11\%$$

A simpler way is:

$$\frac{\text{coupon rate}}{\text{asked price \%}} = \frac{9.5}{85.5} = .1111 = 11.11\%$$

If it is a serial bond sometimes more than one coupon rate is quoted, as in the following example. The first quotation for the Illinois Chicago-Calumet Skyway shows a 3⅜ coupon due in 1995 with a bid of 33 ($1,650 for a $5,000 bond). The "a" qualifier means "ex-coupon," the significance of which is that there will be practically no accrued interest if purchased immediately, since there will not be time for significant accrued interest to build.

The second coupon rate shown is immediately underneath the first: a 4⅜ rate with a bid price of 38.

Illinois Chicago-Calumet Skyway bond with a 3⅜ coupon

and the same with a 4⅜ coupon ("Do" stands for ditto).

Public authority bond issues

Issue Rate Maturity	Bid	Ask
Bi-St Dev Agcy 4⅛-'93	48	53
Chgo Cal Skywy 3⅜-'95	(a)33	36
Do, 4⅜-'95	38	..
Chgo O'Hare Air 4¾-'99	90	..
Do,6.80-'99	86	
Chgo Reg Ports 4-'95	38	
Cook Co.Met Fair 4¼-'95	57	
Do,5-'95	62	
Ill.StateTollHwy6¾-'10	55½	
Do,4¾-'98	45½	
Do,3¾-'95	72	75
Ind.Toll Rd. 3½-'94	87	..
LivoniaMichIDR.6-4'97	37	..
Mackinac Bridge 4 04	95	99
Do,5¼ 11 '94	67	..
Okla.Tpke 4.70-'06	47	50
TexTpke 4-11'05	91	..
W Va St Tpke 3¾-12 1'99	50	53
Do, 4⅛-12 1 '99	52	55

(a) ex-coupon
Source: Bonniwell & Co. Inc., Chicago.

more than one coupon rate shown for some coupon bonds

(Chicago Tribune)

A qualifier that sometimes follows the name or date is "F," indicating that the bond trades "flat," without accrued interest. This means that the municipality has missed an interest payment. Such a bond will be deeply discounted, and although there may be a possibility for capital gains, such bonds are highly speculative.

"F" means the bond trades flat, without accrued interest.

Bonds	Bid	Ask	Chng
Battery Prk 6⅞ s 2014	46	50	......
Chelan Co 5 s 2013	48½	50½	+ ½
Ches Bay 5¾ s 2000F	59	63	......

(The New York Times)

Municipal bonds do not trade as frequently as corporate bonds and are sometimes less liquid. In general, they are bought by investors for current income and retained for a long period of time. They usually pay interest twice a year.

Even though a newspaper does not regularly carry quotations for municipal bonds, one will often find announcements for pending new issues.

announcement for new
issue of municipal bonds

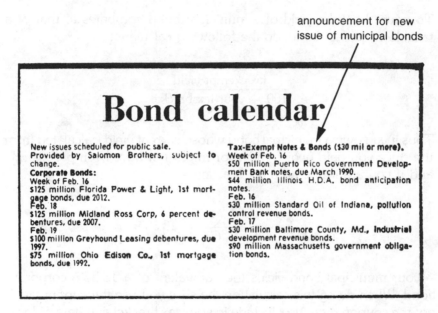

Bond calendar

New issues scheduled for public sale. Provided by Salomon Brothers, subject to change.

Corporate Bonds:

Week of Feb. 16
$125 million Florida Power & Light, 1st mortgage bonds, due 2012.
Feb. 18
$125 million Midland Ross Corp, 6 percent debentures, due 2007.
Feb. 19
$100 million Greyhound Leasing debentures, due 1997.
$75 million Ohio Edison Co., 1st mortgage bonds, due 1992.

Tax-Exempt Notes & Bonds ($30 mil or more).

Week of Feb. 16
$50 million Puerto Rico Government Development Bank notes, due March 1990.
$44 million Illinois H.D.A. bond anticipation notes.
Feb. 16
$30 million Standard Oil of Indiana, pollution control revenue bonds.
Feb. 17
$30 million Baltimore County, Md., Industrial development revenue bonds.
$90 million Massachusetts government obligation bonds.

(The Miami Herald)

C. What the Quotations Don't Tell You

Because there are so few municipal bonds quoted in the newspapers, one cannot consider the examples discussed here as representative of the range and variety offered in this area of fixed-income investing. Before considering the purchase of municipals, you should discuss your tax situation and your investment objectives with a broker or bank representative.

When considering specific bonds, ask for their rating by Moody's or Standard & Poor's. (The definition of the ratings by both these companies for long- and short-term debt obligations is given in Appendix 2.)

You will also want to know the specific type of bond, whether it is callable, and its yield to maturity (defined in the previous chapter). For purposes of comparison, you may also want to calculate the comparable yield (given your tax bracket) from a taxable corporate bond.

D. Figuring Comparable Yields in Taxable Securities

To figure how the yield of a municipal bond compares to that of a taxable corporate bond, do the following calculation:

$$\frac{\text{tax-exempt yield}}{100 - \text{your tax bracket}}$$

Thus if you own a municipal bond whose current yield, calculated from the price you paid (which might or might not have been par), is 8%, and if you are in the 40% tax bracket—

$$\frac{8\%}{100 - 40\%} = \frac{8}{60} = 13.33\%$$

—your municipal bond yields the equivalent of a 13.33% corporate bond. When doing this calculation, be sure you use the current yield, not the coupon rate. Also, include in your tax bracket any state or local income taxes from which your municipal bond may be exempt.

E. State Taxation of Municipal Bonds

As mentioned before, municipal bonds are not always exempt from state income taxes. With the following list, you can verify the tax status of municipal bonds within your state.

A check in the first column indicates that currently the state's own bonds are tax-exempt within that state. A check in the second column indicates that currently the state has also exempted the bonds of other states.

Even in states where municipals are generally taxable, there are exceptions. You may want to check for them with a bond broker.

TAX STATUS OF MUNICIPAL BONDS BY STATE

State's municipal bonds are tax-exempt within that state.	Municipal bonds of other states are tax-exempt within that state.	State
✓		Alabama
✓	✓	Alaska
✓		Arizona
✓		Arkansas
✓		California
		Colorado
✓	✓	Connecticut
✓		Delaware
✓	✓	District of Columbia
✓	✓	Florida
✓		Georgia
✓		Hawaii
✓		Idaho
		Illinois
✓	✓	Indiana
		Iowa
		Kansas
✓		Kentucky
✓	✓	Louisiana
✓		Maine
✓		Maryland
✓		Massachusetts
✓		Michigan
✓		Minnesota
✓		Mississippi
✓		Missouri
✓		Montana
✓	✓	Nebraska
✓	✓	Nevada
✓		New Hampshire
✓		New Jersey
✓	✓	New Mexico
✓		New York
✓		North Carolina
✓		North Dakota
✓		Ohio
		Oklahoma
✓		Oregon
✓		Pennsylvania

TAX STATUS OF MUNICIPAL BONDS BY STATE *(cont'd)*

√		Rhode Island
√		South Carolina
√	√	South Dakota
√		Tennessee
√	√	Texas
√	√	Utah
√	√	Vermont
√		Virginia
√	√	Washington
√		West Virginia
		Wisconsin
√	√	Wyoming

*In California, other state bonds are not exempt from state income tax but they are exempt from state franchise tax.

(courtesy New York City Office of the Controller)

Municipal Bond in Registered Form

This is the famous 3s of 80 issued by New York City in 1940 for the unification of the subway system. Although the bond matured in 1980 there are many of these certificates outstanding that have never been redeemed. In both registered and bearer form, the bond certificate represents the principal amount and must be returned to the issuer (or agent) for the return of principal.

Municipal Bond in Bearer Form

Each coupon, on the right, is dated and printed with the interest amount. If mailed, the coupon should be sent registered or certified to the paying agent specified on the bond. The name and address of the person to whom the check is to be sent should be included.

9 U.S. Treasury Bonds and Notes

A. Background

The U.S. government issues two kinds of public securities:

1. Nonmarketable (that is, they cannot be traded among brokers or individuals). These include Series E and H savings bonds.
2. Marketable. These include:
   a) Treasury bonds which mature in 10–30 years; available in minimum denominations of $1,000.
   b) Treasury notes which mature in 1–10 years; available in minimum denominations of $5,000 (some $1,000).
   c) Treasury bills which mature in 1 year or less; available in minimum denominations of $10,000.

Interest on Treasury bills, bonds, and notes is exempt from state and local income tax but not from federal income tax.

The *marketable* securities are quoted in larger newspapers under various headings, including:

Treasury Bills, Bonds & Notes
Treasury Issues: Bonds, Notes & Bills
US Bonds/Notes
Treasury Bonds
Government Securities

Do not confuse these listings with U.S. agency bonds such as those of the Government National Mortgage Association (GNMA called "Ginnie Maes") or the Federal Land Bank. The above headings are for bonds, bills, and notes that are direct obligations of the U.S. Treasury.

Agency bonds, discussed in chapter 11, are listed in separate quotations.

New issues of Treasury bonds, bills, and notes can be purchased by individuals through noncompetitive bidding. The price, in a noncompetitive bidding system, will be the average of the institutional bids. You may have a broker or a bank place the bid for you, or you may submit it yourself. Information may be obtained from the nearest Federal Reserve Bank. (Ask your local bank for the address of the nearest branch; you must submit bids to the branch of the Federal Reserve Bank that services your area.) Both bonds and notes are available in coupon or registered form.

This chapter is concerned only with U.S. bonds and notes. Quotations for U.S. Treasury bills will be discussed in the next chapter. All newspaper quotations are for bonds and notes trading on the secondary market; that is they have already been purchased from the original source (in this case, the government) and are now being traded among individuals and institutions.

B. The Quotations

1. Date and Rate

Bonds and notes are identified by their date and rate. An "n" between the date and rate indicates a note, while the absence of an "n" indicates that the security is a bond.

security identified
by the date and rate

	BONDS & NOTES						BONDS & NOTES				
May 90	8⅛	98-22	98-26+	02	9.08	Aug 94 n	12⅝	114-30	115-02—	05	9.10
May 90	11⅜	102-16	102-20—	04	9.14	Oct 94	9½	101-19	101-23—	07	9.10
Jun 90	7¼	97-14	97-18—	01	9.12	Nov 94 n	10⅛	104-08	104-12—	08	9.13
Jun 90	8	98-13	98-17—	01	9.12	Nov 94	11⅝	111-01	111-05—	05	9.10

The absence of an   An "n" indicates a note.
"n" indicates a bond.

(The New York Times)

The first quotation in the example above indicates a Treasury *bond* (no "n") maturing in May of 1990 with a coupon rate of 8½%. The first quotation in the second column indicates a Treasury *note* maturing in August of 1994 with a coupon rate of 12⅝%. Sometimes a "k" or "p" is used to indicate that non-U.S. citizens are exempt from withholding taxes.

Some quotation formats give the rate in decimal points. The first note quoted below is shown as 15.87%, but it is actually 15⅞ (which is 15.875%); the second, a bond, is 11¾. The rates are followed by the month and year of maturity.

The rates of some Treasury securities are quoted in ——▶ decimals instead of fractions.

Rate	Mat. date	Bid	Ask	Yld	Ch
15.87	Sep	n 102.13	102.17	14.96	— .06
11.75	Nov	91.20	91.28	14.59	— .04
14.12	Dec	n 98.02	98.10	14.71	— .02

(San Francisco Chronicle)

Since U.S. Treasury securities are among the most liquid in the world, it is assumed that, for each quotation, bonds or notes are available in every denomination ($1,000, $5,000, $10,000, etc.). However, there will be cases where the minimum denomination available will be $5,000 or even $10,000. Your securities agent can determine this for you.

2. Bid—Asked—Bid Change

There are three things to remember about the prices of U.S. notes and bonds:

1. They are quoted in percentage of par value.

2. The decimal places indicate thirty-seconds (only for bid, asked, and bid change).
3. Accrued interest must be added.

GOVERNMENT SECURITIES

Rate	Mat.	date	Bid	Asked	Bid Chg	Yld	Rate	Mat.	date	Bid	Asked	Bid Chg	Yld
11.88	Sep	1982 n	98.6	98.10—	.10	14.66	14.00	Dec	1984 n	98.5	98.13—	1.11	14.69
12.13	Oct	1982 n	98.6	98.10—	.8	14.61	8.00	Feb	1985 n	83.30	84.6	—1.19	14.64
7.13	Nov	1982 n	94.24	94.28—	.10	14.27	13.38	Mar	1985 n	96.10	96.18—	1.10	14.98
7.88	Nov	1982 n	95.4	95.8	— .10	14.51	3.25	May	1985	82.24	83.24—	.8	9.09
13.88	Nov	1982 n	99.6	99.8	— .22	14.87	4.25	May	1975-85	82.24	83.24—	.22	10.20
9.38	Dec	1982 n	95.18	95.22—	.12	14.61	10.38	May	1985 n	88.24	89	—1.15	14.72

Numbers to left of decimal point of bid
and asked prices are percent of par value.   Numbers to right are 32nds.

(The Washington Post)

In this type of quotation each point represents $10 for each $1,000 of face value. In the above example, the December 1984 note (second column) has a bid price of 98.5%. The decimal points in Treasury quotations indicate thirty-seconds of a point, so that the 98.5 is 98% + $5/32$%. For a $1,000 note, that would be $980.00 + $1.5626, which rounded off is $981.56. Should par be $5,000, the bid price would be $4,907.80. *Caution:* Decimal places in "rate" and "yield" quotations are still 100ths (i.e., normal percentage).

"Change" or "bid change" is the change from the bid of the previous trading period. It is also expressed as percent of par, with the decimals representing thirty-seconds. The first quote in the second column above shows a change of -1.11, which is $1\% + {}^{11}/{}_{32}\% = 1.34375\%$. For a $1,000 note, that would be $13.43.

VALUE OF THIRTY-SECONDS

The following chart gives the value for thirty-seconds in decimals and in tens of dollars (applicable to $1,000 par).

32nds		in decimals	of $10 (applicable to $1,000 par)
1/32		.03125	$ .3125
2/32	(1/16)	.0625	- $ .625
3/32		.09375	$ .9375
4/32	(1/8)	.125	$1.25
5/32		.15625	$1.5625
6/32	(3/16)	.1875	$1.875
7/32		.21875	$2.1875
8/32	(1/4)	.25	$2.50
9/32		.28125	$2.8125
10/32	(5/16)	.3125	$3.125
11/32		.34375	$3.4375
12/32	(3/8)	.375	$3.75
13/32		.40625	$4.0625
14/32	(7/16)	.4375	$4.375
15/32		.46875	$4.6875
16/32	(1/2)	.5	$5.00
17/32		.53125	$5.3125
18/32	(9/16)	.5625	$5.625
19/32		.59375	$5.9375
20/32	(5/8)	.625	$6.25
21/32		.65625	$6.5625
22/32	(11/16)	.6875	$6.875
23/32		.71875	$7.1875
24/32	(3/4)	.75	$7.50
25/32		.78125	$7.8125
26/32	(13/16)	.8125	$8.125
27/32		.84375	$8.4375
28/32	(7/8)	.875	$8.75
29/32		.90625	$9.0625
30/32	(15/16)	.9375	$9.375
31/32		.96875	$9.6875

3. Yield

The last column, labeled "yield," is the *yield to maturity* based on the asked price. The yield to maturity may be greater or lesser than the current yield.

The current yield is obtained by dividing the annual interest by the current price (the asked price). In the following example, the current yield of the November 1984 note is 14.29%.

```
| Rate  Mat.  date   Bid  AskedBidChgYld |
| 12.13 Sep  1984 n  95.26 96.2 + .2 13.97 |
|→14.38 Nov  1984 n  100.14 100.18+ .4 14.09 |
| 16.00 Nov  1984 n  103.24 104  + .2 14.15 |
```

(Chicago Tribune)

$$\frac{\text{annual interest}}{\text{current price}} \quad \frac{\$143.80}{(\$1{,}000 + \$5.625)} = 14.29\% \text{ current yield}$$

However, the yield to maturity, shown in the quotation, is 14.09%.

4. Weekly Quotations

Some weekly quotations are more extensive than the daily quotations seen earlier. The following example provides a 52-week high and low in addition to a weekly high and low.

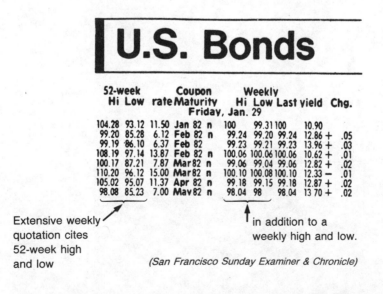

U.S. Bonds

52-week		Coupon		Weekly				
Hi	Low	rate	Maturity	Hi	Low	Last	yield	Chg.
			Friday, Jan. 29					
104.28	93.12	11.50	Jan 82 n	100	99.31	100	10.90	
99.20	85.28	6.12	Feb 82 n	99.24	99.20	99.24	12.86 +	.05
99.19	86.10	6.37	Feb 82	99.23	99.21	99.23	13.96 +	.03
108.19	97.14	13.87	Feb 82 n	100.06	100.06	100.06	10.62 +	.01
100.17	87.21	7.87	Mar 82 n	99.06	99.04	99.06	12.82 +	.02
110.20	96.12	15.00	Mar 82 n	100.10	100.08	100.10	12.33 −	.01
105.02	95.07	11.37	Apr 82 n	99.18	99.15	99.18	12.87 +	.02
98.08	85.23	7.00	May 82 n	98.04	98	98.04	13 70 +	.02

Extensive weekly
quotation cites
52-week high
and low

in addition to a
weekly high and low.

(San Francisco Sunday Examiner & Chronicle)

C. What the Quotations Don't Tell You

There is not a great deal of information necessary for the investor to know in addition to the quotations. U.S. securities are not rated since they are considered the safest in the world. Knowing the 52-week high and low (as shown in the "extensive" weekly quote above) could be of use if timing were a factor in your investment program.

One item of information you should verify upon purchase of a U.S. bond or note is the day of the month it matures. This will also be the day of the semiannual interest payments. It will usually be on the fifteenth or at the end of the month.

10 U.S. Treasury Bills

A. Background

Treasury bills (T-bills) are short-term debt obligations of the U.S. government. They are issued in minimum denominations of $10,000 (and in $5,000 increments above that) and in maturities of thirteen, twenty-six, and fifty-two weeks.

Treasury bills, unlike most debt instruments, are sold at discount and redeemed at par. This means that the price you pay for a bill is less than its face value but the total you receive at maturity is the full face value. The difference between these two amounts is your interest. No other interest payments are made.

The quotations for Treasury bills often appear in securities lists that also include longer-term government obligations such as bonds and notes. These lists are entitled variously:

Treasury Securities
Treasury Bills, Bonds, and Notes
Government Agency and Miscellaneous Securities

Sometimes they are quoted separately under their own headings:

Treasury Bills
T-Bills

Treasury bills are enjoying increasing popularity with the investing public because

1. they pay high interest
2. they are short-term
3. they are easy to buy
4. they are probably the safest of all securities
5. in most instances the yields are not taxable by state or local governments

For the last 30 years, the yields of Treasury bills have averaged 75% (more or less) of the prime rate. This is an attractive return for an almost riskless, partially tax-free investment.

One can purchase T-bills directly from a Federal Reserve Bank, thereby saving a commission charge. The procedures differ slightly from (Federal Reserve) branch to branch, but basically it involves sending a personal certified check or banker's check to the branch of the Federal Reserve Bank serving your area for the par value of the bill denomination wanted. A form such as the one shown on page 130 is not a necessity provided all the information requested is given and procedures required are followed.

Currently, new issues with maturities of three months (91 days) and six months (182 days) are sold at weekly Monday auctions; new issues for twelve months (actually, 364 days) are usually sold every fourth Tuesday. The price the individual eventually pays at the auction will be the average of the prices paid by the institutional bidders. This procedure, set up for small investors, is called a "noncompetitive bid." The amount of the discount (the par value minus the price of the bill) will be mailed back to you in a few days. Note that this is the interest which you receive immediately. On maturity you will receive the par value. You may reinvest it in a new bill (called "rolling over") by so instructing the Federal Reserve Bank (Form PD 4633-1) 20 business days before maturity. If it is possible that you might need to sell a bill before maturity, then you should purchase it through a bank or broker. Resale will be less trouble since a certificate transfer will not be necessary.

The rest of this chapter concerns the purchase and sale of T-bills on the secondary market, as it is only these bills that appear in the newspaper quotations. Prices are the result of over-the-counter bargaining among a few dozen dealers who make a market in Treasury bills and other U.S. securities.

B. The Quotations

1. Maturity Date

Treasury bills are identified by the maturity date, which will always fall on a Thursday. As you can see from the following example, they are available at maturities for every week up to six months and for every month beyond that up to one year.

Treasury Bills

Treasury bills
are identified
by the dates
of maturity.

Due	Bid	Ask	Yld	Due	Bid	Ask	Yld
				4-29	11.86	11.74	12.35
1- 7	12.06	11.52	0.00	5- 6	11.90	11.76	12.41
1-14	11.74	11.38	11.56	5-13	11.89	11.75	12.42
1-21	11.59	11.27	11.48	5-20	12.01	11.87	12.59
1-28	11.38	11.14	11.37	5-27	12.07	11.89	12.64
2- 4	11.04	10.84	11.08	6- 3	12.18	12.00	12.79
2-11	10.97	10.77	11.04	6-10	12.19	11.95	12.77
2-18	11.22	11.04	11.34	6-17	12.34	12.22	13.11
2-25	11.25	11.07	11.40	6-24	12.29	12.17	13.08
3- 4	11.43	11.25	11.61	7- 1	12.41	12.31	13.28
3-11	11.41	11.23	11.61	7-15	12.41	12.31	13.31
3-18	11.60	11.42	11.84	8-12	12.48	12.34	13.38
3-25	11.66	11.48	11.93	9- 9	12.46	12.36	13.45
4- 1	11.70	11.58	12.07	10- 7	12.54	12.40	13.57
4- 8	11.72	11.68	12.20	11- 4	12.54	12.40	13.66
4-15	11.74	11.58	12.12	12- 2	12.48	12.38	13.73
4-22	11.85	11.67	12.25	12-30	12.37	12.31	13.75

(The Washington Post)

As with U.S. bonds and notes, the original date of the issue of the bill is unimportant and therefore not indicated in the quotations. There is a slight difference in price between new bills and outstanding bills maturing on the same date (the new bills are very slightly lower), but here a more substantial saving could be realized by purchasing the bill directly from a Federal Reserve Bank and saving the commission.

2. Bid and Asked Prices

Treasury bills are not quoted like other government securities in percent of par value; instead the prices are quoted as a *percent of discount from par value*. For a $10,000 T-bill maturing in 52 weeks the asked price of 10.00 would mean 10%; 10% of $10,000 is $1,000, so the price would be roughly $9,000 (although, unfortunately, it's never quite so simple).

If the 10% price of a 52-week bill amounted to $9,000 ($10,000 − $1,000), then a 6-month bill would cost $9,500 ($10,000 − $500) and a 3-month bill would cost $9,750 ($10,000 − $250). In each of these cases, however, the price is still quoted as 10%, since prices quoted in this fashion always annualize the percent figure.

From the above examples, one can see that the actual *yield* from a T-bill is more than the *discount percent* that is stated as the asking price. Obviously, $1,000 is more than 10% of $9,000; it's 11.11%.

The principle of T-bill quotations is, in itself, relatively easy. However, translating the discount percentages into dollars and cents is more complicated.

EXAMPLE: It is early January; from a real-estate transaction you have about $10,000, which you will not need for over two months. In such a case, a T-bill maturing on March 25 would offer a high yield with absolute safety. Here is the quotation for the March 25 T-bill from the previous example:

date	bid	ask	yield	
3-25	11.66	11.48	11.93	*12th quote from the earlier example*

The price of a T-bill is the par value minus the dollars and cents discount. The point is that one must translate the discount percent into a dollars and cents amount by means of the following formula:

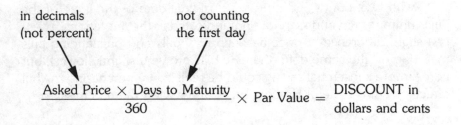

$$\frac{\text{Asked Price} \times \text{Days to Maturity}}{360} \times \text{Par Value} = \frac{\text{DISCOUNT in}}{\text{dollars and cents}}$$

in decimals (not percent) — Asked Price

not counting the first day — Days to Maturity

If one wished to buy the T-bill quoted above, the figures would look like this:

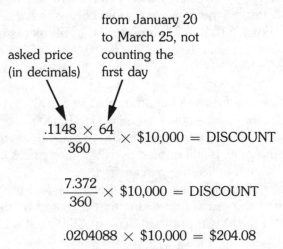

asked price (in decimals) — .1148

from January 20 to March 25, not counting the first day — 64

$$\frac{.1148 \times 64}{360} \times \$10,000 = \text{DISCOUNT}$$

$$\frac{7.372}{360} \times \$10,000 = \text{DISCOUNT}$$

$$.0204088 \times \$10,000 = \$204.08$$

Subtracting the discount from the par value, we get the price of the Treasury bill:

$10,000.00 par value
 −204.08 discount
$ 9,795.92 price of the T-bill

If one were selling the same T-bill, one would do the above calculations using the bid price instead of the asked price. A sale would also incur a commission since one would have to sell on the secondary market. The average commission is $25.

3. Yield

The yield is stated in an annualized percent of the asked price. However, that is not the amount that would be received unless the bill being purchased were a 52-week bill. Obviously, a T-bill at a 10% annual-rate discount would not yield $1,000 if it had only 21 days left; it would yield $21/_{360}$ of that amount. Referring back to the previous example, $204.08 is only 2.08331% of $9,795.92, but this 64-day yield annualizes to 11.93%.

The above yield figure, known as the "bond equivalent yield," adjusts the percentage to a 365-day year (as opposed to the 360-day year used by T-bills). The intricacies of this calculation are many, but suffice it to say that the figure enables one to compare the yield of Treasury bills to other fixed-rate securities.

4. Change

Some quotations show the change in bid price from the previous trading period. The first quotation in the example below shows a −.12 in the "change" column. This means the bid price from the preceding trading period was .12% higher.

TREASURY BILLS					
Date	Bid	Ask	Chg.	Yield	
Jan 28	12.38	12.12	−0.12	12.30	
Feb 4	11.90	11.60	−0.11	11.80	
Feb 11	11.85	11.61	−0.16	11.84	

Some T-bill quotations show change from previous trading period.

(The New York Times)

Quotations of this type are said to be in basis points.

A *basis point,* simply put, is one ten-thousandth (.0001) or, if you prefer, 1% of 1%. Such a system is useful for describing small movements in the interest of fixed-income securities. Fifty basis points are ½%, and 100 basis points are 1%. In the above example, it simply means that the percentage is carried out to two decimal points.

GB 254 1 (6-81)
GOVERNMENT BOND DIVISION

**TENDER FOR TREASURY BILLS
IN BOOK-ENTRY FORM AT THE
DEPARTMENT OF THE TREASURY**
13-WEEK BILLS ONLY

FOR OFFICIAL USE ONLY
FRB REQUEST NO
ISSUE DATE
DUE DATE
CUSIP NO   912793

ACCOUNT NO.

MAIL TO:
Bureau of the Public Debt Securities Transactions Branch
Room 2134, Main Treasury, Washington, D.C. 20226

Federal Reserve Bank or Branch of your District at:

**BEFORE COMPLETING THIS FORM READ THE
ACCOMPANYING INSTRUCTIONS CAREFULLY**

Pursuant to the provisions of Department of the Treasury Circular, Public Debt Series No. 27-76, the public announcement issued by the Department of the Treasury, and the regulations set forth in Department Circular, Public Debt Series No. 26-76, I hereby submit this tender, in accordance with the terms as marked, for currently offered U.S. Treasury bills for my account. (Competitive tenders must be expressed on the basis of 100, with three decimals. Fractions may not be used.) I understand that noncompetitive tenders will be accepted in full at the average price of accepted competitive bids and that a noncompetitive tender by any one bidder may not exceed $500,000.

TYPE OF BID
NONCOMPETITIVE   or   COMPETITIVE   at Price _____

AMOUNT OF TENDER $ _____
(Minimum of $10,000. Over $10,000 must be in multiples of $5,000.)

ACCOUNT IDENTIFICATION: (Please type or print clearly using a ball-point pen because this information will be used as a mailing label.)

DEPOSITOR(S)▶

ADDRESS▶

PRIVACY ACT NOTICE
The individually identifiable information required on this form is necessary to permit the tender to be processed and the bills to be issued, in accordance with the general regulations governing United States book-entry Treasury bills (Department Circular PD Series No. 26-76) The transaction will not be completed unless all required data is furnished

ALPHA-CROSS-REF.

DEPOSITOR(S) IDENTIFICATION NUMBER
SOCIAL SECURITY NUMBER
FIRST
NAMED   EMPLOYER IDENTIFICATION NO
                                    OR
SOCIAL SECURITY NUMBER
SECOND
NAMED

DISPOSITION OF PROCEEDS

The par amount of the account will be paid at maturity unless you elect to have Treasury reinvest (roll-over) the proceeds of the maturing bills. (See below)

I hereby request noncompetitive reinvestment of the proceeds in book-entry Treasury bills

METHOD OF PAYMENT
TOTAL   Maturing
SUBMITTED $_____ Cash $_____ Check $_____   Treasury
                                              Securities $_____

DEPOSITOR'S AUTHORIZATION

Signature_____ Date _____ Telephone Number
                                     During Business Hours _____
                                     Area Code

FOR OFFICIAL USE ONLY

**Form for the Submission of a Noncompetitive Bid for 13-week
Treasury Bills**

11 Government Agency and International Bonds

A. Background

Bonds and notes of government agencies and international agencies are not widely quoted in the newspapers. Federal-agency bonds that sometimes appear are:

Banks for Cooperatives (loans to farmers' cooperative associations) $5,000 minimum, noncallable, exempt from state and local income taxes.

Federal Home Loan Bank (regulates and makes loans to savings and loan associations) $10,000 minimum, noncallable, exempt from state and local income taxes.

Federal Intermediate Credit Bank (loans to banks that loan to agricultural concerns) $5,000 minimum, recent issues noncallable, exempt from state and local income taxes.

Federal Land Banks (real-estate and other loans to farmers) $1,000 minimum, some callable, exempt from state and local income taxes.

Federal National Mortgage Association "Fannie Mae" (purchases residential mortgages from banks and savings and loans during periods of, and in order to ease, tight credit) secondary market notes and capital debentures, $10,000 minimum, most noncallable, some convertible into FNMA common stock, subject to taxes at all levels. (Technically this is a privately-owned corporation but it is regulated by the Secretary of Housing and Urban Development.)

Government National Mortgage Association "Ginnie Mae" (finances residential housing where established funding inadequate) $25,000 usual minimum depending on type, taxable at all levels, noncallable, usually liquidated early (approximately 12 years).

International agencies, which combine the obligations of several different countries, include:

World Bank Bonds (loans in certain areas of the world) $1,000 minimum, taxable at all levels.
Inter-American Development Bank (loans in North and South America) $1,000 minimum, taxable at all levels.
Asian Development Bank (loans in Asia) $1,000 minimum, taxable at all levels.

Quotations for government-agency and international bonds are found in *The Wall Street Journal* under the heading "Government Agency and Miscellaneous Securities" and in *The New York Times* under "Government Agency Bonds." Most newspapers do not quote agency bonds but do occasionally list international bonds at the beginning of the NYSE bond quotations.

B. The Quotations

1. Rate and Maturity

The individual issues are known by their rates and maturity dates. The first quotation in the following example would be known as the Inter-American 8⅝% due in '95.

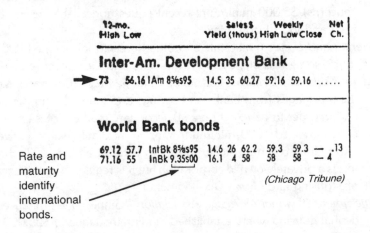

12-mo. High Low		Sales $ Yield (thous)	Weekly High Low Close	Net Ch.
Inter-Am. Development Bank				
➤ 73 56.16	IAm 8⅝s95	14.5 35	60.27 59.16 59.16	......
World Bank bonds				
69.12 57.7	IntBk 8⅝s95	14.6 26	62.2 59.3 59.3	— .13
71.16 55	InBk 9.35s00	16.1 4	58 58 58	— 4

(Chicago Tribune)

Rate and maturity identify international bonds.

Shorter-term bonds given the month of maturity; one must find out from a broker the exact day.

FNMA Bonds

Some securities list the month of maturity.

Rate	Bid	Ask Chg. Yield
7.30	89.26	91.10— .6 14.22
8.10	91.18	92.2 — .6 14.44
10.85	94.30	95.14— .6 14.30
9.70	93.2	93.18— .6 14.34
6¾	88.12	88.28— .6 14.41
8½	90.30	91.14— .6 14.38
9¼	91.24	92.8 — .6 14.36
8	89.8	89.24......... 14.24
8.40	90	90.14......... 14.18
14.05	99.16	99.24-- .4 14.19

(The Washington Post)

As is shown in both the above examples, the rate is sometimes quoted in fractions and sometimes in decimals.

2. Bid and Asked Prices

Bid and asked prices are in percent of par. As with Treasury bonds and notes, the decimal places indicate thirty-seconds. At one time a "+" or "−" indicated plus or minus a sixty-fourth, but this convention is no longer widely used. (See p. 122 or Appendix 1 for the table listing the decimal values of thirty-seconds.) In the last quote of the following example, the FNMA October bond has a bid price of 91.12, which, for a $10,000 bond, would be $9,137.50. Accrued interest must also be added.

FNMA Bonds

Bid and asked prices in percent of par; accrued interest must be added.

Decimals indicate 32nds.

Rate	Bid	Ask Chg. Yield
9½	93.21	94.5 .... 14.67
18	103.12	103.20......... 14.70
6¾	89.28	90.12......... 14.84
7.30	89.18	91.2 .... 14.81
8.10	91.16	92 .... 14.82
10.85	94.18	95.2 .... 14.77
9.70	92.26	93.10......... 14.77
6¾	88.10	88.26......... 14.81
8½	90.20	91.4 .... 14.89
9¼	91.12	91 28......... 14.85

(The Washington Post)

3. Yield

Yield is yield to maturity based on the asked price.

4. Weekly Quotations

The high, low, and last prices of weekly quotations are bid prices.

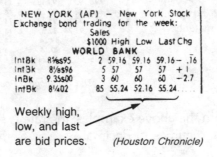

Weekly high,
low, and last
are bid prices.   *(Houston Chronicle)*

5. GNMA Quotations

"Ginnie Mae" quotations are different from other government-agency quotations in several ways. Although the stated maturity of a Ginnie Mae mortgage pool is 30 years, statistically they are expected to last approximately 12. This is a result of prepayments into the pool from the sale of houses under the mortgage. Since the exact date of liquidation of a mortgage pool cannot be known, no maturity date is given in the quotations.

One should also be aware that the stated yields are estimates based on past performance. Earlier-than-expected prepayment would raise the effective yield, and later-than-expected prepayment would lower it. Ginnie Maes pay interest (and part of the principal) monthly.

PART THREE

HOW TO READ
MUTUAL FUND
QUOTATIONS

12 Mutual Funds

A. Background

There are two major types of mutual-fund quotations that regularly appear in newspapers. They are listed under the headings:

Mutual Funds (or **Investment Funds**)
Money-Market Funds

They are both mutual funds.

A *mutual fund* is an investment company that sells an unlimited number of its own shares in order to invest the proceeds in a diversified group of other companies. After costs and reasonable management charges, the returns from these investments are funneled back to the original investors.

Another characteristic of mutual funds is that they redeem their own shares. The investor thus has the advantage of liquidity in addition to investment diversity, convenience, and professional management.

The difference between a mutual fund and a money-market fund is that mutual funds invest in a wide variety of investment vehicles, including stocks and/or bonds, whereas money-market funds invest *only* in money-market instruments, which are, by definition, short-term.

Money-market instruments are short-term debt obligations with maturities ranging from overnight to one year. They include Treasury bills, certificates of deposit, commercial paper (from corporations), banker's acceptances, and others.

In money-market funds, the average maturity of the total investment portfolio is surprisingly short, anywhere from one day to a few months. Since assets are invested in short-term obligations, such funds may take immediate advantage of any rise in interest rates. However, at least a brief amount of time is required before such increased interest rates are reflected in the yields of the funds.

In order to obtain more perspective on mutual funds, let us consider them in a broader context. A mutual fund is a type of *investment company*.

Investment companies, in the broadest sense, are entities in which individuals or institutions pool their funds with other individuals or institutions for investment purposes.

An advantage of an investment "pool" is that larger amounts of money are created with which to invest. This will bring within reach larger investment vehicles that pay higher interest. Commissions and other transactions also constitute a smaller percentage of larger investment costs. More significant, however, is the increased possibility for investment diversity. The "risk" is spread over many investments so that if any one or two do not perform up to expectations, they will not ruin the entire investment plan. The safety of diversity is probably the most attractive feature of investment companies beyond that of the expertise of the management.

There are two types of investment companies: open-end funds and closed-end funds.

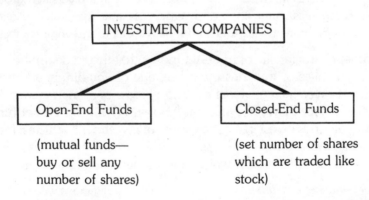

Open-end funds will sell or buy back any number of shares of the fund; thus, the number of shares outstanding is always fluctuating (open-ended). The redemption price of the shares is always the net asset value (defined later).

Closed-end funds, or publicly traded investment funds, maintain the same number of shares and consequently their shares are traded on exchanges in the same manner as common stock.

Closed-end funds are companies with stock like any other company. Their business is investing, and since they have low production costs (no factories or raw materials required), they can funnel a large percent of their yields on to their investors. A number of such companies are listed on the national exchanges as well as over the counter. Weekly, major newspapers list the quotations of a few of these companies separately under the heading "Publicly Traded Funds." See p. 144 for an example.

A special type of closed-end fund is the "dual" fund. It consists of a single pool of investments, but its investors may choose whether to purchase capital-gains shares or income shares. Major weekly newspapers carry a brief list of dual funds under the heading "Dual-Purpose Funds" although these funds, like the publicly traded funds above, are listed elsewhere on other exchanges and over the counter. See p. 145 for an example.

There are two kinds of open-end funds: load and no-load.

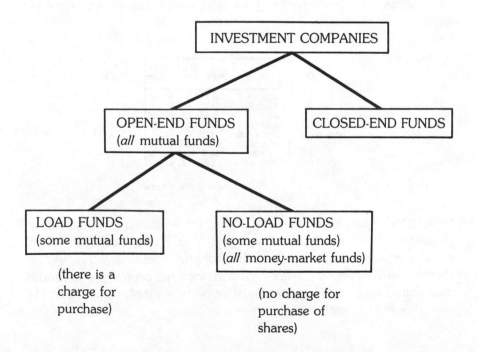

"Load" is a commission charge for the purchase of the shares of a mutual fund. It is *not* a management fee. It can vary from 3% to 8½%.

From the above diagram, we can see that all mutual funds are a type of open-end investment fund. Some charge a fee for investing (load) and some do not. There is no appreciable difference between the performance of the two types; however, mutual funds in general *do* vary considerably in other ways. Some specialize in capital growth, some in income. Some limit themselves to specific types of invesments, such as government securities, bonds, or gold. Some are relatively speculative and others conservative. In deciding which fund to choose, one should examine carefully its investment goals, its methods, and its past record.

B. The Quotations

1. Name of the Fund

The first column lists the name of the fund, sometimes abbreviated and sometimes spelled out.

	Funds	NAV	Offer Price	NAV Chg.
	Able	23.48	NL +	.04
	Acorn F	28.32	NL +	.04
name of	ADV	15.54	NL +	.16
the fund	Afuture	15.66	NL +	.07
	AIM Funds:			
	CvYld	15.51	16.59 +	.09
	Edson	14.77	15.80 +	.18
	HiYld	9.00	9.63 +	.02

(Los Angeles Times)

Note in the example above that AIM has three different mutual funds: Convertible Yield, Edson Fund, and High Yield Fund. A company often establishes several different funds in order to provide investors with a choice of investment strategies (growth, income, capital preservation, speculation, etc.) or different areas of investment emphasis (convertible securities, bonds, etc.).

2. Net Asset Value (NAV)

The second column lists the NAV, which stands for the "net asset value" per share. It is quoted in dollars and cents.

Net asset value per share is determined by taking the current market value of all the holdings of the fund and dividing it by the number of shares. This is the amount—sometimes listed as the sell price or bid price—at which the company will redeem its shares.

In the following example, the first mutual fund, 44 Wall Street, shows a NAV of $26.55 per share.

"Net Asset Value" per share: the price at which shares may be redeemed (quoted in dollars and cents)

Funds	NAV	Offer Price	NAV Chg
44 Wall	26.55	NL +	.27
Fnd Gth	5.40	5.90 +	.04
Founders Group:			
Grwth	9.38	NL +	.10
Incom	15.75	NL +	.04
Mutal	9.58	9.98 +	.07
Specl	23.88	NL +	.23
Franklin Group:			
AGE	3.37	3.63 +	.01
Brown	6.12	6.50 +	.07
DNTC	14.62	15.76 +	.19
Grwth	8.42	9.08 +	.09

(Los Angeles Times)

Many papers are beginning to use "sell" instead of NAV, since this is the price at which one can sell one's shares back to the fund.

mutual funds

Latest approximate closing price ranges as quoted by the National Association of Securities Dealers.

"Sell" is often used instead of NAV.

Descp	Sell	Buy	Descp	Sell	Buy
Able	14.10	NL	Boston Co:		
Acorn F	22.57	NL	IPI Inc	9.50	10.27
ADV	13.47	NL	CapAp	19.74	NL
Afuture	12.26	NLO	Bost Fnd	9.31	10.17
AIM Funds:			Bull & Bear	Gp:	
CvYld	11.94	12.77	Capm	9.24	NL
Edson	11.38	12.17	Capit S	11.23	NL
HiYld	8.23	8.80	Golcn	11.51	NL
Alpha F	16.64	NL	Calvin Bullock:		
A BirthT	10.76	11.76	Bullck	14.08	15.39

(St. Louis Post-Dispatch)

3. Buy Price

The next column lists the "buy" price, sometimes called the "offer" price. This is what the shares will cost the buyer.

MUTUAL FUND PRICES

purchase price of shares in dollars and cents

	Sell	Buy		Sell	Buy		Sell	Buy
Delaw	14.93	16.32	Inv Indic	1.23	NL	NELife Fund:		
Delch	6.22	6.80	InvQual	8.42	8.82	Equit	17.44	18.96
Tx Fre	5.17	5.41	Inv Bos	10.01	10.79	Grwth	12.85	13.97
Delta	9.20	10.05	Investors Group:			Incom	8.96	9.74
Dir Cap	2.37	NL	IDS Bd	3.85	3.99	Ret Eq	17.28	18.78
DodCx Bl	21.64	NL	IDS Dis	5.31	5.78	TaxEx	5.06	5.30
DodCx St	18.90	NL	IDS Grt	12.47	13.56	Neuberger Berm:		

(The Washington Post)

In the above example, the column on the right shows the mutual funds of New England Life. The sell price (NAV) of the NEL Equity Fund is $17.44 and the buy price is $18.96. The difference between these two prices is the charge or commission (load) for the purchase of the shares. In this case it is $1.52 per share or about 8%. For the Growth Fund, the charge is $1.12.

When an "NL" appears in the "buy" column, the fund is a "no-load" and there is no charge for the purchase of shares. In this case the NAV is both the purchase and redemption price. In the following example, the four funds in the left-hand column and eight of those in the right-hand column are no-load funds.

NEW YORK (AP) —The following quotations, supplied by the National Association of Securities Dealers, Inc., are the prices at which these securities could have been sold (Net asset value) or dought (value plus sales charge) Monday.

	Sell	Buy
Able	16.07	NL
Acorn F	24.59	NL
ADV	14.38	NL
Afuture	14.02	NL

	Sell	Buy
TaxM	14.24	15.27
Beac Gth	11.37	NL
Beac Hill	12.78	NL
Berger Group:		
100 Fd	13.38	NL
101 Fd	10.52	NL
Boston Co:		
IPI Inc	10.31	11.15
CapAp	25.39	NL
Bost Fnd	9.54	10.43
Bull & Bear Gp:		
Capm	10.50	NL
Capit S	12.80	NL
Golcn	13.48	NL
Calvin Bullock:		
Bullck	14.95	1634
Candn	7.59	8.30
Divid	2.61	2.85

"NL" indicates no-load funds.

(Cincinnati Enquirer)

There is always a minimum amount necessary for the initial investment and ordinarily a lesser minimum for subsequent investments. Each fund has different restrictions and minimums.

4. Change

The last column is sometimes the "change" or "NAV change" column, which is the difference, in dollars and cents, between the NAV or purchase price of the current quotation and that of the previous trading period (or week if the quotations are weekly). In the following example, which shows funds from the Dreyfus Corporation, the A Bond Fund is up $.01, the Dreyfus is up $.07, the Leverage Fund is up $.03, etc.

	N.A.V.	Buy	Chg.
Dreyfus Grp:			
A Bnd	12.57	NL +	.01
Dreyf	14.90	16.28 +	.07
Levge	17.31	18.92 +	.03
N Nine	10.23	NL +	.01
Spl Inc	6.82	NL	......
Tax Ex	9.45	NL +	.02
Thrd C	7.05	NL +	.07

change from previous NAV or sell price in dollars and cents

(The New York Times)

5. Weekly Quotations

Weekly quotations such as those in a Sunday paper often list "high," "low," and "last" (or "bid") prices. These are the weekly range and final price of the NAV.

"High," "low," and "bid" (last) are the NAV prices for the week.

Mutual funds

"n" = no-load

NEW YORK (AP) — Weekly investing Companies giving the high, low and last prices for the week with the net change from the previous week's last price. All quotations, supplied by the National Association of Securities Dealers, Inc., reflect net asset values, at which securities have been sold.

	High	Low	Last	Chg.
AbleAsc n	17.12	16.38	16.60 —	.05
AcornFd n	24.95	24.68	24.95 +	.23
ADV Fund n	14.80	14.56	14.64 —	.02
AfutureFo n	14.59	14.46	14.51 +	.05

IDS Bond	4.19	4.13	4.15 —	.04
IDS Disc	5.55	5.54	5.55 +	.03
IDS Growth	13.16	13.00	13.04 —	.07
IDS HiYield	3.29	3.27	3.27 —	.01
IDS NewDim	6.95	6.92	6.95 +	.05
IDS Progr	4.49	4.37	4.46 —	.01
InvMutl	9.38	9.23	9.33 —	.01
IDS TaxEx	2.92	2.89	2.89 —	.01
Inv Stock	18.63	18.41	18.53 +	.05
Inv Select	6.85	6.71	6.77 —	.09
Inv Variabl	8.50	8.44	8.46 —	1.38
Investrs Resh	5.17	5.13	5.13 —	.02

(Arizona Republic—Phoenix)

In this format, an "n" after the name of the fund indicates that it is a no-load fund.

6. Income and Capital Gains

The weekly listings in Barron's provide additional information about each mutual fund: income and capital gains.

| Fund | 52-Weeks | | | | Dividend | |
	High NAV	Low NAV	Close NAV	Week's Change	In-come	Cap. Gains
AbleAsc n	24.66	11.89	12.65+	.17	.12	2.33
AcornFd n	28.65	21.38	21.67+	.28	.94	.04
ADV Fund n	15.71	12.62	13.50+	.33	.46	
AfutureFd n	15.98	12.26	12.48+	.16	.4069	3.094

(Barron's)

The income figure is the quarterly dividend paid to the shareholders out of dividends and interest received by the fund. The capital gains figure is a yearly amount, the total of which may be paid in one sum or in installments. It is also the less stable of the two figures. A blank in either column means that dividends or capital-gains disbursements have yet to be declared.

Both the income and the capital gains annualized constitute the total returns performance (or what is labeled "Dividend" in the above example). This is helpful in providing a picture of the past activity of the fund. However, it can be no guarantee of future performance.

7. Quotations of Closed-End Funds

As described earlier, closed-end funds (labeled here "publicly traded funds") are quoted weekly in major newspapers. The purchase price (here labeled "Stk Price," or stock price) is usually less than the net asset value.

Publicly Traded Funds

Following is a weekly listing of unaudited net asset values of publicly traded investment fund shares, reported by the companies as of Thursday's close. Also

Closed-end fund: Shares trade at discount from net asset value.

shown is the closing listed market price or a dealer-to-dealer asked price of each fund's shares, with the percentage of difference.

difference between stock price at Thursday's close and stock price one week earlier in percent

	N.A. Value	Stk Price	% Diff		N.A. Value	Stk Price	% Diff
Diversified Common Stock Funds				Castle	26.33	22⅞	−13.1
				CentSec	10.98	8	−28.2
AdmExp	17.74	15⅛	−14.7	ChaseCvB	14.59	13⅝	−6.6
aBakerFen	91.50	66½	−27.3	Claremont	27.69	19⅞	−28.2
GenAInv	20.51	21¾	+6.0	CLAS	(−3.56)	9/16	.....
Lehman	15.54	14⅞	−4.3	CLAS PFD	26.05	.....	.....
Madison	22.90	18¼	−20.3	Cyprus	.28	9/16	+100.9
NiagaraSh	19.05	19⅛	+0.4	Engex	14.67	8⅝	−41.2
OseasSec	5.76	6¼	+8.5	Japan	z	z	z
Source	26.82	22½	−16.1	Mexico(b)	z	z	z
Tri-Contl	26.08	20¾	−20.4	Nautilus	22.57	20¼	−10.3
US&For	27.24	21¾	−20.1	NewAmFd	30.47	22	−27.8
Specialized Equity and Convertible Funds				Pete&Res	38.95	34⅝	−11.1
				PrecMet	15.18	12¼	−19.3
aAmGnCv	29.43	26	−11.7	a-Ex-Dividend. b-As of Wednesday's close. z-Not available.			
bASA	54.81	43⅜	−20.8				
BancrftCv	25.91	23⅝	−8.8				

(The Wall Street Journal)

On the exchange on which the fund is traded, the stock price appears as the closing price. The net asset value is the only additional information provided by weekly quotations such as the one above.

The percentage difference in the last column is simply another way of quoting the week's net change of the stock (that is, as opposed to quoting it in points).

8. Quotations of Dual-Purpose Funds

Dual-purpose fund: prices are only for capital-gains shares.

Dual-Purpose Funds

difference between current capital shares and capital shares one week ago shown in percent

Following is a weekly listing of the unaudited net asset values of dual-purpose, closed-end investment funds' capital shares as reported by the companies as of Friday's close. Also shown is the closing listed market price or the dealer-to-dealer asked price of each fund's capital shares, with the percentage of difference.

	Cap. Shs. Price	N.A. Val Cap. Shs.	% Diff.
Gemini	37¼	41.27	−9.7
Hemisphere	3⅜	2.69	+25.5
Income and Cap	11	11.64	−5.5
Putnam Duo Fund	13	14.48	−10.2

(The Wall Street Journal)

A small number of dual-purpose closed-end mutual funds are listed separately once a week in major newspapers. These funds have two kinds of shares: those for capital gains and those for income. The weekly listings provide the price for the capital-gains shares (like common stock) and the net asset value. The difference between the current price and the price a week ago is shown in percent.

The information the above listing provides, beyond that of the exchange or OTC listing, is the net asset value. However, the *exchange* listing quotes two types of shares. The shares for capital gains are shown in the following example as "GenCa" and the income shares are shown as "GenIn."

capital gains shares and income shares of a dual-purpose fund listed on the NYSE							
37	27½	GemCa		73	5 u37¼	37¼	37¼ + ¼
16⅜	13⅝	GemIn	2.40a	15.	26 15⅝	15⅝	15⅝ + ⅛

(The Wall Street Journal)

Income shares of a dual-purpose fund have a definite life-span. At expiration, the fund turns into an ordinary closed-end fund and the income shares are paid off or converted into ordinary shares. The investor should know the date of termination and the conversion terms of the income shares.

13 Money-Market Funds

Background information on money funds and their place in the structure of mutual funds was given in the previous chapter, and much of the material there applies to the present chapter.

A. The Quotations

Money-market-fund quotations are among the most direct and easy-to-read quotations printed. Some newspapers do not carry these quotations daily but list them in a weekend edition or on a Monday when there is usually less financial news. Money-market yields, although variable in the long run, are not as volatile from day to day as most other investment vehicles.

1. Name and Assets

The quotations used by many papers *(Donoghue's Money Fund Table)* begin with the name of the fund, seldom abbreviated, and then usually list the assets in millions of dollars.

MONEY MARKET FUNDS

Funds with assets of $100 million or more that are available to individual investors.

Fund	Assets ($ million)	Average maturity (days)	7-day average yield (%)	30-day average yield (%)
Alliance Capital Rsrvs	1,166.2	24	15.8	14.6
American General	208.1	20	16.5	15.6
American Liquid Trust	279.6	26	15.8	14.9
Boston Co. Cash Mgmt.	123.0	23	15.7	14.7
Capital Preservation	1,025.3	27	15.3	14.7
Cap. Prsvtion Fund II	248.5	2	16.6	15.8
Cardinal Govt Secs	148.5	14	15.0	14.0

(The Boston Globe)

2. Average Maturity (Days)

Because money-market funds invest exclusively in short-term obligations, the average maturity time of the various investments is quite
short. This column lists, in days, the *average* maturity time for the entire
holdings of the fund. The shorter the time, the quicker the fund re-
sponds to changing interest rates, both higher and lower.

average maturity,
in days, of all
investments

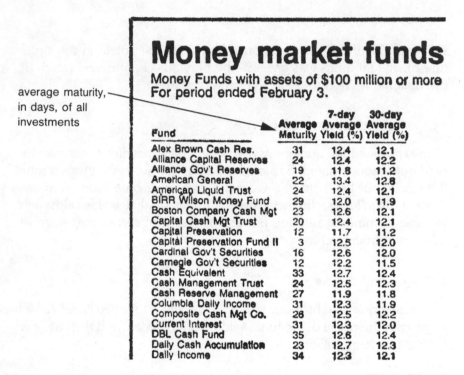

Money market funds

Money Funds with assets of $100 million or more
For period ended February 3.

Fund	Average Maturity	7-day Average Yield (%)	30-day Average Yield (%)
Alex Brown Cash Res.	31	12.4	12.1
Alliance Capital Reserves	24	12.4	12.2
Alliance Gov't Reserves	19	11.8	11.2
American General	22	13.4	12.8
American Liquid Trust	24	12.4	12.1
BIRR Wilson Money Fund	29	12.0	11.9
Boston Company Cash Mgt	23	12.6	12.1
Capital Cash Mgt Trust	20	12.4	12.1
Capital Preservation	12	11.7	11.2
Capital Preservation Fund II	3	12.5	12.0
Cardinal Gov't Securities	16	12.6	12.0
Carnegie Gov't Securities	12	12.2	11.5
Cash Equivalent	33	12.7	12.4
Cash Management Trust	24	12.5	12.3
Cash Reserve Management	27	11.9	11.8
Columbia Daily Income	31	12.3	11.9
Composite Cash Mgt Co.	26	12.5	12.2
Current Interest	31	12.3	12.0
DBL Cash Fund	35	12.6	12.4
Daily Cash Accumulation	23	12.7	12.3
Daily Income	34	12.3	12.1

(Chicago Tribune)

3. Yield Averages

The next two columns, as in the above example, give the yield averages
(total returns minus costs and management fees) for the previous 7
days and the previous 30 days. The 30-day average is obviously the
more reliable for projecting the longer-term performance of the fund.

Interest is calculated daily. In the quotations, the yields are annualized so that when a 7-day average yield is stated, it means that if this
rate held all year, the amount of money accrued would equal that
percentage of the total invested.

4. Associated Press Quotations

Money-market-fund quotations from the Associated Press list first a yearly high and low. After the name of the fund, the average maturity of all investments is given in days. The average yield is annualized from a 7-day period, and the change from the previous 7-day period is given in dollars and cents.

Money-market funds

NEW YORK (AP) — The following quotations, collected by the NASD Inc., are the average of annualized yields and dollar-weighted portfolio maturities for the seven day period ending Friday, Dec. 4. Realized and unrealized gains or losses are not taken into account.

YHi	YLw	Name	Avg Mat	Avg Yld	Chg
16.24	13.87	AlexBrwn	30	13.35	— .52
17.94	13.45	AlliaCpRs f	27	12.73	— .72
16.87	12.10	AlliaGvRs f	27	11.53	— .57
18.69	13.93	AmGenRs b	32	13.86	— .11
18.74	12.89	AmLiqTr	23	12.39	— .50
17.63	13.73	Babson	33	15.12	+ 1.39
17.78	13.21	BirrWil	31	12.42	— .79
17.59	12.47	BostonCo	32	12.52	— .66
17.94	10.97	CapPresrv	15	10.78	— .19
19.25	10.82	CapPresv II	5	10.41	— .41
17.27	11.76	CardinGvt	20	11.58	— .18
17.94	11.36	Carnegie		.00	
18.12	13.17	CashEquiv f	39	14.31	— .42
17.95	13.69	CshMgtA b	12	12.71	— .98
19.31	12.72	CashRsM bf	27	14.16	+ .62
18.26	13.07	CentCapCsh	13	11.30	— 1.77
17.99	13.38	ColDln bf	30	12.72	— .66
18.48	13.85	CompCsh	27	12.99	— .86
17.42	13.30	CurrentIntr	34	12.77	— .53
17.75	13.89	DBL CshFd		.00	
17.90	13.51	LehmanCsh	28	12.80	-- .71
18.43	13.58	Lexington	28	12.81	-- .77
7.85	7.08	LexingTxFr	58	6.94	-- .14
17.95	12.96	LiqCapital		.00	
18.48	10.72	LiqdCshTr	3	10.97	+ .18
17.82	12.97	LordAbCsR	28	12.52	— .45
18.18	12.27	LuthernBr c	42	13.16	— .55
17.26	13.29	MIF Natw c	27	13.32	— .44
37.62	13.22	MassCash	35	13.10	— .70
18.41	13.37	McDonald f	31	13.03	— .34
17.08	13.67	MerLyGv bf	34	11.91	— 1.87
17.58	13.03	MerLyln bf	26	13.42	-- .67
17.78	12.72	MidwIncTr	35	12.17	— .55
17.92	12.38	MonMMgt f	44	13.08	— .51
17.64	12.11	MonMkTrst	40	13.42	— .45
18.45	14.02	MonMtA bd	24	13.46	— .56
17.72	13.56	MorganK f	41	13.01	— .55
8.04	6.54	MuniCshR e	68	7.69	— .26
8.12	4.64	MuniTInv e	49	7.41	-- .09
17.73	13.68	MutlOma c	27	12.35	— 1.33
17.66	13.91	NEL Csh c	38	13.97	+ .06
17.71	12.58	NRT AA f	52	12.46	— .12
17.74	13.54	NatLiqRes	34	13.25	— .94
18.55	14.17	OppMoney		.00	
15.99	13.91	PIA Asset f	24	13.18	— .73
17.29	13.17	PaineWCs f	29	13.19	— .73
18.57	13.48	Phoenix	30	12.76	— .72
17.45	13.39	Plimoney	29	13.11	— .32
17.79	13.84	PutDDiv b	41	13.57	— .27

(Arizona Republic—Phoenix)

PART FOUR

HOW TO READ OPTION QUOTATIONS

14 Stock Options

A. Background

Options are traded on the following exchange, which is exclusively an options exchange:

Chicago Board Options Exchange (CBOE)

They are also traded on four stock exchanges:

American Stock Exchange
Philadelphia Stock Exchange
Pacific Stock Exchange
New York Stock Exchange

All five are considered national exchanges. The headings for their newspaper quotations are shortened to "Chicago Board," "Pacific Options," "American Exchange Options," etc.

Stock options listed on exchanges have standardized dates and exercise prices (defined later). This standardization, more than any other factor, has contributed to the high level of trading volume necessary for the liquidity of options.

Liquidity refers to the ease of purchase and sale.

There are two things to keep in mind about options. First of all, unlike stock, they are a kind of contract. The option owner (called "holder") does not own any part of the underlying security or receive dividends; there is only an agreement that the holder has the *right* to buy or sell stock. (That is a right the holder may or may not choose to exercise.) Second, all listed options transactions are cleared through and guaranteed by the Options Clearing Corporation (OCC). That is, after the buyer and seller arrive at an agreement on the exchange floor, both sides of the transaction are sent to the OCC. The OCC then interposes itself as seller for all buyers and as buyer for all sellers. In this way, an orderly and efficient market is maintained. Because of the records kept by the OCC, there may be no direct link between the purchaser and the seller (called "writer") of options. Options thus become a kind of contract with the OCC.

In most cases, stock options do not trade on the same exchange as their underlying securities. Furthermore, options on the same security may be traded on more than one exchange.

Listed options are not available for all stocks. The following are some of the minimum requirements imposed on a company before an exchange can offer options on their stock. These requirements guarantee that a corporation is of sufficient size and stability before options on its stock are offered to the public.

a)   at least 8 million shares already in public hands
b)   at least 10,000 shareholders
c)   trading volume of at least 2 million shares for each of the two previous years
d)   a price of $10 or more per share for six months prior to the proposed option listing
e)   net income after taxes of at least $1 million for three of the four preceding years

Options may also be purchased over the counter. However, the terms are negotiated (between brokers) and are thus not likely to be standard. This, combined with the fact that they are not listed, makes over-the-counter options far less liquid than options on the exchanges; in fact, they are seldom traded beyond the initial transaction. The discussion here applies primarily to options listed on national exchanges.

There are only two kinds of options, calls and puts.

A *call* is the right to purchase ("call in") 100 shares (usually) of a specific stock, at a specific price, within a specified time period. One can *buy* a call, giving one the right to buy the stock from another person; or one can *sell* a call, giving another person the right to buy the specified stock *from you*. (In either case, the purchaser of the option is not required to exercise it but may do so if desired.)

A *put* is the right to sell 100 shares of a specific stock, at a specific price, within a specified time period. (You can "put it to" someone.) One can *buy* a put, giving one the right to sell the stock to someone else; or one can

sell a put, giving someone else the right to sell the specified stock *to you.*
(Again, the purchaser decides whether or not to exercise the option.)

A diagram of the above possibilities looks something like this:

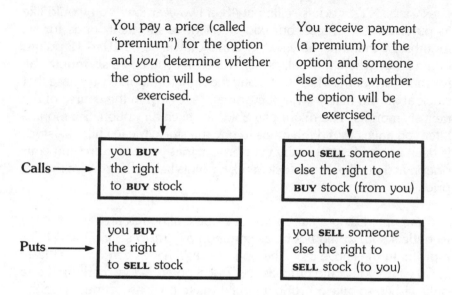

You pay a price (called "premium") for the option and *you* determine whether the option will be exercised.

You receive payment (a premium) for the option and someone else decides whether the option will be exercised.

Calls ———▶

| you **BUY** the right to **BUY** stock |

| you **SELL** someone else the right to **BUY** stock (from you) |

Puts ———▶

| you **BUY** the right to **SELL** stock |

| you **SELL** someone else the right to **SELL** stock (to you) |

Options are usually for 100 shares, so that one multiplies the exercise price, in points, times 100, the same as for the purchase of any round lot.

The *exercise price* (sometimes called the "strike price") is the price per share guaranteed by an option at which one can buy or sell a specific stock.

Thus a call option for XYZ stock at 25 guarantees that one can purchase 100 shares of XYZ for $2,500. If a guarantee for 400 shares is desired, then four options would have to be purchased.

Let us consider the above options one at a time.

You may *buy* this:

| **CALL OPTION** |
| Right to buy: |
| XYZ stock |
| at ($ *exercise price*) |
| until (*expiration date*) |

You will pay a price, called a "premium," for this option and you may exercise it during the time period for which it is valid if you wish to do so. Your basic position: *You want the price of the underlying stock to rise.*

EXAMPLE: XYZ stock is selling at 48, a two-year low. You would like to purchase 100 shares, but you won't have sufficient funds for six months. By that time, however, you think it will be up 10 to 12 points, in the range where it usually sells. Therefore, you buy a six-month call for that stock at 50. That is, you buy the right (option) to purchase that stock at 50 (no matter what it eventually sells for) in the course of the next six months. You might pay $300 for such an option. Six months later you have cleared the funds to buy the stock. Meanwhile the stock is back up to 58. You notify your broker that you are exercising your option and purchase the stock at 50, 8 points below the current market price.

Caution: Using a call to acquire stock, although an easy strategy to understand, would not be as common as simply selling the call for a profit. In the above case, the option would have been worth at least $800 (since you could purchase XYZ at 8 points below market). If one only wished to take a profit, it would make no sense to purchase the stock and resell it (thus incurring two stock commissions) when one could sell the option and incur only one option commission. Also, option commissions are much lower than stock commissions.

To continue our consideration of the various options . . .

One could also *sell* this:

```
┌──────────────────────────┐
│  CALL OPTION             │
│  Right to buy:           │
│  XYZ stock               │
│  at ($ exercise price)   │
│  until (expiration date) │
└──────────────────────────┘
```

Since, in this case, you have *sold* a call option, you are giving someone else the right to exercise the option during the time for which it is valid. You will receive a premium for the sale of this right, but for that price you obligate *yourself* to fulfill the terms of the option should the other person exercise it.

EXAMPLE: You own 400 shares of XYZ stock at 48. It has been between 45 and 50 for a while and you do not expect much movement in the next six months. You would like to supplement your income, so you decide to sell (called "write") options against it. In the case of XYZ, you might write six-month call options at 50, which would grant someone else the right to "call in" that stock, from you, at 50. Assuming that the market price for these options is $300, your total return for four options would be $1,200.

What you are hoping is that the stock will not go above 50 and the options will never be exercised. In that case, you keep the $1,200 and can write more options against the same stock six months later. Of course, should the price of the stock rise, there are things you can do to protect your stock, but more about that later.

To continue the option description . . .

One could buy:

> **PUT OPTION**
> Right to sell
> XYZ stock
> at ($ *exercise price*)
> until (*expiration date*)

You will pay a premium for this option and you may exercise it during the time period for which it is valid if you wish to do so. Your basic position: *You want the price of the underlying stock to fall.*

EXAMPLE: You do not own XYZ stock, but you expect the price to drop in the next six months. It is now selling at 48. You buy a put option for $200 at 45. In five months the stock drops to 40. Your option is now worth more than $500. If the actual price is (for example) $600, then you can sell for a 300% profit.

And finally . . .

One could also sell this:

```
┌─────────────────────────┐
│                         │
│   PUT OPTION            │
│   Right to sell         │
│   XYZ stock             │
│   at ($ exercise price) │
│   until (expiration date)│
│                         │
└─────────────────────────┘
```

You will receive a premium for the sale of this option, but for that price you obligate *yourself* to fulfill the terms of the option should the other person exercise it. Your basic position depends on your strategy:

STRATEGY 1: The price of XYZ stock is at 48, a two-year low. It is a quality stock and you expect it to go up. You sell a put at 45 for $300. If the price never goes down, the option is never exercised and you keep $300.

STRATEGY 2: You do *not* own XYZ stock. It is at 48, a two-year low. It is a quality stock. If you like it at 48, then you certainly would like it at 45. You sell a put at 45 for $300. If the price never goes down, you will keep the $300. If the price drops sufficiently, the option will be exercised and you buy XYZ for 45. However, if you subtract the $300 you received from the option, you are actually getting it for 42.

There are many different ways to use options. It is possible for an investor to make a profit whether the price of a stock goes up *or* down. The correct combination of options can yield a profit under any imaginable movement of the underlying stock price. Options may be used conservatively with little risk or speculation; or they may be employed in such a way that one's gains or losses can theoretically be limitless.

The strategies of selling ("writing") options or of buying options are briefly outlined in the charts given in the next chapter. The strategies differ depending on one's investment goals and on whether one actually owns the underlying stock. In reading the charts, keep in mind that one can cancel one's position at any time (assuming the option has not been exercised) by buying or selling another option, called a "closing transaction."

An *opening transaction* is the initial sale or purchase of an option.

A *closing transaction* is a transaction that reverses the opening transaction (i.e., cancels it). Except for the price paid for the option, it must have exactly the same terms as the option it closes. If you buy a call, you close by selling a call; if you sell a put, you close by buying a put.

A diagram of opening and closing positions is as follows:

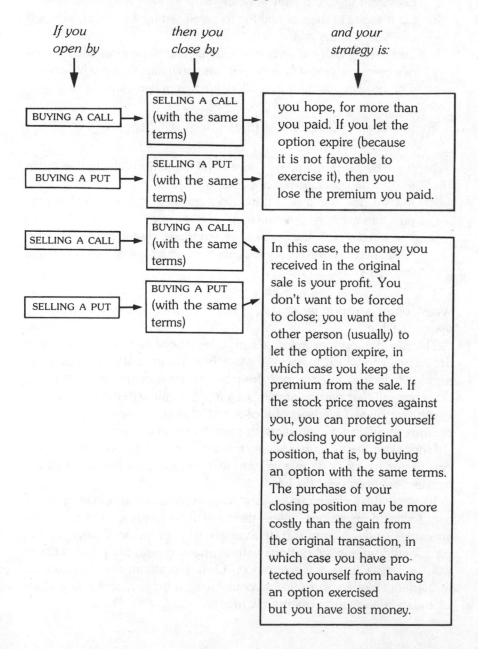

*If you
open by*

*then you
close by*

*and your
strategy is:*

BUYING A CALL → SELLING A CALL (with the same terms) →

BUYING A PUT → SELLING A PUT (with the same terms) →

you hope, for more than you paid. If you let the option expire (because it is not favorable to exercise it), then you lose the premium you paid.

SELLING A CALL → BUYING A CALL (with the same terms) →

SELLING A PUT → BUYING A PUT (with the same terms) →

In this case, the money you received in the original sale is your profit. You don't want to be forced to close; you want the other person (usually) to let the option expire, in which case you keep the premium from the sale. If the stock price moves against you, you can protect yourself by closing your original position, that is, by buying an option with the same terms. The purchase of your closing position may be more costly than the gain from the original transaction, in which case you have pro-tected yourself from having an option exercised but you have lost money.

If you purchase an option (*not* in combination with other options—that will be discussed later), you will eventually do one of three things:

1. Exercise it (if it is to your advantage).
2. Let it expire (if there is nothing to be gained by #1 or #3), in which case you lose the premium.
3. Terminate it with a closing transaction. (This is the most likely.) If the sale premium is more than the purchase premium, then you have made a profit—but you must also allow for two option commissions.

If you sell an option, one of three things will happen:

1. It will be exercised and you must fulfill the terms of the option (often to your disadvantage but not always).
2. It will expire (not likely if it still has intrinsic worth) and you keep the premium minus the commission.
3. You will terminate the option by purchasing a closing option. The cost of this purchase will reduce the gain from your original transaction and perhaps exceed it.

When options expire worthless, it is small consolation that they are tax-deductible.

The fact that options are, in a sense, less tangible than stocks affects the manner in which they are traded. For instance, if one buys a call and later decides to close out the position (at a profit or a loss), one does not sell *that* particular call but simply *a* call with the same terms, except for price. One way of looking at closing transactions is not as options at all, but as contracts to cancel options.

Under ordinary circumstances, there are no option certificates like certificates for stock. However, you will receive a confirmation of the transaction from your broker.

In general, stockbrokerages are conservative about allowing investors to trade in options unless they are fully aware of the risks and strategies, and can demonstrate a certain level of financial solvency. No one should buy or sell options without having read the prospectus of the Options Clearing Corporation. Option trading also requires an individual to open an option account with a broker, and many types of trades also require opening a margin account.

A *margin account* is a highly regulated credit account with a brokerage for the purpose of trading securities; it enables the investor to make certain types of transactions requiring the borrowing of money or stock from the brokerage. Minimum amounts of money or securities (margin) that must be on deposit in the account are regulated by the Federal Reserve Board. Interest is charged by the brokerage for money or securities utilized by the investor in such a manner.

The components of an option are:

1. name (of the underlying security)
2. type (put or call)
3. expiration (listed as a month)
4. exercise price

As mentioned before, the OCC processes all options transactions. It therefore falls to the OCC to assign options when the owners desire to exercise them. This is done in the following way.

Assume that for a specific call option there have been a total of 10,000 opening transactions. (For every transaction there must be both a sale and a purchase, thus 10,000 were bought and 10,000 were sold.) Also assume that on a particular day a significant movement in the stock price caused persons owning 1,000 calls to exercise them. They notify their brokers, who in turn notify the OCC. The OCC then decides on a random basis who among the brokers (of those who had sold this option for their clients) will receive the exercise notices. The brokers who receive those notices will then decide among their clients (who had sold that option) who will receive the notice of exercise. Different brokerages decide in different ways, sometimes on a random basis, sometimes on a first-in, first-out basis. In this example, for a person who sold such an option, the chances of exercise the next day would be one in ten.

Once you have been notified that an option you sold has been exercised, you cannot "get out" of it by buying a closing option. You must buy or sell securities according to the terms of the option, except in cases where you can deliver short (i.e., deliver stock through a short delivery).

Delivering short is delivering stock you have borrowed from your broker in order to fulfill the requirements of an option exercised against you.

The strategy of option writers depends on whether they own the underlying stock or not, that is, whether they are writing "covered" or "naked" options.

A *covered option,* in the case of a call, is a call you write on stock you own. Should the option be exercised, you can deliver your own stock; you are "covered."

A *naked option,* in the case of a call, is a call you write on stock you don't own. Should the option be exercised, you have no protection from theoretically limitless loss (unless you buy a closing option); you are "naked."

The point of writing covered calls is to receive a guaranteed return. This can be achieved whether the call you sell is exercised or not. If the call is not exercised, your gain is the entire premium you received minus commission. If the call is exercised, you still gain a percentage return provided the strike price of the option was higher than the price at which the stock was currently selling. Your return consists of the option commission and the higher price for your stock minus commission. (When you must sell stock because an option is exercised against you, you must still pay your broker's usual stock commission.) Your loss, of course, is the difference between the strike price and the even higher price at which your stock is currently selling.

When you buy an option, *you* are in control at all times; you decide whether you will exercise the option. You are not in danger of someone *else* deciding to exercise an option. You need only react to the price of the underlying stock, and it, in general, can do only one of three things: It may go up; it may go down; or it may not move significantly in either direction. Any of these situations can be favorable and any can be unfavorable, depending on the option or option combinations you have bought or sold.

There is one other term that is necessary for understanding options: "in the money."

In the money means that an option has intrinsic value with respect to the current price of the stock. To be "in the money," the strike price of a *call* must be below the current price of the stock. To be "in the money," the strike price of a *put* must be above the current price of the stock.

For instance, if a stock is selling at 52 and you have a call at 50, then the call is "in the money" 2 points (and thus its price will usually be in excess of 2 points). The opposite is true for a put: If the stock is at

52, you would have to have a put with a strike price at, for example, 55 in order for it to be in the money. If an option is "in the money" more than ⅛ point on the expiration date, in the majority of cases it will be exercised.

B. The Quotations

1. Two Formats

There are two formats in which options quotations appear. Daily quotations subdivide the list by the *month cycles in which the options expire.* The following example shows segments from the same daily listing for two different cycles. The first segment is the beginning of the list, showing options that expire in the February-May-August cycle. The second segment shows the beginning of the March-June-September cycle. If this listing appeared in October, the list would offer three different options that expired respectively in one month, four months, and seven months. The second cycle offers options that expire in two, five, and eight months. The third cycle is not shown, but its months would be April, July, and October for options expiring in three, six, and nine months. Nine months is the longest time period for which options are available.

EXAMPLE OF DAILY OPTIONS QUOTATIONS

name of the exchange · first cycle of terminating months for which the following options are available · second cycle of months for which the following options are available

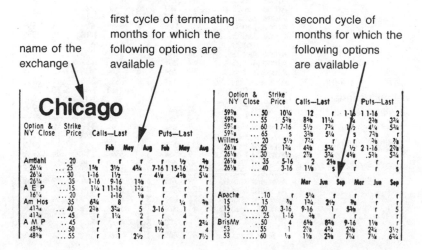

(Chicago Tribune)

There are always three different cycles available, although the third isn't shown in the example above. Options for a particular stock appear in only one of the current cycles.

Although the listings indicate only the month, the last day for *trading* expiring options (not to be confused with *exercising* expiring options) is always the third Friday of the month. On that day trading ceases at 3:00 EST. (Legally, the moment of expiration is the next day, Saturday, at 11:59 P.M. EST.)

There is an earlier deadline for *exercising* expiring options, 5:30 P.M. on the previous Thursday. However, brokerages have their own deadlines for customer orders to ensure sufficient time for execution before the deadline. A customer should verify these deadlines with his broker.

Example of Weekly Options Quotations

Weekly quotations are listed in a single alphabetic list that contains all the options together, such as the beginning of the example below. Note that a volume column is added. This format will be discussed later in "Weekly Quotations."

weekly quotations list; all options in alphabetical order (not by month cycle)

Option	Sales (100s)	Open Int.	High	Low	Last	Net Chg.	Stock Close
Alcoa Jan20...	5	528	5¾	5¾	5¾	......	25½
Alcoa Jan25...	84	1460	1⅜	1	1	− ½	25½
Alcoa Jan25 p..	71	907	7-16	¼	¼ − 3-16		25½
Alcoa Jan30...	54	1317	1-16	1-16	1-16	......	25½
Alcoa Jan30 p..	2	98	4⅞	4½	4½+	¼	25½
Alcoa Jan35...	10	887	1-16	1-16	1-16	......	25½
Alcoa Apr20...	2	510	6	6	6	......	25½
Alcoa Apr25...	38	614	2¼	2⅛	2⅛	......	25½
Alcoa Apr25 p..	68	264	1½	1	1¼+	⅛	25½
Alcoa Apr30....	292	666	⅝	½	½ − 1-16		25½
Alcoa Jul25.....	4	292	3¼	3⅛	3⅛	......	25½
Alcoa Jul25 p..	23	90	2 1 11-16	1 11-16 − 5-16			25½
Alcoa Jul30.....	21	168	1 3-16	1	1 3-16+3-16		25½
Amdahl Feb25..	180	1283	6	5¾	5¾+	⅞	29½
Amdahl Feb25 p	333	2053	11-16	⅜	⅜ −	¼	29½
Amdahl Feb30..	457	2742	2¾	1¾	1⅞ −	¼	29½
Amdahl Feb30 p	454	1527	2⅜	1¾	2⅛+1-16		29½
Amdahl Feb35..	233	1573	¾	5-16	½ − 1-16		29½
Amdahl Feb35 p	19	44	6	5¼	5¾ −	½	29½
Amdahl Feb40..	47	549	⅜	¼	¼ − 3-16		29½
Amdahl May25	10	533	7	7	7 + 1		29½
Amdahl May25 p	20	705	1½	1¼	1¼ −	⅝	29½
Amdahl May30	107	1227	4	3¼	3½ −	⅛	29½
Amdahl May30 p	5	629	3	3	3 −	¼	29½
Amdahl May35	41	326	1⅞	1⅝	1⅞	......	29½
Amdahl Aug30.	2	25	5	5	5 + 1		29½
Amdahl Aug35.	7	4	3½	2½	2½	......	29½
A E P Feb15...	62	2480	1½ 1 7-16	1½	......	16⅛	

(The New York Times)

2. Daily Options Quotations

a) *Name and NY Close*

The following is an example of options on the American Stock Exchange. The first column lists the name of the option (which is the name of the security on which the option is issued) and the closing price of the underlying stock on the New York Stock Exchange. Each option is for 100 shares of stock (unless otherwise indicated).

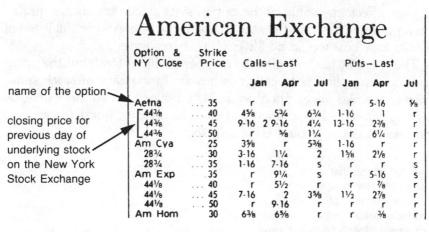

name of the option

closing price for previous day of underlying stock on the New York Stock Exchange

American Exchange

Option & NY Close	Strike Price	Calls – Last			Puts – Last		
		Jan	Apr	Jul	Jan	Apr	Jul
Aetna	... 35	r	r	r	r	5-16	⅝
44⅜	... 40	4⅝	5¾	6¾	1-16	1	r
44⅜	... 45	9-16	2 9-16	4¼	13-16	2⅜	r
44⅜	... 50	r	⅝	1¼	r	6¼	r
Am Cya	25	3⅝	r	5⅜	1-16	r	r
28¾	.. 30	3-16	1¼	2	1⅝	2⅛	r
28¾	... 35	1-16	7-16	s	r	r	s
Am Exp	35	r	9¼	s	r	5-16	s
44⅛	... 40	r	5½	r	r	⅞	r
44⅛	... 45	7-16	2	3⅝	1½	2⅞	r
44⅛	... 50	r	9-16	r	r	r	r
Am Hom	30	6⅜	6⅝	r	r	⅜	r

(The Wall Street Journal)

All four of the above lines are Aetna option quotations, and the New York closing price is applicable to each even though it does not appear in the first line. The New York close has a direct effect on the price (premium) of each option and also determines the amounts of the strike prices available. (This is explained in the next section.)

When only one option is listed, the New York close is not given. This happens when an option is being phased out, as is the case with the following Evans option.

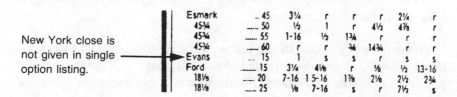

New York close is not given in single option listing.

Esmark	.. 45	3¼	r	r	r	2¼	r
45¾	—— 50	½	1	r	4½	4⅞	r
45¾	—— 55	1-16	½	1¾	r	r	r
45¾	—— 60	r	r	¾	14¾	r	r
Evans	... 15	1	s	s	r	s	s
Ford	—— 15	3¼	4⅛	r	⅛	½	13-16
18⅛	—— 20	7-16	1 5-16	1⅞	2⅛	2½	2¾
18⅛	—— 25	⅛	7-16	s	r	7½	s

(The Dallas Morning News)

An "o" following the option name indicates that the option, due to a stock dividend or a stock split, no longer permits the holder to purchase exactly 100 shares of the underlying stock. (The new number may be more or less than 100 shares.) These are "old" options trading at the time of the split or stock dividend and adjusted for the new value of the stock.

EXAMPLE: If you bought an option at 2 points ($200) and later (while the option was still in effect) the company declared a 4% stock dividend, then your option would automatically be worth 104 shares. This, in turn, affects the value of the option since prices are always quoted on a per-share basis. In the above case, if the option were still listed at $2, its total cost would be $208 (104 shares times $2).

The only way to determine the number of shares (and thus the price) for such an option is to call your broker. In the case of stock splits, fractional strike prices often occur. New options would, of course, be written for only 100 shares, and the old options, good for an odd number of shares, would eventually expire.

An "o" means that a stock dividend or split has caused the option to represent a number of shares other than 100. Strike prices are also affected. One cannot determine the premium of this option until it is known how many shares are represented.

Litton	 45	9⅛	r	r	⅛	¾	1¼
53½	 50	4¾	7⅜	r	⅞	1⅞	r
53½	 55	1 13-16	3⅞	r	2⅞	3¾	r
53½	 60	9-16	2¼	3⅞	6⅜	r	r
[illegible]½	 65	⅛	1	2⅜	11¼	r	r
Litn o	 49	5⅜	s	s	9-16	s	s
53½	.. 53⅞	2¾	s	s	2⅛	s	s
53½	.. 63¾	¼	s	s	r	s	s
53½	.. 68⅝	1-16	s	s	r	s	s

(The Washington Post)

b) *Strike Price*

The ***strike price,*** also known as the *exercise price,* is the price at which the option can be exercised, that is, the price at which a purchase or sale of the designated stock can be made.

The strike price is one of the terms of the option contract standardized by the OCC. In the example below, note that three different strike prices are available for Abbott Laboratories and that these are the strike prices for both the puts and the calls.

PHILADELPHIA

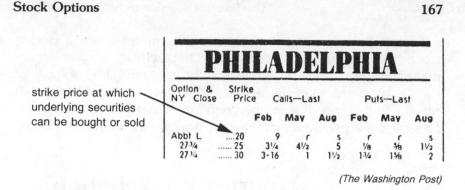

strike price at which underlying securities can be bought or sold

Option & NY Close	Strike Price	Calls—Last			Puts—Last		
		Feb	May	Aug	Feb	May	Aug
Abbt L	20	9	r	s	r	r	s
27¾	25	3¼	4½	5	⅛	⅝	1½
27¾	30	3-16	1	1½	1¾	1⅝	2

(The Washington Post)

Typically, there will be three or more strike prices available: one or two above and one or two below the price at which the stock closed. Below $50 per share, the spread between strike prices is usually $5; from $50 to $200 per share, the difference is usually $10; above $200, it is $20. When the New York close reaches the highest or lowest strike price available, another is opened up. Some exchanges open a new price if the stock moves halfway between one strike price and the highest or lowest strike price.

c) *Price (Calls—Last, Puts—Last)*

The price for each option is shown beneath the applicable month. These are always the last prices paid. As with stock, they are shown in points (dollars) per share and divisions thereof: ½, ¼, ⅛, 1⁄16. (Appendix 1 gives the decimal equivalents of these and other commonly used fractions.) Another term for the price of the option is the *premium.*

American Exchange

Option & NY Close	Strike Price	Calls – Last			Puts Last		
		Jan	Apr	Jul	Jan	Apr	Jul
Aetna	.. 35	r	r	r	r	5-16	⅝
44⅜	.. 40	4⅝	5¾	6¾	1-16	1	r
44⅜	45	9-16	2 9-16	4¼	13-16	2⅜	r

prices or "premiums" of options (in points)

(The Wall Street Journal)

In the above example, the six options listed on the last line are as follows: The Aetna January 45 call is 9⁄16; April 45 call is 2 9⁄16; July 45 call is 4¼. The Aetna January 45 put is 13⁄16; April 45 put is 2⅜; July 45 put ("r" means) did not trade.

It might be helpful to point out that the premium for a closing transaction is found in the same place as the premium for the opening transaction. For instance, if one bought an Aetna July 45 call at 4¼ shown in the example below, and if one wanted to close that transaction one month later, the premium in that same spot (i.e., for the same strike price and month) is the price for the sale of the closing call.

premiums are for opening or closing transactions. Aetna July 45 is 4¼ whether opening or closing, buying or selling.

American Exchange

Option & NY Close	Strike Price	Calls – Last			Puts Last		
		Jan	Apr	Jul	Jan	Apr	Jul
Aetna	... 35	r	r	r	r	5-16	⅝
44⅜	... 40	4⅞	5¾	6¾	1-16	1	r
44⅜	... 45	9-16	2 9-16	4¼	13-16	2⅜	r
44⅜	... 50	r	⅝	1¼	r	6¼	r
Am Cva	... 25	3⅝	r	5⅜	1-16	r	r
28¾	... 30	3-16	1¼	2	1⅝	2⅛	r
28¾	... 35	1-16	7-16	s	r	r	s

(The Wall Street Journal)

There are a number of factors that affect the premium of an option:

1. the current price of the underlying security
2. the exercise price on the option (in relation to the current price of the underlying security)
3. the time remaining until the option expires (As expiration nears, the option loses value.)
4. the volatility of the underlying stock (Greater volatility means a higher premium.)
5. other forces of supply and demand on that particular option

Large dividends also sometimes affect the price of an option. (In this case, it is a matter of the stock itself being slightly devalued after a large dividend payment.) Option holders, of course, do not receive dividends.

As you have noted by now, options are cheaper than stock. Obviously, an attraction of options is that relatively small amounts of money can control large amounts of stock. (This is an example of "leverage.") Also, as mentioned before, option *commissions* are lower than stock commissions.

d) *Qualifiers*

Two abbreviations that commonly appear in option quotations supplied by the Associated Press are:

r = did not trade during the trading period covered. If the quotation is in a daily paper, then the option did not trade the previous day; if weekly, then it did not trade the previous week. Price quotations, however, are available through a broker.

s = not offered. For a variety of reasons the OCC is not offering the option for sale or purchase.

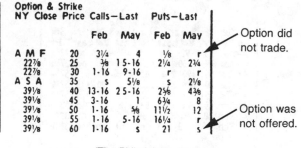

(The Philadelphia Inquirer)

The qualifiers used by the United Press International are:

nt = did not trade during the trading period covered
no = was not offered

A space-saving abbreviation used by UPI is "s" for sixteenths.

Option did
not trade.

An "s" stands for
16ths (1s15 =
1 15/16).

Option &		CALLS			
		Apr	Jul	Oct	Stk
Strike	Pr	Vol Last	Vol Last	Vol Last	Pr
Aetna 40	35	6 nt	nt	nt nt	45⅝
Aetna 50	25	⅝	52 1½	2 2¼	45⅛
ACyan 25	33	2⅞	1 3¾	3 4½	27½
ACyan 30	282	½	184 1s3	28 1s15	27½
ACyan 35	2	s3 no	no	no no	27½

Option was
not offered.

(The Tampa Tribune)

e) *Volume*

Although volume is not usually listed in daily quotations, it is generally included in weekly quotations. Liquidity is an important consideration in the buying or selling of options. Obviously, the higher the volume in a particular option, the easier it will be for one to close out a position. It is possible to be stuck with options that, for a variety of reasons, may be difficult or impossible to close. In the following quotation, the heaviest volume is in AT&T options.

Here is an example of a daily quotation that includes volume:

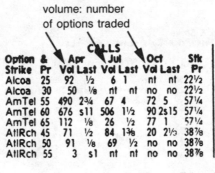

volume: number
of options traded

Option & Strike	Pr	CALLS Apr Vol Last	Jul Vol Last	Oct Vol Last	Stk Pr
Alcoa	25	92 ½	6 1	nt nt	22½
Alcoa	30	50 ⅛	nt nt	no no	22½
AmTel	55	490 2¾	67 4	72 5	57¼
AmTel	60	676 s11	506 1½	90 2s15	57¼
AmTel	65	112 ⅛	26 ½	77 1	57¼
AtlRch	45	71 ½	84 1⅜	20 2⅓	38⅞
AtlRch	50	91 ⅛	69 ½	no no	38⅞
AtlRch	55	3 s1	nt nt	no no	38⅞

(The Tampa Tribune)

Volume in weekly quotations is covered in the next section.

2. Weekly Quotations

a) *Format*

Sunday newspapers and other weeklies that cover option transactions for the entire week list the options on each exchange in alphabetical order without subdividing the entire list by monthly cycles. When there is no qualifier after the strike price, the option is a call. A "p" indicates a put.

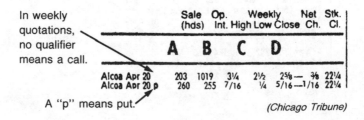

In weekly quotations, no qualifier means a call.

	Sale (hds)	Op. Int.	Weekly High	Low	Close	Net Ch.	Stk. Cl.
	A	**B**	**C**		**D**		
Alcoa Apr 20	203	1019	3¼	2½	2⅝ —	⅜	22¼
Alcoa Apr 20 p	260	255	7/16	¼	5/16 —1/16		22¼

A "p" means put.

(Chicago Tribune)

b) *Volume*

The number of sales is listed in hundreds (in weekly quotations) so that in the example above there were 28300 Alcoa April 30 calls traded.

c) *Open Interest*

Open interest is the total number of contracts for that particular option that are outstanding (i.e., that have not been closed). This number, listed in hundreds, in conjunction with the volume gives a picture of the liquidity of the option.

Open interest: total number   Note that column
of options not closed out   headings are not
                                 aligned properly.

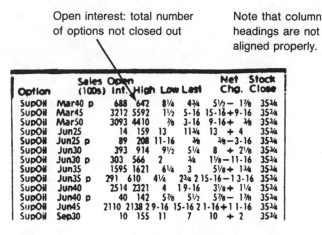

Option	Sales (100s)	Open Int.	High	Low	Last	Net Chg.	Stock Close
SupOil	Mar40 p	688	642	8¼	4¾	5½ − 1⅞	35¾
SupOil	Mar45	3212	5592	1½	5-16	15-16 +9-16	35¾
SupOil	Mar50	3093	4410	⅞	3-16	9-16 + ⅜	35¾
SupOil	Jun25	14	159	13	11¾	13 + 4	35¾
SupOil	Jun25 p	89	208	11-16	⅜	⅜ −3-16	35¾
SupOil	Jun30	393	914	9½	5¼	8 + 2⅛	35¾
SupOil	Jun30 p	303	566	2	¾	1⅛ −11-16	35¾
SupOil	Jun35	1595	1621	6¼	3	5⅛ + 1¾	35¾
SupOil	Jun35 p	291	610	4¼	2¾	2 15-16 −1 3-16	35¾
SupOil	Jun40	2514	2321	4	1 9-16	3⅛ + 1¼	35¾
SupOil	Jun40 p	40	142	5⅞	5½	5⅞ − 1⅞	35¾
SupOil	Jun45	2110	2138	2 9-16	15-16	2 1-16 +1 1-16	35¾
SupOil	Sep30	10	155	11	7	10 + 2	35¾

(The Philadelphia Inquirer)

It is typical that the column labels for option quotations and other securities quotations are out of place. Note that in the above example "Open Int." is above the volume column and "High" is above the open-interest column.

d) *Remainder of Quotation*

The "high/low/last/net change" is in the same format as stock quotations. The prices are actual transactions so that the bid prices could have been slightly lower. "Stock Close" is the NYSE weekly close.

C. Options on Commodities, Indexes, and Other Instruments

Recent years have seen an explosion of new financial instruments, and options have not been spared this plethora of creativity. Options based on commodities are quoted essentially the same as stock-based options. Their prices move in direct relation to the underlying commodities just as with ordinary puts and calls.

Options on silver and gold have been particularly popular because, unlike futures contracts, one's risk is limited to the amount invested. You will never get a margin call or be forced to liquidate a position as can happen with futures contracts.

Options based on stock indexes are complex and require a thorough knowledge of security indexes. For a description of the New York Stock Exchange Composite Index see section C, "Stock Index Futures," at the end of chapter 17.

15 Option Combinations and Strategies

A. Opening Transactions

Investment strategies are beyond the subject of this book; however, some detail is given here concerning option combinations because these strategies either directly apply to or indirectly affect a number of other financial instruments. Also, the major types of option combinations derive their names from the manner in which the applicable premiums are positioned in the newspaper quotations (i.e., "vertical," "horizontal," "diagonal").

Consider chart 1, "Strategies of an Opening Transaction." If you think a particular security is overpriced and feel that the price will soon drop, you have two possible courses of action as far as single opening transactions are concerned: You can buy a put or sell a call. By examining the three consequences shown in the chart, you can decide which course of action, which risk, which gain, would be most suitable for you. For practice, trace the following course of action through the chart:

EXAMPLE: You own 300 shares of XYZ at 61. The market in general is at a high and you feel it will drop within the next six months, taking XYZ with it. However, you are reluctant to sell XYZ, so you decide to buy 3 puts in order to lock in its high price. You buy 3 puts at 60 for 2½ each ($750 total). In four months the market is down and XYZ is at 53, a drop of 8 points. You don't see it recovering in the near future, so you exercise your option, selling 300 shares of XYZ at 60, 1 point below where your stock *was* but 7 points above the current market price. This gives you a profit (from the current price) of $2,100 not counting commissions. Overall, you have lost $1,050 ($750 + (3 × $100)) from the time your stock was 61, but you saved yourself from a possible loss of $2,400 (3 × $800). For further practice, you should compare this outcome with the other possible courses of action (e.g., selling 3 calls).

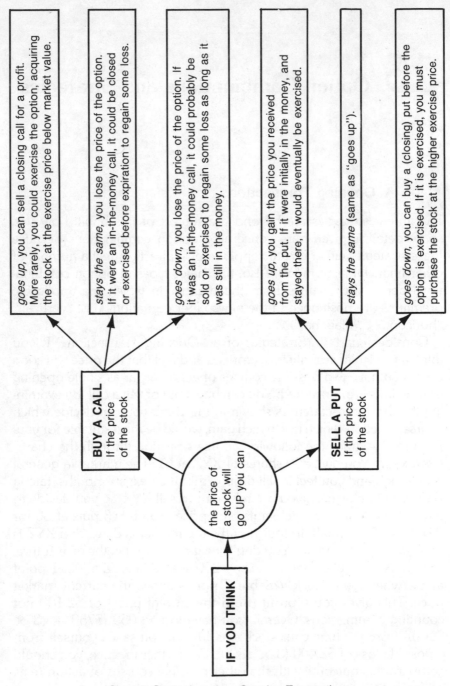

Chart 1: Strategies of an Opening Transaction

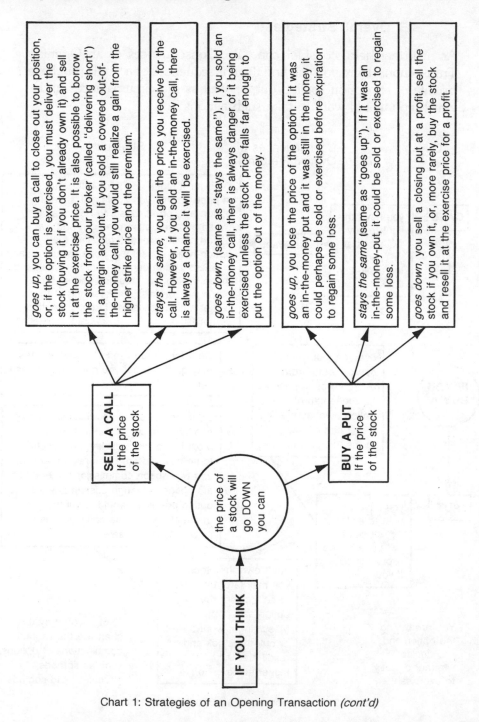

goes up, you can buy a call to close out your position, or, if the option is exercised, you must deliver the stock (buying it if you don't already own it) and sell it at the exercise price. It is also possible to borrow the stock from your broker (called "delivering short") in a margin account. If you sold a covered out-of-the-money call, you would still realize a gain from the higher strike price and the premium.

stays the same, you gain the price you receive for the call. However, if you sold an in-the-money call, there is always a chance it will be exercised.

goes down, (same as "stays the same"). If you sold an in-the-money call, there is always danger of it being exercised unless the stock price falls far enough to put the option out of the money.

goes up, you lose the price of the option. If it was an in-the-money put and it was still in the money it could perhaps be sold or exercised before expiration to regain some loss.

stays the same (same as "goes up"). If it was an in-the-money-put, it could be sold or exercised to regain some loss.

goes down, you sell a closing put at a profit, sell the stock if you own it, or, more rarely, buy the stock and resell it at the exercise price for a profit.

SELL A CALL
If the price
of the stock

BUY A PUT
If the price
of the stock

the price of
a stock will
go DOWN
you can

IF YOU THINK

Chart 1: Strategies of an Opening Transaction *(cont'd)*

B. Overall Strategies

As a further help, consider chart 2, "Consequences of an Opening Transaction." Here you will find the consequences of a single purchase or sale of an option spelled out, as well as the circumstances under which you would want to take such actions.

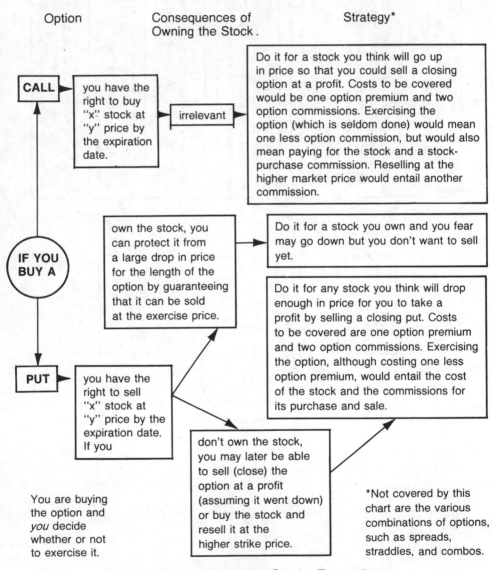

Option   Consequences of   Strategy*
                      Owning the Stock.

CALL — you have the right to buy "x" stock at "y" price by the expiration date. — irrelevant → Do it for a stock you think will go up in price so that you could sell a closing option at a profit. Costs to be covered would be one option premium and two option commissions. Exercising the option (which is seldom done) would mean one less option commission, but would also mean paying for the stock and a stock-purchase commission. Reselling at the higher market price would entail another commission.

IF YOU BUY A

own the stock, you can protect it from a large drop in price for the length of the option by guaranteeing that it can be sold at the exercise price. → Do it for a stock you own and you fear may go down but you don't want to sell yet.

Do it for any stock you think will drop enough in price for you to take a profit by selling a closing put. Costs to be covered are one option premium and two option commissions. Exercising the option, although costing one less option premium, would entail the cost of the stock and the commissions for its purchase and sale.

PUT — you have the right to sell "x" stock at "y" price by the expiration date. If you

don't own the stock, you may later be able to sell (close) the option at a profit (assuming it went down) or buy the stock and resell it at the higher strike price.

You are buying the option and *you* decide whether or not to exercise it.

*Not covered by this chart are the various combinations of options, such as spreads, straddles, and combos.

Chart 2: Consequences of an Opening Transaction

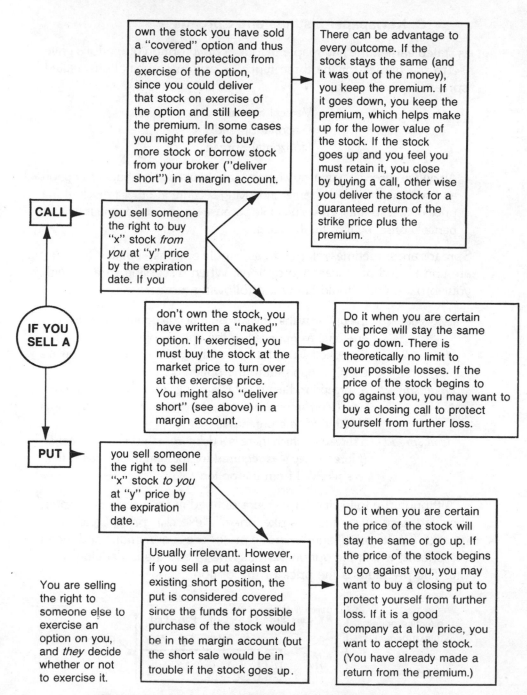

own the stock you have sold a "covered" option and thus have some protection from exercise of the option, since you could deliver that stock on exercise of the option and still keep the premium. In some cases you might prefer to buy more stock or borrow stock from your broker ("deliver short") in a margin account.

There can be advantage to every outcome. If the stock stays the same (and it was out of the money), you keep the premium. If it goes down, you keep the premium, which helps make up for the lower value of the stock. If the stock goes up and you feel you must retain it, you close by buying a call, other wise you deliver the stock for a guaranteed return of the strike price plus the premium.

CALL

you sell someone the right to buy "x" stock *from you* at "y" price by the expiration date. If you

IF YOU SELL A

don't own the stock, you have written a "naked" option. If exercised, you must buy the stock at the market price to turn over at the exercise price. You might also "deliver short" (see above) in a margin account.

Do it when you are certain the price will stay the same or go down. There is theoretically no limit to your possible losses. If the price of the stock begins to go against you, you may want to buy a closing call to protect yourself from further loss.

PUT

you sell someone the right to sell "x" stock *to you* at "y" price by the expiration date.

You are selling the right to someone else to exercise an option on you, and *they* decide whether or not to exercise it.

Usually irrelevant. However, if you sell a put against an existing short position, the put is considered covered since the funds for possible purchase of the stock would be in the margin account (but the short sale would be in trouble if the stock goes up.

Do it when you are certain the price of the stock will stay the same or go up. If the price of the stock begins to go against you, you may want to buy a closing put to protect yourself from further loss. If it is a good company at a low price, you want to accept the stock. (You have already made a return from the premium.)

Chart 2: Consequences of an Opening Transaction *(cont'd)*

C. Newspaper Listings and Spreads

As stated earlier, the newspaper layout of *daily* option quotations gave rise to the names for the three types of option combinations, called "spreads":

> Vertical Spread
> Diagonal Spread
> Horizontal Spread

An ***option spread*** is a strategy whereby one simultaneously buys one option and sells another on the same underlying security in order to lock in the price of that security. This is possible because loss on one option is at least partially offset by gain on the other.

Spreads are sometimes referred to as "single options," but in effect they are constituted of at least two options. When discussing spreads with your broker, you should know the following terms:

long side: the option within the spread that you bought (in which you are long) as opposed to the option sold

short side: the option within the spread that you sold (in which you are short) as opposed to the option bought

credit spread: a spread in which there is a credit from the initial transaction (More money was received from the sale than was required for the purchase.)

debit spread: a spread in which there is a debit from the initial transaction (More money was required for the option purchased than was received from the option sold.)

Although the following terms were defined in the previous chapter, they are easy to confuse: "strike price," "exercise price," and "premium." "Strike price" and "exercise price" are synonymous and mean the price at which the option permits one to buy the underlying security. The premium is the price of the option.

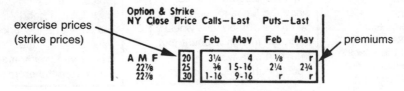

(The Philadelphia Inquirer)

Before detailing the strategies of spreads, here are some more definitions with example quotations.

Vertical spread is the simultaneous purchase/sale of options (on the same security) with the same expiration dates but different strike prices.

			CALLS		PUTS	
			Mar	Jun	Mar	Jun
two options that	Apache	10	r	5¼	r	r
could constitute a	15	15	⅞	1¾	⅞	r
vertical spread	15	20	3-16	9-16	5⅜	r
	15	25	1-16	⅜	r	r

(The Miami Herald)

In the quotations above, note that the premiums (5¼ and 1¾) are in the same vertical column. Any two (different) prices in the same column can make up a vertical spread.

Diagonal spread is a simultaneous purchase/sale of options (on the same security) with different strike prices and different expiration dates.

Option & NY Close	Strike Price	Calls—Last			Puts—Last		
		Feb	May	Aug	Feb	May	Aug
A M F	.. 20	3¼	3½	4¾	⅛	⅝	r
23	 25	7-16	1¼	2⅛	2⅜	r	3⅜
23	 30	1-16	⅜		r	r	r

two options that could constitute a diagonal spread

(Chicago Tribune)

In the quotations above, the premiums are on a diagonal.

Horizontal spread is the simultaneous purchase and sale of options (on the same security) with the same strike price but different expiration dates.

Option & NY Close	Strike Price	Calls—Last			Puts—Last		
		Feb	May	Aug	Feb	May	Aug
Amdahl	.. 25	2	4	4¾	9-16	1 15-16	2½
26½	___ 30	¼	1⅞	r	3¾	4⅝	5
26½	___ 35	r	¾	1⅞	r	r	r

two options that could constitute a horizontal spread

(The Dallas Morning News)

In the quotations above, the premiums are in the same horizontal lines.

D. Examples of Spread Strategies

1) Vertical Bull Spread: *"Buy low, sell high" (that is, buy the option with the low exercise price, sell the option with the high exercise price).*

a. *With Calls (debit spread)*

buy a call at lower exercise price

		Mar	Jun	Sep	Mar	Jun	Sep
Apache	10	r	6¼	r	r	r	r
15⅝	→ 15	1½	2½	2 13-16	½	1¼	1½
15⅝	→ 20	3-16	13-16	1⅜	r	4⅛	r
15⅝	 25	r	r	¾	r	r	r
15⅝	 30	1-16	s	s	r	s	s

sell a call at higher exercise price

(The Dallas Morning News)

buy an Apache June 15 call	$-2^{13}/_{16}$	(premium)
sell an Apache June 20 call	$+1^{3}/_{8}$	(premium)
net debit	$-1^{7}/_{16}$	

risk: net debit

break-even point: the exercise price of the lower call plus the net debit

lower exercise price	15
net debit	$+\ 1^{7}/_{16}$
break-even point	$16^{7}/_{16}$

range within which profit can be taken (not counting commissions): anywhere above the break-even point

maximum profit: the exercise price of higher call minus the exercise price of the lower call minus the net debit

exercise price of higher call	20
exercise price of lower call	-15
	5
net debit	$-\ 1^{7}/_{16}$
maximum profit	$3^{9}/_{16}$

b. *With Puts (credit spread)*

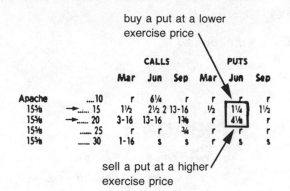

buy a put at a lower
exercise price

		CALLS			PUTS		
		Mar	Jun	Sep	Mar	Jun	Sep
Apache	10	r	6¼	r	r	r	r
15⅝	→..... 15	1½	2½ 2 13-16		½	1¼	1½
15⅝	→..... 20	3-16	13-16	1⅜	r	4⅛	r
15⅝	 25	r	r	¾	r	r	r
15⅝	 30	1-16	s	s	r	s	s

sell a put at a higher
exercise price

(The Dallas Morning News)

buy an Apache June 15 put   −1¼ (premium)
sell an Apache June 20 put   +4⅛ (premium)

net credit   +3⅛

risk: difference between the strike prices minus the net credit

difference between strike prices   5
net credit   −3⅛
                                    ─────
maximum risk   1⅞

break-even point: higher strike price minus net credit

higher strike price   20
net credit   − 3⅛
                       ─────
break-even point   16⅞

range within which profit can be taken (not counting commissions):
anywhere above the break-even point

maximum profit: initial net credit

2) Vertical Bear Spread: *"Buy high, sell low" (that is, buy the option with the high exercise price and sell the option with the low exercise price).*

a. *With Calls (credit spread)*

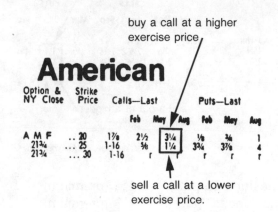

buy a call at a higher
exercise price

American

Option & NY Close	Strike Price	Calls—Last			Puts—Last		
		Feb	May	Aug	Feb	May	Aug
A M F	.. 20	1⅞	2½	3¼	⅛	¾	1
21¾	... 25	1-16	⅝	1¼	3¾	3⅜	4
21¾	... 30	1-16	r	r	r	r	r

sell a call at a lower
exercise price.

(Chicago Tribune)

buy an AMF August 25 call   −1¼ (premium)
sell an AMF August 20 call   +3¼ (premium)

net credit   +2

risk: the difference between the strike prices minus the net credit

difference between strike prices   5
net credit   − 2

maximum risk   3

break-even-point: the lower strike price minus the net credit

lower strike price   20
net credit   − 2

break-even point   18

range within which profit can be taken: any point below the break-even point. If the stock closes below 18 on the expiration day, a profit will be made (not counting commissions).

maximum profit: net credit

3) Diagonal Bull Spread: *"Buy low, sell high."*

a. *With Calls (debit spread)*

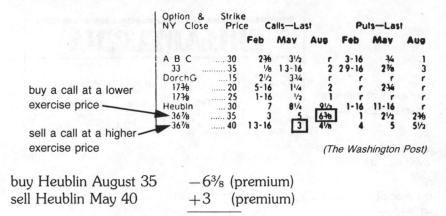

buy a call at a lower exercise price ⟶

sell a call at a higher ⟶ exercise price

Option & NY Close	Strike Price	Calls—Last			Puts—Last		
		Feb	May	Aug	Feb	May	Aug
A B C	30	2⅜	3½	r	3-16	¾	1
33	35	⅛	13-16	2	29-16	2⅞	3
DorchG	15	2½	3¾	r	r	r	r
17⅜	20	5-16	1¼	2	r	2¾	r
17⅜	25	1-16	½	1	r	r	r
Heubln	30	7	8¼	9½	1-16	11-16	r
36⅞	35	3	5	6⅜	1	2½	2⅜
36⅞	40	13-16	3	4⅛	4	5	5½

(The Washington Post)

buy Heublin August 35   −6⅜ (premium)
sell Heublin May 40   +3   (premium)

          net debit   −3⅜

risk: net debit

break-even point: the exercise price of the lower call plus the net debit

     lower exercise price   35
     net debit   + 3⅜

       break-even point   38⅜

range within which profit can be taken: anywhere above the break-even point

maximum profit: the exercise price of the higher call minus the exercise price of the lower call minus the net debit

     exercise price of higher call   40
     exercise price of lower call   −35

                            5
     net debit   − 3⅜

       profit (but see below)   1⅝

Within a certain range, the diagonal spread can yield more than the vertical spread. When the short position expires, one also has a call that can usually be sold, or it can be retained on the chance of further profit. The diagonal spread has a greater profit potential but a greater risk than a vertical spread.

4) Calendar Spread, Horizontal: *"Buy long, sell short."*

a. *With Calls (debit spread)*

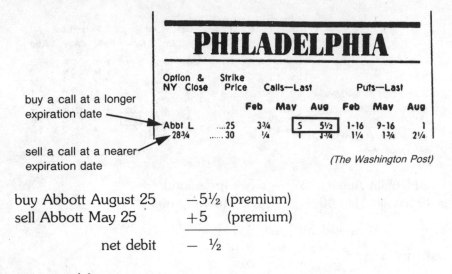

buy a call at a longer
expiration date

sell a call at a nearer
expiration date

(The Washington Post)

buy Abbott August 25	−5½	(premium)	
sell Abbott May 25	+5	(premium)	
net debit	− ½		

risk: net debit

break-even point: There is a break-even point on either side of the
strike price. If the short call expires, the long call can be sold at
face value or held for further possible gains.

PART FIVE

HOW TO READ
FUTURES
QUOTATIONS

16 Commodity Futures

A. Background

The term "commodity" has come to mean anything on which futures are sold on an exchange.

In the past, a *commodity* was thought to be a farm product such as cotton or grain, or it was thought to be a mineral, an oil, or a forest product. More recently, the term has been applied to financial instruments such as Treasury bills and certificates of deposit.

Several features are required of a commodity in order for it to be suitable for trading on an exchange. The first is that there be sufficient supply and demand. The second is that the commodity be divisible into standard units. The third is that the commodity be gradable with respect to quality. The necessity of these qualities for exchange trading is obvious.

Within commodities trading there are two types of markets: cash (spot) markets and futures markets. Transactions on cash markets involve the acquisition of the physical commodity (or at least a warehouse receipt). Transactions on futures markets involve the writing or exchange of contracts—specifically, *futures* contracts.

Commodities that are ready for delivery are termed "actuals," and their prices called "cash prices" (for grains) or "spot prices" (for other commodities). Taking delivery is complex and handled by specialists. Inspection and grading is often necessary, and cash payments or other financial arrangements must be made.

However, 98% of all commodity-futures transactions never involve delivery. Granted, a future delivery date is specified, but before that eventuality, a contract may change hands many times. Commodities are even less likely to be delivered as a result of futures transactions than stocks are likely to be traded as a result of an option transaction.

The concept of "futures" should not be entirely new at this point since there are some similarities with options. For instance, like options, futures are highly leveraged and require far less capital than the acquisition of the commodity itself.

The basic vehicle of the futures market is the futures contract:

A *futures contract* is a delivery agreement that specifies the quantity, the quality, the price, and the approximate time (usually a month) for the delivery of a commodity.

One can buy or sell a futures contract. If one buys a futures contract, one is *buying a delivery*. (This is called "going long.") Until the contract is liquidated, the holder is obligated to take delivery of, and pay the stipulated price for, the designated commodity.

If one sells a futures contract, one is *selling a delivery*. (This is called "going short.") Until the contract is liquidated, the seller is obligated to make a delivery of, and receive the stipulated price for, the designated commodity.

The individual exchanges have standardized the contract sizes with respect to quantity. For instance, copper on the Commodities Exchange of New York trades at 25,000 pounds per contract. If 73,000 pounds are needed, one must buy three contracts.

Once a contract has been bought or sold in an opening transaction, you must either:

a) offset it before maturity with another contract
b) make or accept delivery at maturity.

As with options, a contract may be offset (closed) by the *purchase* of a contract with the same terms as the one originally *sold,* or by the *sale* of a contract with the same terms as the one originally *bought.*

Futures contracts are bought and sold through commodity brokers. The usual commission is more than $60–$100 per round trip.

Round trip refers to the practice of charging commission on commodity futures *only* on the liquidating transaction.

Various types of limit orders are possible on commodity exchanges as on stock exchanges. However, there are some important differences. For instance, on a stock exchange a stop order is an order to buy or sell at the market when a specific price is reached. However, on some commodity exchanges the order will be triggered when that price is *quoted,* and on others only when there is a *trade* at that price. Obviously, differences of this kind make it important to know the regulations of the exchange on which you are trading.

There is a separate clearinghouse for each commodity exchange. These houses serve similar functions as the option clearinghouse. They are the buyers for all sellers and the sellers for all buyers. Commodities are graded and deliveries are guaranteed by the clearinghouse.

Before proceeding with commodity futures, here are a few sensible rules:

1. You should not begin trading in commodity futures without $30,000 to $40,000. This amount will permit the diversification necessary for protection in a market as volatile as commodity futures.
2. You should not begin trading without the guidance of a commodity broker or registered trading adviser who is a specialist in the area in which you are trading. A commodity broker does not necessarily have the training required of the registered adviser.
3. It is important to remember that 75% of commodity speculators end a year with overall losses.
4. Most trades are unprofitable. The point is to cut your losses immediately but to let the winners ride.

There are two kinds of commodity traders: hedgers and speculators.

A *hedger* in commodities is a person who either produces a commodity or utilizes a commodity. Futures are used by the hedger to lock in a guaranteed future price for a commodity being produced or to guarantee the future price of a commodity that will be needed.

For example, a farmer might sell commodity futures on his crop in order to guarantee a fair price by the time he is ready to harvest or sell. Or a dentist might buy gold futures in order to protect himself from widely fluctuating gold prices during the coming year. The object of hedging is not so much to make money as it is to avoid losing it.

The other kind of commodity trader is the speculator.

A *speculator* is a person who is willing to assume the risks that the hedger is trying to avoid. For taking these risks, the speculator expects the potential for high profits.

Speculators are an essential part of futures contracts trading. Most commodity-futures traders are speculators. Without them there would not be sufficient liquidity in the commodity-futures market.

Trading in futures involves some of the same kinds of strategies as options. Margin requirements for trading are generally 5% to 10% of the market value. One may buy a contract with the expectation that the price of the underlying commodity will rise, thus making the futures contract more valuable. One would then close the position by selling a contract, at a profit, with the same terms as the one bought. If one expected the price of a commodity to drop, one would sell a contract, as an opening position, just like options. One closes at a future date by buying a closing position at a (hopefully) lower price. The profit to the speculator is the difference between the two prices. As with options, spreads and straddles are also available.

The following is a list of the commodity-futures exchanges in the United States and some of the commodities they trade:

Chicago Board of Trade (CBT)—corn, oats, soybeans, soybean meal, soybean oil, wheat, plywood, gold, silver, commercial paper, GNMA mortgages, Treasury bonds

Chicago Mercantile Exchange (CME) including the International Monetary Market (IMM)—broilers, cattle (feeds), cattle (live), eggs, hogs (live), lumber, pork bellies, potatoes, gold, silver coins, currencies, Treasury bills, certificates of deposit, Eurodollars, S & P 500 Futures

Coffee, Sugar & Cocoa Exchange, Inc., New York (NYCSCE or CSCE)—cocoa, coffee, sugar

Commodity Exchange, Inc., New York (NYCX or CMX or COMEX)—copper, gold, silver, aluminum

Kansas City Board of Trade (KCBT or KC)—wheat, Value Line stock index futures

Mid-America Commodity Exchange—corn, oats, soybeans, wheat, gold

Minneapolis Grain Exchange (MPLS)—sunflower seeds, wheat

New York Cotton Exchange (NYCTN or CTN) including the Citrus Associates of NYCTN (NYCTN, CA)—cotton, orange juice, propane

New York Futures Exchange (NYFE)—NYSE composite index, options on futures (This is a subsidiary of the New York Stock Exchange.)

New York Mercantile Exchange (NYM)—imported beef, potatoes, no. 2 heating oil, no. 6 heating oil, gasoline, gold, silver coins, palladium, platinum.

Commodity brokers also have access to the Winnipeg Commodity Exchange in Canada and to commodity exchanges in Europe, Asia, and Australia.

There are more than 50 different types of commodity futures traded on exchanges in the United States. Each has its own trading requirements and its own patterns of price volatility. In the next chapter we will discuss financial futures. The subject of this chapter will be futures on commodities in the farm/forest/mining sense.

B. The Quotations

1. The Commodity, Unit Size, Manner of Pricing

Whether the commodity quotations are listed by exchange or simply grouped by commodity type, the headings for the prices of each commodity state:

1. the commodity
2. perhaps the exchange (sometimes the city)
3. the size of the standard contract
4. manner of pricing per unit

For example:

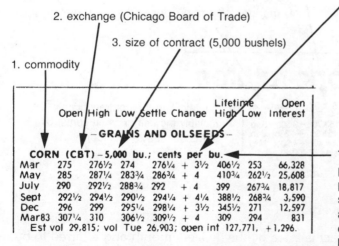

4. manner in which price is quoted (cents per bushel)

2. exchange (Chicago Board of Trade)

3. size of contract (5,000 bushels)

1. commodity

	Open	High	Low	Settle	Change	Lifetime High	Low	Open Interest

— GRAINS AND OILSEEDS —

CORN (CBT) – 5,000 bu.; cents per bu.

	Open	High	Low	Settle	Change	Lifetime High	Low	Open Interest
Mar	275	276½	274	276¼	+ 3½	406½	253	66,328
May	285	287¼	283¾	286¾	+ 4	410¾	262½	25,608
July	290	292½	288¾	292	+ 4	399	267¾	18,817
Sept	292½	294½	290½	294¼	+ 4¼	388½	268¾	3,590
Dec	296	299	295¼	298¼	+ 3½	345½	271	12,597
Mar83	307¼	310	306½	309½	+ 4	309	294	831

Est vol 29,815; vol Tue 26,903; open int 127,771, +1,296.

(The Wall Street Journal)

To calculate contract prices, multiply the unit price (in cents) by the size (5,000). Note that a price such as 276¼ cents = $2.7625 per bushel, making a contract price of $13,812.50.

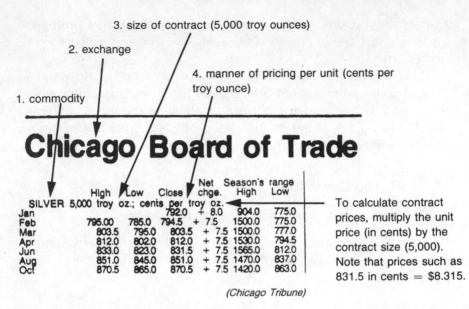

3. size of contract (5,000 troy ounces)

2. exchange

4. manner of pricing per unit (cents per troy ounce)

1. commodity

Chicago Board of Trade

	High	Low	Close	Net chge.	Season's range High	Low
SILVER 5,000 troy oz.; cents per troy oz.						
Jan			792.0	+ 8.0	904.0	775.0
Feb	795.00	785.0	794.5	+ 7.5	1500.0	775.0
Mar	803.5	795.0	803.5	+ 7.5	1500.0	777.0
Apr	812.0	802.0	812.0	+ 7.5	1530.0	794.5
Jun	833.0	823.0	831.5	+ 7.5	1565.0	812.0
Aug	851.0	845.0	851.0	+ 7.5	1470.0	837.0
Oct	870.5	865.0	870.5	+ 7.5	1420.0	863.0

To calculate contract prices, multiply the unit price (in cents) by the contract size (5,000). Note that prices such as 831.5 in cents = $8.315.

(Chicago Tribune)

The manner of pricing per unit is the most frequently misunderstood part of commodities quotation headings. If the price is in cents, then 374.5 = $3.745; but if it is in dollars, then 374.5 = $374.50.

Here is another example:

3. size of contract (15,000 pounds)

2. city of exchange   4. manner of pricing per unit (cents per pound)

1. commodity

New York futures

ORANGE JUICE (15,000 lbs.; cents per lb.) closed: March 149.50 +2.25c; May 151.30 +2.60c; July 153.70 +3.50c; Sep. 154.90 +4.00c; Nov. 155.30 +4.30c; Jan. 155.80 ...; March 156.40 +4.90c; May 156.80 +4.80c. Est. sales 2,400.

To calculate the contract prices, multiply the unit price (in cents) by the contract size (15,000)

(Chicago Tribune)

2. Month of Delivery

Each future contract is listed by the delivery month and referred to by that month (for example, "March corn" or "July soybeans"). Not all commodities are available for delivery every month.

ORANGE JUICE
15,000 lbs.- cents per lb.

futures contracts available every other month

Mar	145.60	148.00	145.60	147.25	+	.35
May	147.80	149.75	147.40	148.70	−	.20
Jul	149.25	151.00	148.50	150.20	−	.80
Sep	150.90	152.00	150.25	150.90	−	1.35
Nov	151.00	152.00	150.75	151.00	−	1.75
Jan	151.00	153.00	151.00	151.00	−	2.25
Mar	152.00	152.00	150.50	151.50	−	2.35
May	153.00	153.50	151.00	152.00	−	2.45

Est. sales: 3,000 Prev. sales 3,661
Prev. day's open int 9,836, Chg. + 557

SILVER
5,000 troy oz.- cents per troy oz.

futures contracts available irregularly

Jan	790.0	790.0	790.0	782.5	−	8.0
Feb				785.2	−	8.5
Mar	800.0	802.5	792.0	793.0	−	9.0
May	822.0	822.0	812.5	811.8	−	9.1
Jul	841.0	841.0	832.0	831.1	−	9.1
Sep	860.0	860.0	851.0	850.4	−	9.1
Dec	880.0	888.0	880.0	879.6	−	8.9
Jan				889.2	−	8.9
Mar	920.0	920.0	918.0	908.5	−	8.9
May				927.8	−	8.9
Jul	954.0	954.0	954.0	947.1	−	8.9

Est. sales: 5,100 Prev. sales 5,628
Prev. day's open int 27,208, Chg. − 181

(San Francisco Chronicle)

The quotations specify only the month of delivery. The last actual trading day for each commodity future (within the month of delivery) is specified by the individual exchanges. All outstanding contracts must be settled on or before that day.

Near the end of the month prior to delivery, or in the first part of the month of delivery, is a day specified as the *first notice day.* Again, it is designated separately for each commodity by each exchange. This is the beginning of the period during which *notices of intention to deliver* can be assigned through the commodity clearinghouses. These assignments resemble in many ways the assignments of options by the Options Clearing Corporation. Most speculators will try to close their positions before this day. Should individuals wish to keep positions in the market but not make or accept delivery, they may always liquidate their positions, even after a notice of intent to deliver, in the coming expiration month and simultaneously acquire an equivalent contract in the next available month. This is known as "switching forward" or a "rollover." Commodity brokerages usually request instructions from their clients during the month preceding delivery regarding their open positions.

3. Prices

Some quotations begin with the high and low of the "season," which means the high and low for the "lifetime" of that particular contract. In the following example, the lifetime high and low are the first and second items of the quotation.

Some quotations
begin with the
high and low prices
for the lifetime
of the contract.

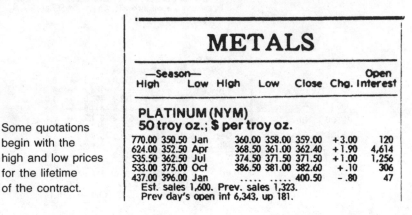

(The New York Times)

In the above example January platinum is quoted at a lifetime high of 770.00 and a lifetime low of 350.50. The heading (50 troy oz.; $ per troy oz.) tells us the price is in dollars and the contract size is 50 troy ounces. The lifetime high in dollars was therefore $38,500 (770 × 50), and the low was $17,525 (350.50 × 50).

In other formats, the lifetime high and low appear later in the quotation.

high and low
prices for the
lifetime of
the contract

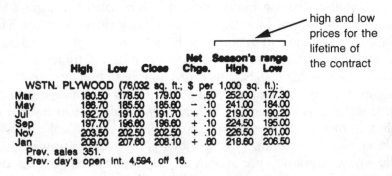

(Chicago Tribune)

The "high," "low," and "settle" (or "close") give the complete picture of trading for the previous trading period (which may be a day or a week, depending on whether the quotations are daily or weekly). Sometimes the opening price is also given.

high, low, and
close of the
previous week's
trading

	High	Low	Wk. Close	Wk. Chg.	Open Interest
WHEAT					
5,000 bu minimum; lars per bushel					
Mar	3.85	3.68¾	3.70½	—.06½	25,065
May	4.00½	3.84¼	3.86¼	—.05½	13,698
Jul	4.09	3.94½	3.96½	—.02½	18,974
Sep	4.22	4.10¼	4.12¼	—.00¼	3,360
Dec	4.41½	4.29½	4.35	+.04	2,431
Mar	4.58	4.45½	4.51½	+.04½	294

Total sales 72,610.
Total open interest 63,822.

(The Washington Post)

opening price
of the previous
day's trading
in addition to
the high, low,
and settle
(close)

NEW YORK (AP) — Futures trading on the New York Commodity Exchange Friday.

	Open	High	Low	Settle	Chg.
GOLD					
100 troy oz.; dollars per troy oz.					
Feb	384.00	387.60	381.70	384.50	—1.60
Mar	387.00	387.50	387.00	387.40	—1.70
Apr	392.00	392.60	389.10	392.00	—1.80
Jun	401.00	402.00	398.40	401.40	—1.60
Aug	409.50	411.00	408.00	410.90	—1.60
Oct	420.00	420.00	420.00	420.70	—1.60
Dec	429.00	430.90	428.10	430.80	—1.50
Feb	440.50	440.90	440.20	441.20	—1.50
Apr	451.50	451.50	450.50	451.70	—1.50
Jun				462.30	—1.50
Aug				472.90	—1.50
Oct				483.60	—1.50

Prev. sales 35,699.
Prev day's open int 143,424, off 4,645.

(The Dallas Morning News)

Some quotations, in order to save space arrange the quotations in strings. This is less convenient to read, but it is still clear. The second line of the following example reads: January copper closed at $.719, down $.006; February copper closed at $.7215, down $.006; March copper closed $.731, down $.0055; etc.

price quotations in continuous string rather than in columns

New York futures

COPPER (25,000 lbs.; cents per lb.): Jan, 71.90 –.60c; Feb, 72.15 –.60c; March, 73.10 –.55c; May, 74.95 –.50c; July, 76.80 –.40c; Sep, 78.60 –.35c; Dec, 81.25 –.40c; Jan, 82.15 –.40c; March, 84.05 –.25c; May, 85.80 –.25c; July, 87.55 –.25c; Sep, 89.30 –.25c. Prev. sales 3.788.

(Chicago Tribune)

There are two important aspects of the price quotations for most commodities:

1. the smallest amount by which the price can fluctuate
2. the largest amount by which a price can change *in a single day*

Each exchange separately specifies the above limits for every commodity. For example, the New York Mercantile Exchange specifies the minimum price fluctuation for potatoes as $.01 per 100 pounds. When a $.01 price change is quoted, it means a $5 change per contract since contracts are for 50,000 pounds.

The minimum price fluctuation is called a "tick." It can usually be determined by looking at all the quotations for a specific future. In the following example, one can see that the prices for copper on the Commodity Exchange, New York, vary by increments of .05 of a cent ($.0005, and that is, in fact, the minimum fluctuation specified by the Exchange). Since a contract is for 25,000 pounds, a $.0005 fluctuation means that a "tick" in a copper future is $12.50.

From examining all prices, one can usually determine the minimum price fluctuation. Here, it is .05, which in cents is $.0005.

COPPER
25,000 lbs.; cents per lb.

	Open	High	Low	Settle	Chg.
Feb	......	......	......	72.20	+1.20
Mar	72.35	72.95	72.35	72.70	+1.20
Apr	73.10	73.10	73.10	73.75	+1.15
May	74.40	75.00	74.40	74.80	+1.15
Jul	76.50	76.95	76.50	76.80	+1.20
Sep	78.60	78.80	78.60	78.70	+1.25

(The Miami Herald)

The maximum price fluctuation per day, called a "limit move," cannot be determined from the quotation as can the tick; a speculator should get this information from a commodity broker or the exchange itself. To give some examples: On the International Monetary Market, the limit move in gold futures is $5,000 per contract. On the Chicago Mercantile Exchange, the limit move in feeder cattle (steers averaging between 575 and 700 pounds) is $660 per contract.

The intention of the maximum price fluctuations is to slow down, somewhat, extreme changes in commodity-futures prices and thereby promote an orderly market. However, this restriction in price movement does not necessarily protect one from severe loss. For instance, if, after a limit move in price, one decides to liquidate, it is possible there will be no buyers. In extreme cases, one might have to wait out several days of limit moves before prices bottom and buyers once again appear.

There are standard circumstances under which limitations in maximum price fluctuation are removed. This usually happens during the course of the delivery month. Also, there are cases where the exchanges do not set limit moves at all. There are no limits, for instance, on stock futures.

4. Change

The change from the previous trading period is specified in the same manner as the price quotations. In this example, March wheat (the first quotation) shows a change of $+\$.04$. The quotation is in dollars per bushel, and a contract is 5,000 bushels, so the price of the contract rose during the trading period by $200 ($.04 $\times$ 5,000).

Chicago
Board of Trade

	Open	High	Low	Settle	Chg.
WHEAT					
5,000 bu	minimum;	dollars	per	bushel	
Mar	3.76	3.85	3.72¾	3.81	+.04
May	3.90½	4.00½	3.88	3.96¼	+.04½
Jul	3.98½	4.09	3.96½	4.05½	+.06½
Sep	4.12½	4.22	4.10½	4.20	+.07½
Dec	4.31	4.41½	4.29½	4.39	+.08
Mar	4.46	4.57	4.45½	4.55¾	+.08¾

Prev. sales 11,664.
Prev day's open int 67,174, off 167.
CORN
5,000 bu minimum; dollars per bushel

Change from previous day's settlement is in the same form as the price quotations (in this case, in dollars per bushel)

(Los Angeles Times)

If the "change" column specifies an amount that is at or near the maximum price fluctuation allowed by the exchange, then one should look for reasons. The price of the commodity, for one reason or another, is moving faster than considered normal.

5. Open Interest

Some quotations list the number of contracts open (in the same sense as "open interest" is specified for option contracts). This information, in addition to the volume specified, helps give an idea of the liquidity of the contract.

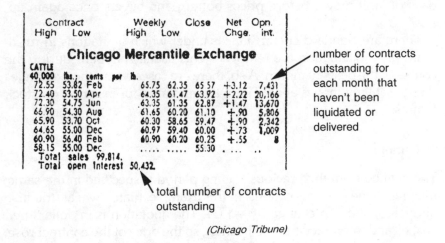

(Chicago Tribune)

The total number of futures contracts with open interest, shown in the bottom line of the above example, can give one an idea of the relative size of the market when compared to similar commodity futures. A heavily traded market (such as for cattle above) is less volatile than a thinly traded market (such as for fresh broilers).

6. Volume

Often the estimated number of transactions for the day is given at the bottom of each futures group, and this is followed by the number of transactions from the previous day for comparison.

	Open	High	Low	Close	Chg.

COCOA
10 metric tons- $ per ton

	Open	High	Low	Close	Chg.
Mar	2142	2164	2140	2150	+ 19
May	2136	2146	2128	2136	+ 22
Jul	2135	2149	2135	2141	+ 16
Sep	2145	2160	2140	2159	+ 24
Dec	2175	2180	2170	2180	+ 17
Mar				2210	+ 17

volume, in number of contracts, and the previous day's volume ——→ Est. sales: 1,945 Prev. sales 1,747
Prev. day's open int 14,746, Chg. + 31

(San Francisco Chronicle)

7. Weekly Quotations

Weekly quotations for commodities are usually identical in format to daily quotations. The high, low, and change, of course, reflect prices for the entire week rather than for the previous day.

8. Advertisement Quotations

Some exchanges guarantee the appearance of quotations by publishing them as advertisements in leading newspapers. This is done particularly for futures contracts in young or emerging markets.

ADVERTISEMENT

Petroleum Associates
NY Cotton Exchange. Inc.

futures quotations appearing as advertisements

Four World Trade Center, New York, New York 10048
January 6, 1982 Futures Prices
LIQUEFIED PROPANE GAS
(cents per gallon in contract units of 42,000 gallons)

	Open	High	Low	Settle	Change
Feb82	34.75b-35.00a	34.50	34.50	34.00	− 75
Mar	35.60b-36.00a	35.40	34.60	34.50	− 90
Apr	35.70b-32.25a	34.81	34.70	34.60	− 80
May :......	35.80b-36.00a	35.00	35.00	34.70	− 50
June	35.80b-36.00a	....	....	34.75	− 45
July	35.90b-36.10a	....	....	34.75	− 55

Est. Vol: 30; Vol.: Tues., 48; Open int. 32, +3.

(The Wall Street Journal)

Here, "b" and "a" are bid and asked prices. They were posted at the opening, but there were no initial transactions.

9. Cash Market

Making or taking delivery is complex and usually handled by specialists. However, an examination of the spot prices (another name for cash prices) is essential for the speculator. They are usually under the heading "Cash Prices" or "Spot Prices" and divided by commodity group. These are current prices, so this is where you would look if you wanted, for instance, the price of gold.

CASH PRICES

Wheat No. 2 hard red winter 3.72¾n; No 2 soft red winter 3.72¾n Corn No. 2 yellow 2.62n. (hopper); unquoted for (box). Oats No. 2 heavy 2.19¾n. Soybeans No. 1 yellow 6.29¾n.

No 2 yellow corn Monday was quoted at 2.64n. (hopper) unquoted for (box).

Copper 77⅝-79½ cents a pound, U.S. destinations.

Lead 28-34 cents a pound.

Zinc 42 cents a pound, delivered.

Tin $7.7665 Metals Week composite lb.

Aluminum 76-77 cents a pound, N.Y.

N.Y. Gold $375.25 per troy ounce, Handy & Harman (only daily quote).

London Gold $374.625 per troy ounce

Silver $7.880 troy ounce, Handy & Harman (only daily quote).

(San Francisco Chronicle)

Cash commodities

Omaha livestock

OMAHA, Neb. (AP)(USDA) — Omaha Livestock Market quotations Tuesday:

Hogs: 3200; barrows and gilts moderately active 50-1.00 lower; some late sales 200-220 lb 1.50 lower; near 300 head sorted; .S. 1-2s 220-245 lb 51.50; U.S. 1-2s 210-250 lb 50.50-51.00; several lots 51.25; U.S. 1-3s 240-260 lb 50.00-50.50; sows under 475 lb 25-75 lower; over 475 lb 1.50-1.75 lower; 300-600 lb 42.00-42.50.

Cattle and Calves: 3700; steers moderately active steady; heifers fairly active fully steady; some sales 25 higher; cows 50-1.00 higher; steers 4 loads choice 1200-1250 lb 66.00, choice including some end of prime 1050-1300 lb 64.50-65.50; occasionally 65.75; heifers 3 loads and part load choice some with end prime 975-1100 lb 63.75-64.00; choice including some

Rice futures

NEW YORK (AP) — Futures trading on the New Orleans Commodities Exchange Tuesday.

	Open	High	Low	Settle	Chg.
MILLED			**RICE**		
120,000 lbs.; dollars per 100 lbs.					
Mar	.....	.....	.....	16.60	—.02
May	.....	.....	.....	16.60	—.02
Sep	.....	.....	.....	17.35	.....
Prev day's open int 153.					
ROUGH			**RICE**		
200,000 lbs.; dollars per 100 lbs.					
Mar	8.10	8.10	8.06	8.08	—.07
May	.....	.....	.....	8.55	.....
Jul	8.91	8.91	8.91	8.91	1.06
Sep	.....	.....	.....	8.95	.....
Nov	.....	.....	.....	8.95	.....
Prev. sales 38.					
Prev day's open int 526, off 19.					
COTTON					
50,000 lbs.; cents per lb.					
Mar	57.70	57.70	57.50	57.50	—.16

(Houston Chronicle)

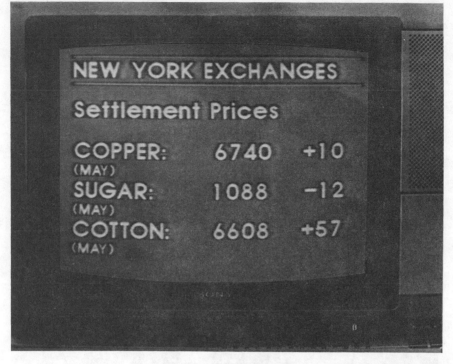

(courtesy The Nightly Business Report/Produced by WPBT-Miami.
Photo: Perry McLamb)

Commodity Futures

Commodity futures prices are shown on the PBS program, The Nightly Business Report. Here we see:

1. May copper futures at 6740. Although copper is quoted in cents per pound it is usual to quote it to a hundredth of a cent. The price 6740 is therefore understood to mean $.674 per pound. The indication +10 means that the price is up $.001 from the previous day's settlement price.

2. May sugar futures at 1088 means $.1088 per pound. This price is down $.0012 from the previous day's settlement price.

3. May cotton futures at 6608 means $.6608 per pound. This price is up $.0057 from the previous day's settlement price.

(courtesy Chicago Board of Trade)

The Chicago Board of Trade

The largest trading floor in the world. There are too many people to see the trading pits clearly but to the left of foreground center may be seen the steps of one trading pit. To the right of center a man and a woman are sitting on the edge of another trading pit.

buy   sell

¼ cent   ½ cent

¾ cent   1 cent

(courtesy Chicago Board of Trade)

Trader's Hand Signals

Hand signals are used in most exchange trading in order for the traders to make themselves understood over the noise and other trading activity around them. These photographs were made at the Chicago Board of Trade.

17 Financial and Stock Index Futures

A. Financial Futures

Financial futures are probably the least understood of all investment vehicles available to the public. The recent growth of the financial-futures market has been largely a result of the need by businessmen, portfolio managers, and investors in general for protection against widely fluctuating interest rates. However, many investors have yet to recognize the advantages of these types of futures.

In the 30 to 40 years prior to 1968, interest rates changed at such a slow pace and within such narrow confines that businesses usually had time to adjust without disruption or adverse consequences. But since 1968, the increasing volatility of interest rates has proven as ravaging to business as any natural disaster to the farm.

Rates of currency exchange are also increasingly volatile. As interest rises within one country, foreign capital is attracted and the value of that country's currency rises against the currency of others. When interest rates fall, there is a resultant outflow of foreign capital. The size and speed of these fluctuations have a dramatic effect (both positive and negative) on all businesses but particularly on those that depend on imports or foreign operations of any kind.

Financial futures are based on (called "written on") fixed-rate instruments such as Treasury bonds or certificates of deposit. It is the fixed-rate component with which hedgers seek to protect themselves against loss and with which speculators seek to make profits. This is possible because the price at which fixed-rate instruments may be bought or sold has an inverse relationship to the movement of interest rates. As interest rates move up, the resale value of a fixed-rate instrument (which has already been issued) moves down; and as interest rates fall, the resale value of the fixed-rate instrument (which has already been issued) rises. Financial futures are based on this simple relationship.

By taking long or short positions in futures, portfolio managers, corporate treasurers, and financial planners seek to protect their investments or future investments against adverse interest-rate movements or changes in foreign currency rates. Thus, hedgers play the same role in financial futures as they do in commodity futures. For instance, a portfolio manager might anticipate falling interest rates just before a large number of CDs become due. By purchasing CD futures, the manager could guarantee a currently profitable rate of return when it is time for the funds from the CDs to be reinvested, no matter what has happened to interest rates in the meantime. Likewise, a larger manufacturer who purchases electronic components abroad might hedge against a future unfavorable currency-exchange rate by buying currency futures. Thus, for the hedger, financial futures are a kind of insurance.

In order for there to be hedgers, there must, of course, be those willing to assume the risks: the speculators. If speculators decide that interest rates will move in a certain direction, they have only to back their opinion with capital and reap substantial rewards if they are correct. The dangers of speculation in financial futures are similar to those of commodity speculation, and the warnings given in the previous chapter are also applicable here. In particular, no one should undertake speculation in financial futures without substantial capital and the guidance of a registered commodity-trading adviser.

Futures transactions are processed by clearinghouses associated with the individual exchanges. As with options, there is no direct link between the buyer or the writer.

The following exchanges trade financial futures:

Chicago Board of Trade (CBT)—Ginnie Mae mortgages, Treasury bonds, certificates of deposit

Chicago Mercantile Exchange (CME) and the International Monetary Market (IMM)—foreign currencies (British pound, Canadian dollar, deutsche mark, Japanese yen, Mexican peso, Swiss franc), Eurodollars, Treasury bills, and certificates of deposit

Kansas City Board of Trade—*Value Line* stock average futures

American Board of Trade—foreign currencies, certificates of deposit, Treasury bills

New York Futures Exchange (NYFE, a unit of the New York Stock Exchange) —certificates of deposit, Treasury bills and bonds

B. The Quotations

1. The Commodity, Contract Size, Manner of Pricing

The headings for the quotations are in the same format as the quotations for other futures: the commodity first, sometimes the exchange (in parentheses), the size of the standard contract, and the manner of pricing per unit.

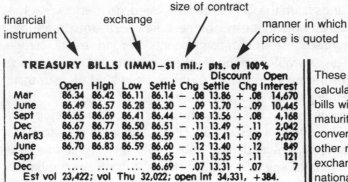

financial instrument — exchange — size of contract — manner in which price is quoted

	Open	High	Low	Settle	Chg	Discount Settle	Chg	Open Interest
TREASURY BILLS (IMM) — $1 mil.; pts. of 100%								
Mar	86.34	86.42	86.11	86.14	− .08	13.86	+ .08	14,670
June	86.49	86.57	86.28	86.30	− .09	13.70	+ .09	10,445
Sept	86.65	86.69	86.41	86.44	− .08	13.56	+ .08	4,168
Dec	86.67	86.77	86.50	86.51	− .11	13.49	+ .11	2,042
Mar83	86.70	86.83	86.56	86.59	− .09	13.41	+ .09	2,029
June	86.70	86.83	86.59	86.60	− .12	13.40	+ .12	849
Sept	....	....	....	86.65	− .11	13.35	+ .11	121
Dec	....	....	....	86.69	− .07	13.31	+ .07	7

Est vol 23,422; vol Thu 32,022; open int 34,331, +384.

(The Wall Street Journal)

These futures contracts are calculated on Treasury bills with 90 days to maturity (there are conversion tables for other maturities): the exchange is the International Monetary Market (a division of the CME); the size of a contract is $1 million; prices are in percent of face value. Notice that both percent of par and percent of discount are given.

US TREASURY BONDS
(8 pct-$100,000;phs & 32nds of 100 pct)◄

Mar	57-9	57-15	56-30	57-3	− 06
Jun	57-18	57-26	57-10	57-15	− 06
Sep	57-30	58-6	57-23	57-28	− 06
Dec	58-12	58-16	58-3	58-8	− 06
Mar	58-21	58-26	58-16	58-19	− 06
Jun	58-31	59-6	58-29	58-29	− 07
Sep	59-13	59-13	59-6	59-6	− 08
Dec	59-23	59-23	59-14	59-14	− 09
Mar	59-28	59-30	59-22	59-22	− 09
Jun	60-4	60-5	59-29	59-29	− 10
Sep				60-4	− 11
Dec				60-11	− 12

Prev. sales 70,861.
Prev day's open int 216,268, up 815.

(St. Louis Post-Dispatch)

These futures contracts are calculated on Treasury bonds with an 8% coupon (there are conversion tables for other rates): the exchange is not shown; the size of the contract is $100,000; prices are in percent and 32nds (the numbers after the dashes are 32nds).

2. Month of Delivery

Most financial futures are available quarterly, as can be seen from this example:

	US T. BILLS $1 million; pts of 100 pct.				
	Mar	85.67	85.75	85.56	85.67	− .09
financial futures	Jun	85.79	85.90	85.67	85.85	− .02
usually available	Sep	85.82	86.05	85.77	86.00	+ .11
	Dec	85.91	86.09	85.87	86.06	+ .08
with quarterly	Mar	86.01	86.18	86.00	86.15	+ .06
	Jun	86.12	86.19	86.12	86.23	+ .05
delivery months	Sep	86.25	86.25	86.25	86.25	+ .02
	Dec				86.25	− .02

Prev. sales 27,421.
Prev day's open int 35,168, up 395.

(St. Louis Post-Dispatch)

The exact delivery time can vary from exchange to exchange and from brokerage firm to brokerage firm. For longer-term instruments (GNMA futures or Treasury bond futures), delivery may be on any business day during the contract's delivery month. In this case, the seller is given the option of initiating the delivery process. As deliveries are initiated, the exchange assigns them to buyers (who hold futures contracts), who will in turn take delivery or liquidate their positions.

Shorter-term instruments may specify an exact day. For example, the last trading day for Treasury bill futures is usually the Wednesday following the third auction of Treasury bills in the delivery month, and the delivery period may be only one day, e.g., the business day following the last trading day. Trading in CD futures may be allowed until the last seven days of the expiring month, with delivery possible any day of the delivery month.

The instruments delivered in fulfillment of a futures contract have a specified maturity. Treasury bond futures, for example, specify that bonds delivered must have at least 15 years to call *or* maturity, whichever comes first. Treasury bill futures require three-month maturity. Thus a March Treasury bill future would require delivery on the delivery day of Treasury bills that matures in 90 days.

3. Prices

The headings for futures quotations give one the necessary information for calculating the dollar price of the contract. The first example below states that prices are in percent with thirty-seconds after the decimal point (a format we have seen before for the actual quotations of U.S. Treasury bonds and notes).

FINANCIAL

—Season—						Open
High	Low	High	Low	Close	Chg.	Interest

LONG-TERM TREAS. BONDS (CBT)
8%-$100,000 prin.; pts. and 32d's of 100% ◄——— Treasury bond futures in percent and 32nds

91-15	55-20	Mar	58-14	58-2	58-4	- 10	64,866
88-8	56-8	Jun	58-26	58-15	58-17	- 10	38,048
84-19	56-23	Sep	59-7	58-30	58-30	- 10	17,774
84-3	57-3	Dec	59-19	59-8	59-10	- 10	19,895
83-19	57-14	Mar	59-29	59-21	59-21	- 10	14,326
74-20	57-28	Jun	60-7	59-31	59-31	- 10	13,334
74-19	58-5	Sep	60-12	60-8	60-8	- 10	14,460
71-15	58-10	Dec	60-20	60-17	60-17	- 10	12,763
70-31	58-20	Mar	.....	.....	60-25	- 10	10,803
66-15	58-28	Jun	61-6	61-1	61-1	- 10	5,064
71-7	59-3	Sep	.....	.....	61-9	- 10	1,921
70-12	59-10	Dec	61-25	61-17	61-17	- 10	875

Est. sales 17,748. Prev. sales 65,223.
Prev day's open int 214,129, off 1,200.

(The New York Times)

The first quotation above, for a March Treasury bond future, shows a closing price of 58-4. (You may want to consult Appendix 1 for the values of thirty-seconds.)

$$58\text{-}4 = 58\% + \frac{4}{32}\% = 58.125\%$$

This means that the closing price for one $100,000 8% Treasury bond futures contract was $58,125. The season high for that same contract was 91-15.

$91\text{-}15 = 91\% + \frac{15}{32}\% = 91\% + .46875\% = 91.46875\% =$ $91,468.75

Treasury bill futures are quoted in an annualized straight percentage. In the following example, the September Treasury bill future closed at 86.15, which is 86.15%. Some quotations, such as the initial example in this chapter, also give the discount percentage, but it is easy enough to calculate (100% − 86.15% = 13.85%). The discount of 13.85%, however, is for an annual return. A 90-day, three-month return is one-quarter of that, 3.4625%. For a million-dollar contract, that is a $34,625 return, making the price of the contract $965,375.

Treasury bill futures are in straight percent but annualized.

US T. BILLS	Open	High	Low	Settle	Chg.
$1 million; pts of 100 pct.					
Mar	86.20	86.27	85.95	86.20	+.04
Jun	86.20	86.26	85.97	86.22	+.08
Sep	86.09	86.21	85.98	86.15	+.06
Dec	86.13	86.27	86.07	86.20	+.06
Mar	86.21	86.26	86.14	86.25	+.03
Jun	86.27	86.35	86.27	86.29	+.05
Sep	86.34	86.34	86.34	86.34	+.04
Prev. sales 27,001.					
Prev day's open int 34,099, off 808.					

(The Dallas Morning News)

The next example is for foreign-currency futures contracts. For some reason, many papers do not print the size of the contract in the headings for foreign-currency futures as they do for other futures quotations. This means that while the prices tell you the exchange rate, they do not tell you how much the contracts cost (in addition to not telling you the amount for which the contracts are written). The following is an example of such a quotation.

International monetary market

	High	Low	Close	Net chge.	Season's Range High	Low
BRITISH POUND ($ per pound; 1 point equals $0.0001)						
Mar	1.8580	1.8475	1.8555	+ 90	2.2570	1.7790
Jun	1.8650	1.8600	1.8635	+ 100	1.9580	1.7950
Sep	1.8675	1.8650	1.8700	+ 95	1.9580	1.8475
Dec			1.8750	+ 110	1.9350	1.8490
Prev. sales 10,449.						
Prev. day's open int. 17,672, up 2,717.						
CANADIAN DOLLAR ($ per dlr.; 1 point equals $0.0001)						
Mar	.8244	.8228	.8239	+ 13	.8525	.7912
Jun	.8252	.8233	.8250	+ 16	.8439	.7901
Sep	.8247	.8236	.8236	+ 6	.8357	.7890
Dec	.8228	.8218	.8228	+ 14	.8350	.8120
Prev. sales 1,438.						
Prev. day's open int 10,846, off 354.						
GERMAN MARK ($ per mark; 1 point equals $0.0001)						
Mar	.4254	.4233	.4245	+ 8	.5460	.4010
Jun	.4317	.4298	.4307	+ 7	.4720	.4100
Sep	.4360	.4347	.4360	+ 10	.4775	.4372
Dec			.4438		.4675	.4430
Prev sales 6,423.						
Prev day's open int. 14,035, off 156.						

Example of foreign-currency futures quotations. Without the size of the contracts specified, it is impossible to calculate the cost of the contracts.

(Chicago Tribune)

On the International Monetary Market, the British pound futures contracts are for £25,000; the Canadian dollar futures are for $100,000 Canadian; and the German mark futures are for DM125,000. In the above example, we see that the June mark futures closed at .4307. Since we know that a contract is for DM125,000, we can calculate that the contract price is $53,837.50 (.4307 × 125,000).

4. Change

The "change" column indicates the amount of change from the previous close in the same mode as the prices are stated. If the fractions are thirty-seconds, as is the case for Treasury bonds, then the change will also be stated in thirty-seconds. If the prices are in straight percent or in U.S. dollars, then the change is stated in the same respectively.

5. Open Interest

Open interest indicates the total number of contracts that have not been offset by delivery or by liquidation.

The total open-interest figure, which is usually last, is the total of open interest for all contracts for *that* quotation, despite the fact that it is sometimes labeled "previous day's" open interest.

6. Volume

Estimated sales indicate the number of contracts sold irrespective of the month of delivery. Do not confuse this with the open-interest figures.

7. Weekly Quotations

The format for weekly quotations is usually the same as that for daily quotations.

C. Stock Index Futures

Stock index futures are not as tricky as they might seem at first. Nevertheless, before attempting an explanation we will review the basic futures contract:

Financial Futures

Financial futures prices are quoted on the PBS program, The Nightly Business Report. Here we see:

1. June Ginnie-Mae futures at 6026. (See chapter 11 for a discussion of GNMA mortgage pools.) The first two numbers are percent of par value (60%) and the second two are thirty-seconds of a percent ($^{26}/_{32}$% which equals .8125%). The settlement price is therefore 60.8125% of par. This price is down $^{5}/_{32}$nds from the previous day's settlement price.

2. June T-bond futures at 6126. The first two numbers are percent of par value (61%) and the second two are thirty-seconds of a percent ($^{26}/_{32}$% which equals .8125%). The settlement price is therefore 61.8125%, down $^{9}/_{32}$nds.

3. June T-bill futures at 8695. This figure is straight percent of par carried to a hundredth of a percent. The price is therefore 86.95%, unchanged from the previous day's settlement price.

A *futures contract* is an agreement to buy (called "going long") or to sell (called "going short") a specific product at a specified price and at a specified time in the future.

In the case of a stock index future the "product" is an intangible (i.e., the numerical value of an index). The product has a dollar value because it is assigned to the index (e.g., $100 per point).

The investor does not actually own any of the stocks that make up the index. When the contract matures the investor who still has an open contract (i.e., is either long or short) pays or takes receipt of the amount at which the index is valued. All settlements are in cash. As it turns out, the settlement price is not exactly the closing value of the index on the last day of trading but it is usually close to that amount. (More will be said about this later.)

Most stock index futures are based on established indexes designed to measure the combined market performance of all the stocks of which they are constituted. The Major Market Index, however, is at least one case where an index was created especially for the purpose of assigning a futures contract to it.

The most well-known stock index is the Dow Jones Industrial Average (DJIA). Obviously, futures on that index would be extremely popular but the Dow Jones & Company, which owns the rights to the DJIA, has refused to permit futures contracts based on it. Among their reasons is concern that futures contracts might eventually begin to assert some influence over the index itself (i.e., the market prices of the stocks contained in the index). Indeed there is evidence that this has happened, although to a relatively small degree, to other indexes on which futures are written.

Be that as it may, stock index futures have developed for most of the other major indexes. The most well-known are:

NYSE Composite Index—made up of all common stock traded on the New York Stock Exchange.
S & P Composite Index (known also as the S & P 500 Stock Index)—made up of Standard & Poor's selection of 500 stocks traded on the NYSE, AMEX, and OTC.
***Value Line* Composite Index**—made up of *Value Line*'s selection of 1,700 stocks traded on the NYSE, AMEX, regional, and OTC markets.

Major Market Index—made up of 20 blue chip stocks whose options are traded on the Chicago Board of Trade.

A stock index future makes it possible for an investor to participate in the overall performance of a market as represented by the stocks in the index. In all but the *Value Line* index the stocks are weighted to reflect the number of shares outstanding. In the *Value Line* index the stocks are rated equally.

Weighting a stock within an index according to the number of shares outstanding reflects the fact that a rise in the security price of a company with a large number of shares outstanding creates more equity dollars than the same increase in the price of shares of a company with fewer shares outstanding. For instance, if the shares of a company with 10 million shares outstanding rises by one dollar, 10 million equity dollars are created whereas if the same price increase occurred for the shares of a company with one million shares outstanding only one million dollars in equity is created.

To illustrate how a contract works we will describe a New York Stock Exchange futures contract. The value assigned to the index (the NYSE Composite Index) is $500 times the number at which the index stands. Thus if the index was at 100, the dollar value would be $50,000. If the index rose one-half point, the value would be $50,250.

Future contracts on the NYSE Composite Index are available for 3 months, 6 months, and 9 months out. Just as with other futures contracts, as one contract matures a new 9-month contract is introduced. NYSE futures are on a March, June, September, December cycle.

Up to this point little has been said about the price of the futures contract. The prices are quoted the same way as the index itself, $500 per point. The price you will pay depends on a number of factors:

1. The current value of the Composite Index.
2. The estimation of the marketplace—that is, other traders—as to the future of the market. Will it go up or down, and how much?
3. The length of the contract. Obviously, a contract for 6 months would bring a higher price than a contract for 3 months since the former would have a longer time to possibly perform as the investor anticipated.

Thus if the NYSE index closed at, for example, 108.75 for a dollar value of $54,375, typical contract prices might be something like the following:

3-month contract at 111.55 = $55,775
6-month contract at 113.55 = $56,775
9-month contract at 115.55 = $57,775

Note that in the preceding example investors will pay (or receive) a $1,400 premium above spot (the current price) for a 3-month contract. For each additional three months traders are paying (or receiving) an additional $1,000. Such a spread between the current level of the index and between the 3-month, 6-month, and 9-month contracts represents a reasonable amount for the market to rise or fall. Don't forget, investors who are bullish are buying contracts and paying those amounts while investors who are bearish are selling contracts and receiving those amounts.

Although the index itself moves in increments of one hundredths, the minimum movement for the futures contract is five hundredths (.05), which is known as a "tick." One tick thus has a value of $25.

Minimum margin is set by the exchange and currently stands at $3,500. Profits and losses are credited or debited to the investor's account every day at the close of trading. If the contract increases in value the profit can be removed and, conversely, if the value of the contract falls the investor will be called to deposit additional funds should the level drop below the "maintenance" level, currently set at $1,500. Since the initial investment per contract can be as low as $3,500, and since the index value can obviously fall more than that amount, investors have the potential to lose even more than their initial investment.

Investors may hold contracts as briefly or for as long a period as they like—until the contracts mature. Contracts may be closed at any time by purchasing or selling, whichever is appropriate, the same contract (just as with options).

If a contract is held until maturity the settlement price is a bit complicated. It is not the closing price on the last day of trading as one would expect but the *difference* between that price and the previous day's close.

The strategy of investors who are bullish on the market would be to buy contracts. If the value of the index rises the value of the contracts rises as if the investor had the same amount of money invested in the stocks. When the investor closes his position by selling a like contract the additional amount received, above what was paid for the initial contract, constitutes the profit (after commissions).

Because of high margin requirements selling short has always been more difficult for small investors. Stock index futures, therefore, almost constitute a new investment tool. For the individual who is bearish on the market, it is much easier to sell a futures contract. Let us say that an individual (as an initial position and without margin considerations) sells a contract for $35,000 and the index falls, say 4.05 points. If the position is closed at that time by the purchase of an identical contract, the 4.05 points difference ($2,025) is kept as profit (after deduction of commission).

D. The Quotations

1. The Index, Exchange, Manner of Pricing

Headings for stock index futures quotations usually list the name of the index first, then the exchange, and finally the manner of pricing. The latter is the dollar amount which, when multiplied by the current futures figure, gives the current market price. In the example at the end of the chapter the manner of pricing is shown as $500 times the futures number.

2. Season High and Low, and Month of Delivery

The standard format for futures quotations places the season high and low first. These are the highest and lowest prices ever paid for that particular futures contract.

Next comes the month of delivery, which is what is used by traders to distinguish among the contracts (e.g., the June S & P, the September NYSE, etc.). Settlement for each contract is the last day of trading in the month indicated.

3. Prices

The three columns after the month of the contract give the high, low, and close for the period covered by the quotation. If it is a daily paper it will be the high, low, and close for the previous day's trading. If it is a Sunday paper then the high and low will be for the entire previous week.

4. Change

The change from the previous close (for the day or week) is quoted in the same manner as the futures prices, i.e., in ticks of .05 of a point. Note that what is being indicated is the change from the previous closing price of that particular futures contract, not the change from the previous close of the Composite Index itself.

5. Open Contracts

The last column shows the number of contracts outstanding.

6. Other Information

At the bottom of the quotations the closing value of the index is given along with the number of sales and the previous trading period's total open interest.

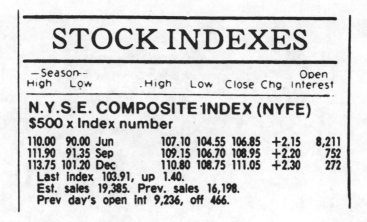

STOCK INDEXES

—Season—							Open
High	Low		.High	Low	Close	Chg	Interest

N.Y.S.E. COMPOSITE INDEX (NYFE)
$500 x Index number

110.00	90.00	Jun	107.10	104.55	106.85	+2.15	8,211
111.90	91.35	Sep	109.15	106.70	108.95	+2.20	752
113.75	101.20	Dec	110.80	108.75	111.05	+2.30	272

Last index 103.91, up 1.40.
Est. sales 19,385. Prev. sales 16,198.
Prev day's open int 9,236, off 466.

Example of stock
index futures quotation.
Prices are determined by
multiplying $500 times
the value indicated.
The March contract is
not yet trading (there
are no open contracts)
and the prices quoted
are preliminary.

(*The New York Times*)

(Edward C. Topple, NYSE photographer)

**TRADING ON THE FLOOR OF THE
NEW YORK FUTURES EXCHANGE**

Appendix 1
Dollar/Decimal Equivalence of Fractions

Dollar/decimal equivalences of fractions are often needed for the price and premium calculations of a variety of financial instruments. THIS PAGE IS PRINTED TWICE SO THAT YOU MAY CUT ONE OUT TO HAVE HANDY FOR REFERENCE.

Fractions				Decimals
1/32				.03125
2/32	1/16			.0625
3/32				.09375
4/32	2/16	1/8		.125
5/32				.15625
6/32	3/16			.1875
7/32				.21875
8/32	4/16	2/8	1/4	.25
9/32				.28125
10/32	5/16			.3125
11/32				.34375
12/32	6/16	3/8		.375
13/32				.40625
14/32	7/16			.4375
15/32				.46875
16/32	8/16	4/8	1/2	.5
17/32				.53125
18/32	9/16			.5625
19/32				.59375
20/32	10/16	5/8		.625
21/32				.65625
22/32	11/16			.6875
23/32				.71875
24/32	12/16	6/8	3/4	.75
25/32				.78125
26/32	13/16			.8125
27/32				.84375
28/32	14/16	7/8		.875
29/32				.90625
30/32	15/16			.9375
31/32				.96875

Appendix 1
Dollar/Decimal Equivalence of Fractions

Dollar/decimal equivalences of fractions are often needed for the price and premium calculations of a variety of financial instruments. THIS PAGE IS PRINTED TWICE SO THAT YOU MAY CUT ONE OUT TO HAVE HANDY FOR REFERENCE.

Fractions				Decimals
1/32				.03125
2/32	1/16			.0625
3/32				.09375
4/32	2/16	1/8		.125
5/32				.15625
6/32	3/16			.1875
7/32				.21875
8/32	4/16	2/8	1/4	.25
9/32				.28125
10/32	5/16			.3125
11/32				.34375
12/32	6/16	3/8		.375
13/32				.40625
14/32	7/16			.4375
15/32				.46875
16/32	8/16	4/8	1/2	.5
17/32				.53125
18/32	9/16			.5625
19/32				.59375
20/32	10/16	5/8		.625
21/32				.65625
22/32	11/16			.6875
23/32				.71875
24/32	12/16	6/8	3/4	.75
25/32				.78125
26/32	13/16			.8125
27/32				.84375
28/32	14/16	7/8		.875
29/32				.90625
30/32	15/16			.9375
31/32				.96875

Appendix 2

Definitions of Ratings by Moody's
and Standard & Poor's

Corporate and municipal bonds are rated by both Standard & Poor's and by Moody's Investor's Service. Their ratings do not constitute a recommendation to buy, sell, or hold bonds. The ratings assess only the ability of the issuer to meet the obligations of the bond. They do not address considerations such as price of the security or its suitability for a particular investor.

Ratings are based on the most current information available, and they may be changed at any time. One should verify that the rating of any bond under consideration is current.

STANDARD & POOR'S Corporate and Municipal

Bond Rating Definitions

AAA Bonds rated AAA have the highest rating assigned by Standard & Poor's to a debt obligation. Capacity to pay interest and repay principal is extremely strong.

AA Bonds rated AA have a very strong capacity to pay interest and repay principal and differ from the highest rated issues only in small degree.

A Bonds rated A have a strong capacity to pay interest and repay principal although they are somewhat more susceptible to the adverse effects of changes in circumstances and economic conditions than bonds in higher rated categories.

BBB Bonds rated BBB are regarded as having an adequate capacity to pay interest and repay principal. Whereas they normally exhibit adequate protection parameters, adverse economic conditions or changing circumstances are more likely to lead to a weakened capacity to pay interest and repay principal for bonds in this category than for bonds in higher rated categories.

BB, B, CCC, CC Bonds rated BB, B, CCC and CC are regarded, on balance, as predominantly speculative with respect to capacity to pay interest and repay principal in accordance with the terms of the obligation. BB indicates the lowest degree of speculation and CC the highest degree of speculation. While such bonds will likely have some quality and protective characteristics, these are outweighed by large uncertainties or major risk exposures to adverse conditions.

C The rating C is reserved for income bonds on which no interest is being paid.

D Bonds rated D are in default, and payment of interest and/or repayment of principal is in arrears.

Plus (+) or Minus (-): The ratings from "AA" to "B" may be modified by the addition of a plus or minus sign to show relative standing within the major rating categories.

Provisional Ratings: The letter "p" indicates that the rating is provisional. A provisional rating assumes the successful completion of the project being financed by the bonds being rated and indicates that payment of debt service requirements is largely or entirely dependent upon the successful and timely completion of the project. This rating, however, while addressing credit quality subsequent to completion of the project, makes no comment on the likelihood of, or the risk of default upon failure of, such completion. The investor should exercise his own judgment with respect to such likelihood and risk.

NR Indicates that no rating has been requested, that there is insufficient information on which to base a rating, or that S&P does not rate a particular type of obligation as a matter of policy.

KEY TO MOODY'S CORPORATE RATINGS

Aaa

Bonds which are rated **Aaa** are judged to be of the best quality. They carry the smallest degree of investment risk and are generally referred to as "gilt edge." Interest payments are protected by a large or by an exceptionally stable margin and principal is secure. While the various protective elements are likely to change, such changes as can be visualized are most unlikely to impair the fundamentally strong position of such issues.

Aa

Bonds which are rated **Aa** are judged to be of high quality by all standards. Together with the **Aaa** group they comprise what are generally known as high grade bonds. They are rated lower than the best bonds because margins of protection may not be as large as in **Aaa** securities or fluctuation of protective elements may be of greater amplitude or there may be other elements present which make the long-term risks appear somewhat larger than in **Aaa** securities.

A

Bonds which are rated **A** possess many favorable investment attributes and are to be considered as upper medium grade obligations. Factors giving security to principal and interest are considered adequate, but elements may be present which suggest a susceptibility to impairment sometime in the future.

Baa

Bonds which are rated **Baa** are considered as medium grade obligations, i.e., they are neither highly protected nor poorly secured. Interest payments and principal security appear adequate for the present but certain protective elements may be lacking or may be characteristically unreliable over any great length of time. Such bonds lack outstanding investment characteristics and in fact have speculative characteristics as well.

Ba

Bonds which are rated **Ba** are judged to have speculative elements; their future cannot be considered as well-assured. Often the protection of interest and principal payments may be very moderate, and thereby not well safeguarded during both good and bad times over the future. Uncertainty of position characterizes bonds in this class.

B

Bonds which are rated **B** generally lack characteristics of the desirable investment. Assurance of interest and principal payments or of maintenance of other terms of the contract over any long period of time may be small.

Caa

Bonds which are rated **Caa** are of poor standing. Such issues may be in default or there may be present elements of danger with respect to principal or interest.

Ca

Bonds which are rated **Ca** represent obligations which are speculative in a high degree. Such issues are often in default or have other marked shortcomings.

C

Bonds which are rated **C** are the lowest rated class of bonds, and issues so rated can be regarded as having extremely poor prospects of ever attaining any real investment standing.

KEY TO MOODY'S MUNICIPAL RATINGS

Aaa

Bonds which are rated **Aaa** are judged to be of the best quality. They carry the smallest degree of investment risk and are generally referred to as "gilt edge." Interest payments are protected by a large or by an exceptionally stable margin and principal is secure. While the various protective elements are likely to change, such changes as can be visualized are most unlikely to impair the fundamentally strong position of such issues.

Aa

Bonds which are rated **Aa** are judged to be of high quality by all standards. Together with the **Aaa** group they comprise what are generally known as high grade bonds. They are rated lower than the best bonds because margins of protection may not be as large as in **Aaa** securities or fluctuation of protective elements may be of greater amplitude or there may be other elements present which make the long-term risks appear somewhat larger than in **Aaa** securities.

A

Bonds which are rated **A** possess many favorable investment attributes and are to be considered as upper medium grade obligations. Factors giving security to principal and interest are considered adequate, but elements may be present which suggest a susceptibility to impairment sometime in the future.

Baa

Bonds which are rated **Baa** are considered as medium grade obligations, i.e., they are neither highly protected nor poorly secured. Interest payments and principal security appear adequate for the present but certain protective elements may be lacking or may be characteristically unreliable over any great length of time. Such bonds lack outstanding investment characteristics and in fact have speculative characteristics as well.

Ba

Bonds which are rated **Ba** are judged to have speculative elements; their future cannot be considered as well-assured. Often the protection of interest and principal payments may be very moderate, and thereby not well safeguarded during both good and bad times over the future. Uncertainty of position characterizes bonds in this class.

B

Bonds which are rated **B** generally lack characteristics of the desirable investment. Assurance of interest and principal payments or of maintenance of other terms of the contract over any long period of time may be small.

Caa

Bonds which are rated **Caa** are of poor standing. Such issues may be in default or there may be present elements of danger with respect to principal or interest.

Ca

Bonds which are rated **Ca** represent obligations which are speculative in a high degree. Such issues are often in default or have other marked shortcomings.

C

Bonds which are rated **C** are the lowest rated class of bonds, and issues so rated can be regarded as having extremely poor prospects of ever attaining any real investment standing.

CON. (...)

Bonds for which the security depends upon the completion of some act or the fulfillment of some condition are rated conditionally. These are bonds secured by (a) earnings of projects under construction, (b) earnings of projects unseasoned in operating experience, (c) rentals which begin when facilities are completed, or (d) payments to which some other limiting condition attaches. Parenthetical rating denotes probable credit stature upon completion of construction or elimination of basis of condition.

Those bonds in the A and Baa groups which Moody's believes possess the strongest investment attributes are designated by the symbols **A 1** and **Baa 1**.

KEY TO MOODY'S SHORT-TERM LOAN RATINGS

MIG 1

Loans bearing this designation are of the best quality, enjoying strong protection from established cash flows of funds for their servicing or from established and broad-based access to the market for refinancing, or both.

MIG 2

Loans bearing this designation are of high quality, with margins of protection ample although not so large as in the preceding group.

MIG 3

Loans bearing this designation are of favorable quality, with all security elements accounted for but lacking the undeniable strength of the preceding grades. Market access for refinancing, in particular, is likely to be less well established.

MIG 4

Loans bearing this designation are of adequate quality, carrying specific risk but having protection commonly regarded as required of an investment security and not distinctly or predominantly speculative.

*Reprinted by permission of
Moody's Investor's Service*

Glossary: Terms and Jargon

Because of the large number of terms from the combined areas of investing whose quotations are covered in this book only those terms are included that directly relate to the production or dissemination of those quotations or that are of major importance and likely to be encountered in newspaper articles. For alphabetic qualifiers and for terms not found here, see the index.

accrued interest   The amount of interest accumulated since the last interest payment. In the case of most bonds, accrued interest must be added to the purchase price (but that amount will be recovered by the purchaser in the next interest payment).

actuals   The physical commodities as distinguished from futures contracts. Actuals, also called cash commodities or spot commodities, are on hand and ready for delivery or storage. They are sold on, and their prices are quoted on, cash markets; also called spot markets.

adjustment bond   *See* income bond.

ADR   *See* American depository receipt.

aftermarket   Trading in a new issue, either OTC or on an exchange, immediately following its initial distribution.

American depository receipt *(ADR)*   A certificate, issued by a U.S. bank, that represents a specific number of foreign securities held by a U.S. banking institution in the country of origin on the behalf of an investor in this country. This practice facilitates the trading of foreign securities by eliminating currency exchange problems, legal obstacles, and the difficulties of bearer-form stock certificates which are not used in this country.

American Stock Exchange *(ASE or AMEX)*   The second largest stock exchange in the U.S. It also handles transactions in bonds and options. Sometimes referred to as the "curb" exchange because it originated as an outdoor market near Wall Street.

AMEX   *See* American Stock Exchange.

annual report   A comprehensive financial statement issued yearly by corporations. The reports are highly regulated and should present a clear picture of the financial condition of a company. Also included are announcements of new products or services, explanations of past performance, and statements of future prospects. Copies are sent to shareholders and are available to other interested parties on request.

arbitrage (pronounced är′b*i*träzh′)   The simultaneous purchase on one exchange and sale on another of the same or equivalent financial instruments (such as stocks, options, futures, etc.) or commodities in order to profit from any price differences between them. Often the differences are so slight that such transactions are profitable only to exchange traders who do not pay the usual commissions.

as agent   The usual role of a brokerage when it undertakes securities transactions for clients. Broker commissions are for this service. *See* as principal.

ASE   *See* American Stock Exchange.

ask or **asked price**   *See* bid and asked prices.

as principal   When a brokerage buys or sells securities for its own account. In the case of a sale to a client there is a reasonable markup but no commission charged.

assets   Everything owned by a corporation and that is due it. Fixed assets include buildings and machinery; current assets include inventory and accounts receivable; intangible assets include patents and even goodwill.

assign   The designation of an option writer for the fulfillment of the terms of an option that was sold. The OCC randomly makes the assignment to brokerages who in turn (and by a variety of methods) must decide to which client the assignment will be given. *See* exercise.

at-the-market   Also called a "market order." An order to buy or sell immediately at the best price available. This is the most common mode of securities transaction.

automatic exercise   A procedure whereby an in-the-money option is automatically exercised just before expiration by the brokerage or the OCC on behalf of the holder.

average down   The purchase of additional shares of the same security after a drop in prices so that the average of the two (or more) purchase prices will be lower than the initial price paid.

baby bond   A bond with less than $1,000 par value, usually $100.

BAN   *See* bond anticipation note.

bankers' acceptances   Negotiable short-term instruments issued by U.S. banks with which U.S. companies pay foreign trade debts. Foreign banks may redeem these certificates (bills of exchange) at the issuing U.S. bank or may sell them to a third party. Their yields are close to those of large certificates of deposit.

banks for cooperatives *(CO-OP)*   See p. 131.

basis grade   A commodity grade specified by an exchange as acceptable for delivery on a futures contract.

basis point   One percent of one percent. Often used in comparing yields of fixed-income securities. 10.15 percent and 10.16 percent differ by 1 basis point.

bear   An investor who expects prices on securities markets to decline, particularly one who invests so as to profit by such a decline.

bearer bond   *See* bearer form.

bearer form   A form in which bonds are issued, also called coupon form, in which coupons are attached to the bond certificate. No record is kept by the issuing company so that the bearer (presumed owner) must clip the coupons and return them to the company or its agent in order to receive interest payments. While out of favor with corporations it is the preferred form for municipal bonds.

bear spread   A specific option strategy that can be implemented by either puts or calls and in which a profit can be realized by a decline in the price of the underlying security. Some risk is also eliminated. See p. 182.

bid and **asked prices**   A bid price is a price at which a broker has offered to purchase a security or commodity; thus it is the price you will receive should you sell. The asked price is the price at which a broker has offered to sell a security or commodity; thus it is the price you will pay should you purchase. Most NAS-DAQ stock quotations list both these prices for OTC stock. In the NASDAQ system these represent firm offers from brokers who are making a market in that particular security. The difference between the two prices is known as the spread and constitutes the current profit for the market maker in transactions of this stock. The more actively the stock is traded the smaller the spread. Bid and asked prices are part of all exchange trading but only the transaction price is usually reported. Sometimes bid and asked prices are reported on the ticker for exchange listed stocks or commodities that did not trade during the period covered by the quotation.

big board   The New York Stock Exchange.

block   A large number of shares, usually over 10,000.

blue chip   Refers to common stock that is throught to be of the highest quality. These are usually higher-priced shares of stable, long-established companies that have paid dividends regularly.

blue-sky law   State laws concerning registration and sale of new securities. Intended to protect the public against fraud, the term refers to the alleged statement of a judge to the effect that a particular stock had about the same value as a patch of blue sky.

bond   A long-term debt instrument (the issuer is the borrower) usually with a fixed interest rate (coupon rate) and a maturity date at which time the face value will be returned to the purchaser. They are issued in either bearer form or coupon form. Bonds may be divided into four broad classifications depending on the issuer: corporate bonds, municipal bonds, government bonds, and government agency bonds. Within these categories there are many varieties of bonds issued. See Part Three, "How to Read Bond Quotations." When compared to other debt obligations bonds are the longest term; notes are generally shorter and bills are the briefest. For bond ratings see Appendix 2.

bond anticipation note (*BAN*)   See p. 109.

book value   The net worth or net assets of a corporation (assets minus liabilities) divided by the number of common shares outstanding after deducting the liquidation price of all preferred stock. An attempt to affix a tangible value to the shares of a company. This is presumably the return to the shareholder if the company were liquidated. Sometimes called equity capital or stockholder's equity, it should not contain preferred share liquidation value.

broker   A licensed agent who executes public orders in securities or commodities for a commission. The term is often applied to, but does not necessarily include, registered representatives within a brokerage.

brokerage   A firm that executes public orders for securities or commodities. Also, the commission received by a broker.

broker's loans   Money borrowed from banks by brokers in order to buy securities, finance new issues, or to carry their clients' margin accounts. The interest rates charged by banks for these loans are watched closely by the securities industry.

bucket shop   Refers to various illegal practices with regard to customers' orders, such as accepting but not executing them, or accepting them but delaying execution in an attempt to obtain lower prices while charging the client the original prices.

bull   An investor who expects prices on markets to rise, particularly one who invests so as to profit by such a rise.

bull spread   An option strategy that can be implemented either by puts or calls in which a profit can be made by a rise in the price of the underlying security and certain risks eliminated. See pp. 180–181, 183.

butterfly spread   An option strategy constructed of either puts or calls that involves both a bull spread and a bear spread. There are three striking prices with the middle one shared by both spreads.

calendar spread   A horizontal option spread in which two options of the same type (puts or calls) are bought or sold with the same strike price but different expiration dates. See p. 184.

call   An option giving the right to purchase 100 shares (usually) of a specific stock, at a specific price, within a specific time period.

callable   A bond or preferred stock which has a call feature.

call feature   (1) A stipulation of a bond issue whereby bonds may be redeemed by the issuer before maturity for a specified price (the call price) and under specified conditions. (2) A similar stipulation for a preferred stock issue whereby the stock may be bought back by the issuer at a price equal to or slightly higher than either the par value or the market price.

call protection   A feature of some bonds and preferred stock whereby they either cannot be called or cannot be called before a specified date.

capital gain or **capital loss**   The profit or loss from the sale of securities over (or under) the original purchase price. Does not include interest. If a bond is sold at a higher price than that for which it was paid, the difference is capital gain. The interest received in the meantime is not. Interest from discounted debt instruments is not capital gains. Capital gains from securities held longer than one year are taxed at a lower rate than those held less than one year.

cash commodity   *See* actuals.

cash cow   A company attractive as a takeover target because of its large cash holdings.

cash forward sale   The sale of a commodity (as opposed to a future) for delivery at a later date.

cash market   Used to designate the purchase or sale of actuals or cash commodities (as opposed to futures). Also called spot market. Sometimes the term is used only for grains and spot market for the actuals of other commodities.

CBOE   Chicago Board Options Exchange.

CBT   Chicago Board of Trade.

certificate of deposit (*CD*)   The negotiable certificate of deposit is a receipt for funds that have been deposited in a bank for a specified period of time and at a fixed rate of interest. Certificates for $100,000 or more may be traded on the secondary market. Their maturities range from one to eighteen months although the 90-day CD is standard. Most are issued with an interest bearing coupon although some are issued at a discount.

CFTC   Commodity Futures Trading Commission.

churning   Frequent buying and selling of securities with little purpose other than to generate commissions.

class   In options it distinguishes puts from calls. Options of the same class would be only puts or only calls.

closed-end investment company   A company formed for the purpose of investing in other securities. It is "closed end" in that there are a set number of shares (as with most companies) which distinguishes it from a mutual fund.

closing price   The last transaction price for a security during a trading day. "Last" price is also used, although the latter can also apply to the price of a security as of a specific time, e.g., as of 12:00 noon.

closing transaction   An options transaction (purchase or sale) that cancels a previous position. Except for the premium, it must have the same terms as the option it closes. If one has sold a put, one closes by buying a put with the same terms.

CME   Chicago Mercantile Exchange.

collateral trust bond   A mortgage or debenture bond issue that is at least in part secured by a stock or bond portfolio.

combination   An option position other than a straddle which is made up of both puts and calls.

COMEX   Commodity Exchange, Inc., of New York.

commercial paper   Short-term unsecured debt obligations issued by corporations. Sold at discount in denominations of $100,000 and over.

commission   A broker's fee for handling securities or commodity transactions.

commodity   A farm product such as grain or cotton; a mineral such as gold or copper; a forest product such as lumber or plywood; and sometimes the term is used for financial instruments such as CDs or Treasury bills. Commodities traded on an exchange must have sufficient supply and demand, be divisible into standard units, and be gradable with respect to quality.

commodity future   *See* futures contract. Sometimes this term is used to distinguish farm product or mineral futures from financial futures.

common stock   A unit of ownership in a corporation. Distinguished from preferred stock as the latter has, among other differences, a set dividend rate.

consolidated tape   A system that continuously reports every transaction on all exchanges linked by the Intermarket Trading System, that is, both national exchanges and five regional exchanges. Network A reports on all stocks listed on the NYSE whether traded on the NYSE or on a regional exchange. Network B reports on all stocks listed on the AMEX whether traded on the AMEX or on a regional exchange. These are commonly known as the ticker tape. Reports are flashed to ticker displays on all exchanges. After a 15-minute delay they are broadcast to all other ticker machines, displays, and on cable television.

conversion   *See* convertible.

conversion price   The resultant value of the underlying security when converted into the common stock at the conversion ratio. If the conversion ratio is 50 (i.e., 50 shares per $1,000 bond) then the conversion price of the underlying stock is $20.

conversion ratio   Indicates the number of shares (usually common stock) of the same company into which a convertible security (bond or preferred stock) may be converted. The conversion ratio is adjusted for stock splits.

convertible   A feature of some bonds, preferred stocks, and shares of mutual funds. For a bond or preferred stock it permits conversion into a stated amount of common stock of the same company under specified conditions. For mutual funds it permits the holder of shares in one fund to exchange them for a comparable amount of shares in another fund managed by the same company.

cornering the market   Control of enough securities, options, or commodity futures to permit price manipulation. In commodities it can mean, in extreme cases, acquisition of more futures contracts than the existing supply of the commodity can meet.

corporate bond   A long-term debt instrument issued by a corporation (including railroads and public utilities); one of the major categories of bonds.

corporation   A form of business organization chartered by, and to an extent regulated by, a state. The shares of closed corporations are owned by relatively few individuals. The shares of public companies are owned by many persons and traded OTC on one or more exchanges. The liability of the owners (the shareholders) is only to the extent of their investment.

coupon bond   *See* bearer form.

coupon rate   The fixed rate of interest paid by a bond.

cover   A closing transaction for an option that was previously sold.

covered option   An option that is sold when the writer (seller) owns the underlying security or has purchased another option with the same terms.

covering   *See* short covering.

cumulative preferred stock   An issue of preferred stock on which the dividends accumulate should any be omitted. The payment of cumulative dividends takes priority over the dividends of common stock.

curb exchange   *See* American Stock Exchange.

current market value   For securities it is assumed to be the most recent transaction price, bid price, or closing price unless news has been released, when the markets are closed or when trading in that security has been halted, that is expected to affect the price once trading has resumed.

current yield   The percent of the purchase price of a stock or a bond returned by the annual dividend or interest payments.

CUSIP number   An identification number appearing on the face of security documents and certificates. Stands for Committee on Uniform Security Identification Procedure. On recent stock certificates it usually appears on the right-hand side preceded by the letters "CUSIP." Each security is assigned its own identification number.

CV   *See* convertible.

date of record   Last day before a stock goes ex-dividend. Shareholders registered in corporate books on that day receive the dividend.

debenture   A commonly issued unsecured bond backed by the full faith and credit of the issuer but not by tangible assets.

default   Failure of the issuer of a bond to pay interest due or principal at maturity or to pay interest due on preferred stock. In commodities it is the failure to make or take delivery as required by a futures contract.

delivery The fulfillment of an option exercise or a futures contract by tendering stock (in the case of options) or a commodity (in the case of futures).

delivery notice Notice from the seller of intent to deliver on a particular date. The notices are assigned to the buyer by the clearing house, and they specify grade and place of delivery.

designated order turnaround *(DOT)* A computerized system which automatically routes small security orders to the appropriate stock specialist.

diagonal spread The simultaneous purchase and sale of calls and of puts on the same security with different strike prices and different expiration dates. See p. 183.

discount (1) The amount bonds and preferred stock are selling below their face value. (2) The pricing of an option below its intrinsic value. (3) Also means "to take into account" in the sense that a current stock price which has dropped could be said to have discounted the news of an expected cut in dividends.

diversification The spreading of one's investments among different companies in different industries, sometimes in different countries, and sometimes among different investment media, such as precious metals, in order to reduce risk.

dividend An amount declared by the board of directors of a corporation to be paid per share to the shareholders. Usually in cash, it is sometimes paid in stock. The amount can vary according to the fortunes of the company, and sometimes it can be paid from past earnings if current earnings are insufficient. For preferred shares the amount is fixed and does not change under ordinary circumstances.

dollar cost averaging A long-term system of buying securities at regular intervals and at fixed dollar amounts no matter what the current price fluctuations. The resulting total price for the investor will be the average of all prices paid.

DOT *See* designated order turnaround.

Dow-Jones averages Market averages from three industry groups: the industrial average taken from thirty industrial stocks; the transportation average taken from twenty transportation stocks; and the utilities average taken from fifteen public utilities stocks. The average within each area is determined by dividing the closing prices of each security by a divisor that compensates for past stock splits. The composite average includes all the above stocks. This is the oldest and most widely used stock market average. Many economists, however, feel that it is misleading because it is constituted of such a small number of stocks.

downside protection Indicates a range through which the security price could fall before there is a loss. Also can refer to protection against a fall in price.

down tick A transaction at a price less than the previous one. Also called a minus tick.

dually listed A security that trades on more than one exchange.

dual purpose company A closed-end investment company that issues initially two classes of stock: income shares and capital shares.

earnings The total net profit of a company per year. In annual reports it is also given as a per-share figure. Earnings are vital in the fundamental evaluation of a stock. Brief earnings reports are often grouped together in the financial pages of the newspapers; they give earnings for the current year (or quarter) and compare them to the earnings for the previous year (or quarter).

equipment trust bond A bond for which machinery or equipment (such as railroad cars) is used as collateral.

equity Commonly used to refer to ownership interest in a company by means of common or preferred stock. It is also used to refer to the excess value of property or stock in a company over and above any indebtedness. When applied to a margin account it refers to the total value of the securities above the debit balance.

ex-distribution The day after a distribution, such as a stock dividend, to which a new purchaser will not be entitled.

ex-dividend The day after a dividend has been paid and to which a new purchaser will not be entitled.

exercise Notification by the holder of an option that he or she requests fulfillment of the terms of the option contract.

exercise limit A limit on the number of options which one holder may exercise within a stated period of time. Set by exchanges to prevent cornering of the market.

exercise notice The document sent to the Options Clearing Corporation by an option holder requiring fulfillment of the terms of the option by the individual to whom it is assigned.

exercise price The price stipulated by the option contract at which the holder can buy or sell the underlying security. Also called a strike price.

ex-rights Refers to securities which formerly traded in units that contained rights but which are now trading without them because they have been removed or they have expired.

extra Often used to mean an extra dividend.

extraordinary item An item of either income or expense which is not expected to recur.

ex-warrants Refers to securities which formerly traded in units that contained warrants but which are now trading without them because they have been removed or they have expired.

face value The price at which a bond is redeemed at maturity and on which the coupon rate is calculated. Also called par value.

Federal Home Loan Bank *(FHLB)* A government-sponsored agency that issues bonds for the purpose of making mortgages available to the home-building industry. Interest is exempt from state and local income tax.

Federal Intermediate Credit Bank *(FICB)* A government-sponsored agency that issues bonds for the purpose of making loans available to farming and production interests. Interest is exempt from state and local income tax.

Federal Land Bank *(FLB)* A government-sponsored corporation that issues bonds for the purpose of making mortgages available to farms and agricultural concerns. Interest is exempt from state and local income tax.

Federal National Mortgage Association *(FNMA)* Known as Fannie Mae. A government-sponsored corporation (publicly owned) engaged in the purchasing and the selling of FHA, FHDA, or VA mortgages. Interest is exempt from state and local income tax.

first notice day The first day that notices of intention to deliver can be sent to sellers (those in short positions) through the various commodity clearing houses.

fiscal year The bookkeeping year for a corporation. It may begin (and end) at any time during the calendar year.

flat The condition under which a bond is traded without accrued interest.

floating-rate notes   Bonds whose interest rates are tied to and periodically adjusted to (a percent of) the rates of some other financial instrument such as Treasury bills.

flower bond   A Treasury bond that may be redeemed at par value upon the death of the owner for the purpose of application to inheritance tax.

fourth market   Direct securities transactions between large institutions without the utilization of a broker.

fully diluted earnings per share   An earnings figure that represents maximum possible dilution, that is, an earnings figure calculated as if all convertible securities had been exchanged for common stock.

fully registered bond   A bond whose holders are registered on the books of the issuing company. Interest payments and redemption of par at maturity are automatically mailed.

fundamental analysis   The study of a company and its securities that employs aspects of accounting, that examines management, and that views the company in the broader context of market conditions.

futures contract   An agreement to deliver a stated quality and quantity of a commodity, currency, or financial instrument. If one buys a futures contract (goes "long"), one is in the position of eventually receiving the commodity and paying the stated price unless the position is liquidated. If one sells a futures contract (goes "short"), one is in the position of eventually delivering the commodity and accepting the stated price.

general obligation bond   A municipal bond backed by the full faith and credit of the issuer.

golden parachute   Benefits designed for company executives should they lose their positions through a takeover. Such provisions usually include severance pay or stock bonuses.

Government National Mortgage Association *(GNMA)*   Called Ginnie Mae. A government corporation that buys mortgages backed by the FHA and VA. Bonds are issued on pools of mortgages. Payments of principal and interest from the mortgages are passed through the corporation to the investor monthly.

growth stock   Stock with prospects for a rapid appreciation in value. Not necessarily smaller or younger companies, these are companies with, for example, increased market potential or new technologies.

guaranteed bonds   Bonds guaranteed by a company other than the issuer.

hedge   The holding of the combination of a long position and a short position in the same security, option, commodity, or future where a loss in one position is offset by a gain in the other. The strategy is not so much for gains as to avoid loss. Such a position can be used to prevent the decline in value of a fixed-income portfolio or to guarantee the price of a commodity to be needed in the future. In commodities a hedger is also one who deals in the physical commodity but who makes use of the price differences between the cash market and futures market for protection and for profit.

holder   One who holds a security.

holder of record   The individual (or institution) who owns the security on the record date, that is, the legal day on which dividends are distributed (the day before the security goes ex-dividend).

holding company   An investment company with holdings (often majority holdings) in other companies.

horizontal spread   A calendar spread.

hot issue   A new issue, available from investment bankers, whose price is expected to rise immediately upon initial trading in the aftermarket (i.e., as soon as it becomes available OTC or on an exchange).

IMM   *See* International Monetary Market.

income bond   A bond whose interest is paid only if earnings permit. Sometimes issued by companies in financial difficulty. For some issues the interest is partially cumulative. The principal is under obligation to be paid at maturity.

income shares   One of a type of shares issued by dual-purpose funds with guaranteed minimum dividends. The other type is capital gains shares.

indenture   The terms of a debt instrument such as a bond.

index   A relative measure of changes in prices, sales, production, etc., calculated from an arbitrary value assigned to a specific year (or years).

industrial revenue bond   A type of municipal bond issued to raise funds for the construction of facilities for corporations. Proceeds from the facility pay interest and principal of the bond.

initial distribution   *See* primary distribution.

insider   A member of the board, an officer, or even a stockholder who is privy to nonpublic information about a company, particularly of a kind that would affect the price of that company's securities. Also includes members of that person's immediate family.

institutional investor   A large organization or a branch of a large organization whose primary function is to invest its assets or assets entrusted to it. Includes mutual funds, pension funds, insurance companies, banks, and many others.

instrument   Synonymous with "security." Sometimes implies a shorter-term vehicle than the latter.

interest   The amount a lender gives a borrower (in addition to the return of the principal) in payment for the use of the principal.

International Bank for Reconstruction and Development   A bank set up to make industrial loans to various countries who are members. The U.S. controls 25 percent interest.

International Monetary Market *(IMM)*   A division of the Chicago Mercantile Exchange on which futures are traded for Treasury bills, gold, silver, copper, and foreign currencies.

in the money   An option that would yield a profit if it were immediately exercised. Either a call with a striking price below the current market price of the underlying security, or a put with a striking price above the current market price of the underlying security.

intrinsic value   The amount that an option is in-the-money.

investment   The use of money in such a way as to yield more money while at the same time protecting capital and minimizing the risk to less than that of gambling.

investment banker   An individual or institution that underwrites new securities. An investment banker buys the securities from the company, thus guaranteeing the company the capital it seeks, and in turn sells the securities, at a markup, to the public or institutions.

investment club   A group of people who pool their resources to invest and to socialize. They are member-managed and not usually constituted of professional investors.

investment company A company that invests in other companies. Investment companies have the advantages of pooled resources and professional management. There are closed-end investment companies and open-end investment companies. The latter are mutual funds.

investment value Applied to a convertible security it is the estimated market price of a security if it had no conversion feature. In other words, the price at which the security would have to sell to bring its yield into line with the yield percent available from comparable nonconvertible securities.

issue Any of the various types of securities of a company that are at least partially in the hands of the public.

job lot In commodity futures (and sometimes other types of transactions) it is a unit of trading less than a round lot.

junk bond A bond with a credit rating below B. Such bonds are often used to raise money for the acquisition of other companies. They are highly speculative.

leverage The use of a small amount of capital or equity in combination with a large amount of debt in order to achieve a higher yield not possible with use of the equity alone.

leveraged buyout Use of borrowed money to acquire another company.

leveraged company A company with more than one third of of its capital in the form of long-term debt.

liabilities All claims against a company such as debts, dividends, salaries, taxes, accounts payable, etc.

life of contract The first to the last trading day in a futures contract.

limit In commodities the maximum price fluctuation permitted by the exchange from the previous session's settlement price. Separate limits are established by the individual exchanges for each commodity.

limit order An instruction to a broker for a purchase at a price not above a specified maximum, or a sale at a price not below a specified minimum.

liquidation The conversion of securities or property into cash. In commodities it is a transaction that closes a former open position.

liquidity The facility with which a market can absorb the buying and selling of a security or commodity.

load A portion of the initial cost of shares in a mutual fund for transaction commissions and other expenses. There is usually no charge of this kind on redemption.

long or **long position** In securities it means ownership. In options it refers to options purchased. In commodities it refers to the ownership of a futures contract or the ownership of the physical commodity.

long-term When applied to capital gains it refers to securities held for more than a year. For debt instruments it refers to obligations of over one year.

M Abbreviation used for 1,000; used to specify face value of bonds.

margin The amount of collateral, in cash or securities, required to be on deposit in a brokerage account to maintain certain credit positions such as short sales. The amount varies depending on Federal Reserve regulations and on the size and number of positions current.

margin account A brokerage account in which the customer leaves the necessary margin on deposit to make use of credit from the broker. A margin account is necessary for short sales, most options, and all futures.

margin call   A demand from a broker that the client deposit additional equity (cash or securities) into a margin account in order to meet Federal Reserve or brokerage requirements.

market   The total facilities for buying or selling a security including the anticipated supply and demand.

market maker   Usually refers to brokers or dealers who actively purchase and sell a specific OTC security for their own accounts and who post their bid and asked prices in the NASDAQ computer system or in the pink sheets. In options and commodities it is an exchange member who trades for his own account but who may be (one of several) assigned to specific securities or commodities.

market order   *See* at-the-market.

market value   The price at which a security can be publicly bought or sold at a given time on an exchange or over the counter. *See also* current market value.

maturity   The day on which a bond is due for redemption. In commodities it is the period during which delivery may be made.

merger   The takeover of one company by another that has the cooperation of the board of directors of the target company.

minus tick   *See* down tick.

money-market funds   A mutual fund that invests exclusively in short-term debt instruments. *See* mutual fund.

money-market instrument   Short-term debt such as Treasury bills and commercial paper. Usually purchased at discount (less than face value) and redeemed at par.

mortgage bond   A bond issue secured by all or part of the real assets of the company.

MSE   Midwest Stock Exchange; also the Montreal Stock Exchange.

municipal bond   Debt obligations issued by states and their political subdivisions and by certain agencies and authorities within the state. Interest is exempt from federal income tax and from the taxes of some states.

mutual fund   An open-end investment company. An unlimited number of shares are sold and the capital is invested in other companies. Mutual funds redeem their own shares. *See* money-market funds.

naked option   An option sold when the writer does not own the underlying stock or an offsetting option position.

NASD   *See* National Association of Securities Dealers.

NASDAQ   *See* National Association of Securities Dealers Automated Quotations.

National Association of Securities Dealers *(NASD)*   An association of brokers and dealers engaged in the transaction of securities in the U.S. It is the regulatory body for all over-the-counter brokers and dealers and is supervised by the SEC.

National Association of Securities Dealers Automated Quotations *(NASDAQ)*   A system operated by the Bunker Ramo Corp. under contract from the NASD. Current bid and asked prices as well as other pertinent data are available for over-the-counter securities by means of quote terminals. *See* National Quotation Service.

National Quotation Service *(NQS)*   Maintained by the National Quotation Bureau, reports on OTC securities not quoted by the NASDAQ system. Pink sheets list OTC stock, their market makers, and bid and asked prices. Yellow sheets contain reports on corporate bonds.

net asset value *(NAV)*   For open-end investment companies (mutual funds and money-market funds) it is the net worth of all securities held by the fund. Per-share net asset value is that amount divided by the total number of shares outstanding. For other types of companies it is the net worth of *all* assets.

net change   The difference between the current price usually a closing price, and the closing price of the previous trading session.

net tangible asset value per share   Book value per share.

new issue   A security which is being offered for the first time. In the stock tables such an issue is specified "n" for one year to indicate that the 52-week high and low are as of the inception of trading and not literally 52 weeks.

New York Cotton Exchange   A futures exchange trading in cotton, orange juice, and propane.

next day contract   A securities transaction requiring payment the following day.

no-load mutual fund   A mutual fund that does not have a sales charge.

noncumulative preferred stock   Preferred stock whose omitted dividends are not cumulative.

nonrecurring item   *see* extraordinary item.

notice day   Any day on and after which a notice of intent to deliver may be issued to the holder of a futures contract.

NQB   National Quotation Bureau, Inc.

NYSE   New York Stock Exchange.

OCC   Option Clearing Corporation.

odd lot   An amount of stock less than a round lot, which is usually 100 shares. Securities that do not trade actively are sometimes traded in 10-share lots and, on the AMEX, in 10, 25, and 50-share lots. In these cases an odd lot is less than the round lot stipulated. In Canada the term "broken lot" is used. For commodities trading it is an amount more or less than the usual contract specification, also called a job lot.

offset   The closing or liquidation of a futures position.

open contract   *see* open interest.

open-end investment company   *see* mutual fund.

open interest   The total number of option or futures contracts outstanding that have not been closed, or, in the case of commodities, liquidated or offset by delivery.

opening transaction   The initial buying or selling of an option contract.

option   A contract granting the right to buy (*see* call) or to sell (*see* put) a specified amount of securities at a fixed price for a designated amount of time. One may buy or one may sell (called write) either type of contract.

Option Clearing Corporation *(OCC)*   The corporation that processes all option transactions. After a transaction is completed between the buyer and seller (writer) on an exchange floor, the OCC interposes itself as seller for the buyer and buyer for the seller. In this way no link is maintained between the original parties in the transaction. The OCC then randomly assigns the exercises to parties in short positions as they are received from parties in long positions.

OTC   *see* over-the-counter.

out of the money An option with no intrinsic value in terms of the relationship between the striking price to the current price of the underlying security.

oversubscribed The condition of a new issue when there have been more securities requested than there are securities available. When this happens each subscription is reduced proportionately until the total equals the amount available. Such issues usually increase in value immediately upon issuance. In takeover bids, or offers to repurchase stock (by the original company), it is the condition whereby more shares are offered than originally requested. Share purchases may then be made on a pro-rata basis or declined altogether.

over-the-counter *(OTC)* The market for securities not listed on a national or regional exchange. Prices of the most active are available from NASDAQ and the less active on the pink sheets. Government and municipal bonds are OTC as well as the stocks of many banks and insurance companies.

paper loss or **profit** An unrealized loss or profit on a security that is still held and which would become real if the security were sold or the position closed.

par (1) A value assigned to stock of a new issue for bookkeeping purposes. It has no relationship to intrinsic worth or market value of the stock. (2) For preferred stock it may be the dollar value on which the dividend percent is calculated. (3) For bonds it is the face value on which the interest percent is calculated.

parity An option trades at parity when the striking price plus the premium equal the current market price of the underlying security.

participating preferred stock An issue of preferred stock that may yield, in addition to the stated dividend, additional dividends once expected common stock dividends have been paid.

PE Philadelphia Stock Exchange.

penny stocks Low-priced issues whose quotations are often stated in cents rather than in fractions of a point. Sometimes used to indicate any low-priced stock.

P-E ratio *see* price-earnings ratio.

pink sheets A list of stocks with their market makers (and sometimes bid and asked prices) that trade over-the-counter but may not appear on NASDAQ newspaper lists or on quote terminals.

pit The trading areas of a futures exchange.

plus tick *see* up tick.

point For stock quotations it is $1; for bond quotations it is $10.

poison pill A measure adopted by a company fearful of a takeover, which is designed to make the company "hard to swallow." Such a measure, often harmful to the target company, might consist of issuing preferred shares at an unusually high dividend rate.

portfolio The total securities held by an investor or institution.

preferred stock Stock with a fixed dividend rate. This dividend (which may be cumulative) must be paid before the dividend of any common stock. Preferred stockholders do not usually have voting privileges.

premium (1) The price of an option. (2) The amount that the strike price and option price combined are above the current market price of the underlying security.

premium, trading at When a bond is priced above the par value.

price-earnings ratio The number of times the per-share price of the stock exceeds the per-share earnings of the company.

price limit The maximum amount which the price of a futures contract can move from the settlement price of the previous trading period.

primary distribution The initial sale of a new issue of securities. Distribution, through an investment banker, is usually over the counter. Also called primary offering or initial distribution.

primary market The market for new issues. Sometimes used to mean the organized stock exchanges.

prime rate The interest rate charged by a bank for loans to its most creditworthy customers.

principal (1) Capital. (2) Face value of a bond. (3) The client for whom a securities transaction is made by a broker (as agent). When a brokerage buys and sells for its own account it acts as principal.

principals The stockholders.

profit-taking Selling stock for capital gain; usually used to describe sales that follow (and sometimes halt) a short rally.

proxy contest The attempt of a person or group of people to obtain the proxies of a sufficient number of shareholders to influence a corporate election or vote.

prudent man rule A standard by which one invests with caution for reasonable income and preservation of capital.

PSE Pacific Stock Exchange.

public, to go For a company to issue stock, available to the public, for the first time. This is called an initial offering.

put An option giving the right to sell 100 shares (usually) of a specific stock, at a specific price, within a specific time period.

quotation or **quote** In investing, a verbal or printed representation of a securities price. It may be a transaction price or it may consist of both a bid and asked price.

ratio strategy Any number of option spreads and combinations in which the short positions exceed the long positions.

real estate investment trust (*REIT*) A closed-end investment company that invests in real estate.

record date *see* holder of record.

redemption price (1) For bonds it is the price at which a bond will be redeemed should it be called before maturity. (2) For mutual funds it is the price at which shares can be redeemed, usually the net asset value.

red herring A preliminary prospectus (description) of a new issue being offered by an underwriter. The caveats must be printed in red on the first page.

registered as to interest only Bonds for which interest is sent automatically to the registered holder but for which face value is returned (at maturity) only to the bearer.

registered as to principal only A coupon bond which will return the face value (at maturity) automatically to the registered holder.

registered bond *see* fully registered bond.

registered representative An employee of a brokerage who has been trained and is registered to handle customer accounts. Also known as an account executive. Such an individual is not, strictly speaking, a broker.

retained earnings That part of the earnings of a company not distributed to the stockholders.

return *See* yield.

revenue anticipation note *(RAN)* A short-term (one year or less) municipal note backed by anticipated revenues. Usually issued at discount in denominations of $25,000.

revenue bonds Municipal bonds of several types which are backed by revenue from a special project or tax.

right Allows the holder to purchase additional shares at a stipulated price for a stipulated time period. See unit.

rollover Reinvesting funds from a maturing security into longer-term securities. Applicable to debt instruments, options and futures.

round lot Standard unit of trading. For stocks it is 100 shares except for some inactive issues traded in 10-share lots. On the AMEX there are also a few that trade in 25 and 50-share lots. For futures the contract size is specified separately for each commodity on each exchange.

roundtrip Both the opening transaction and closing transaction in a futures position. Commission in commodities is charged per roundtrip.

secondary distribution A public offering of a large block of stock held by the issuing company or one or more large stockholders at a time after the primary distribution. Also called secondary offering. *See* special offering.

secondary market The trading of securities any time after their initial distribution. *See* aftermarket. Sometimes used to mean the trading of securities not listed on an exchange.

secondary offering *See* secondary distribution.

securities Sometimes used only to mean stocks and bonds; in a broader sense it includes almost any financial instrument. Sometimes implies a longer-term vehicle than, for example, "instrument."

Securities and Exchange Commission *(SEC)* The government agency that regulates the securities industry.

serial bond Bonds of the same issue but with different maturities and coupon rates.

settlement price The official closing price for a commodity set by the clearinghouse at the end of each trading day. This is the price from which margin requirements and price limits for the next day are calculated. The final transaction price is used whenever possible but often there are a number of simultaneous trades in the closing moments of a session. When this happens a price near the mid-point of the various final transaction prices is selected.

shareholders' equity *see* book value.

shark repellent A measure adopted by a company to ward off takeovers—for example, changing the certificate of incorporation to require an unusually large majority of voters to approve a merger.

short or **short position** When one has made a short sale or when one has sold an option or a futures contract. *See* long.

short-against-the-box Selling a security short that one also owns (in the same quantity).

short covering A purchase on a securities or commodities market in order to close a short position or sale, or to return stock previously borrowed.

short sale   The sale of a security that is borrowed for this purpose from one's broker. It is necessary to have a margin account for this purpose. The expectation is that when the security is purchased at a later date, in order to repay the broker, that the price will have gone down and that the investor will realize the difference between the two prices as profit. A short sale can only take place on an up tick (rise in price) of at least ⅛ point.

sinking fund   Funds set aside by a corporation, usually annually, to retire outstanding bonds and sometimes preferred stock.

specialist   A member of an exchange charged with maintaining an orderly market in one or more securities. To this end the specialist buys and sells for his own account as well as for others, often absorbing temporary disparities between supply and demand.

special offering   A secondary distribution (also called secondary offering) of securities from the issuing company in accordance with plans which the company has registered with the SEC. The plan must specify price, commission, and other terms of the offering.

speculator   An individual willing to assume higher risk in return for higher gain. In some trading situations it is an individual willing to take the risks others are seeking to avoid. In commodities it is an individual who trades in futures but does not intend to make or accept delivery.

split   A division of shares into, usually, a larger number. A 2-for-1 split would double the number of shares held by any investor and each share would be worth half as much as before. Reverse splits are also possible.

spot commodity   *See* actuals.

spot market   *See* cash market.

spot price   Prices quoted for actuals or cash commodities.

spread   The difference between the bid and asked price of a security.

spread option   A strategy whereby one simultaneously buys one option and sells another on the same security in order to lock in a price or so that the gain on one will offset a loss on the other.

stock   A unit of ownership in a corporation. There are two major types: common stock and preferred stock.

stock exchange   An institution that provides the facilities for the trading of stocks, bonds, warrants, and sometimes other securities. The exchanges themselves do not purchase, sell, or set prices for securities. Trading is done by or through members of the exchange and the securities must be registered on that exchange.

stockholder of record   Any party whose name as a shareholder is recorded on the books of the issuing company.

stockholders' equity   *See* book value.

straddle   An option strategy involving a put and a call on the same underlying security. In commodities it is a spread in futures other than grains.

strap option   An option strategy involving one put and two calls on the same underlying security.

street name   Indicates that securities are being held for the purchaser by a brokerage.

strike price *See* exercise price.

subordinated debt instrument A bond whose claim to the assets of a corporation, or whose repayment of principal, is subordinate to another debt instrument.

support A term from technical analysis indicating a price area where buyer demand is expected to keep the price of a security from falling through.

TAN *See* tax anticipation note.

target company A company that is sought in a takeover bid by another company.

tax anticipation note *(TAN)* A short-term (one year or less) municipal note backed by anticipated proceeds from a forthcoming tax collection. Usually issued at discount in denominations of $25,000.

tax-exempt securities *See* municipal bonds.

tax shelter An investment by means of which certain costs can be deducted from taxable income or income from which is tax exempt.

technical analysis An approach to investing based on the examination of the previous price movements of a security. Usually thought of in opposition to fundamental analysis.

technical rally A brief upturn in security prices that is caused by factors other than a fundamental shift in the supply and demand for that security. It is not expected to reverse the prevailing downward trend.

tender offer Large-scale public offers to buy shares of a particular stock sometimes with the intention of taking control of a corporation. The buyer may reserve the right to decline, at a later date, all or a part of the shares subsequently presented.

term bond A bond issue consisting of bonds that mature on the same date and have the same coupon rate. *See* serial bond. Also, a Treasury bond which can be called before maturity.

thin market Lack of trading activity for a specific security, commodity, or an entire market. Prices are somewhat more volatile under these conditions.

third market Over-the-counter trading by brokerages of securities that are listed on an exchange.

tick The minimum price fluctuation for a futures contract. The amount is specified separately for each commodity by each exchange.

ticker Refers to ticker quotations which are trade-by-trade transaction reports that specify the name, price, and usually the volume, of each stock, bond, option, or commodity traded on an exchange. *See* consolidated tape.

time spread *See* calendar spread.

time value premium The amount of an option's premium above its intrinsic value. This is the value which declines with time.

Treasury securities Direct debt obligations of the U.S. government. They are issued in bills, bonds, and notes.

TSE Toronto Stock Exchange.

type Used in option trading to distinguish puts and calls. Options of one type would either be all calls or all puts.

uncovered option *See* naked option.

unit New issues are sometimes initially offered in units each of which may consist of one or more shares of stock and one or more warrants.

underwriter *See* investment banker.

up tick A transaction at a price greater than the previous one. Also called a plus tick.

vertical spread An option strategy consisting of the simultaneous purchase and sale of puts or of calls with the same expiration date and different exercise prices.

volume   The number of shares or contracts traded.

warrant   A certificate granting the long-term privilege (5–10 years) of purchasing more shares of stock from a company at a specified price. Warrants may be traded like stock.

when distributed   A security trading in advance of the printing of the certificate.

when issued   A security trading in advance of its final authorization for issuance. Should the security not be authorized all transactions will be canceled. *See also* p. 34.

white knight   A company to which a target company offers itself in the hope of averting a hostile takeover by another company.

World Bank   *See* International Bank for Reconstruction and Development.

write   To sell an option.

yield   Dividends or interest from a security. Expressed as a percent of purchase price or of par. *See* yield to maturity.

yield to maturity   An annualized yield percent that takes into account the current yield, capital gain or loss at maturity, and reinvestment of all interest payments at the coupon rate.

zero-coupon bond   This type of bond does not pay interest until maturity. It is sold at deep discount and redeemed, upon maturity, at face value (the face value includes the accrued interest). Taxes, however, must be paid each year on the nonpaid interest.

Index